WHY THE MIND HAS A BODY

WHY THE MIND HAS A BODY

BY

C. A. STRONG

PROFESSOR OF PSYCHOLOGY IN COLUMBIA UNIVERSITY

NEW YORK
THE MACMILLAN COMPANY
LONDON: MACMILLAN & CO., LTD.
1908

COPYRIGHT, 1903,
BY THE MACMILLAN COMPANY.

Set up and electrotyped April, 1903.
Reprinted July, 1908.

UNIVERSITY PRESS · JOHN WILSON
AND SON · CAMBRIDGE, U. S. A.

PREFACE

The reader will find in this book (1) a sketch of an explanation of the connection of mind and body; (2) a proposal, based thereon, for a settlement of the controversy between the parallelists and the interactionists.

(1) The explanation of the connection of mind and body is not in substance new. It is that which is implied in the panpsychism of Fechner and Clifford. Brief expositions of it have been given by Paulsen in his *Einleitung in die Philosophie*—indeed, to Paulsen I owe my first acquaintance with it—and, more recently, by Stout in the chapter "Body and Mind" of his *Manual*. What specially characterizes my treatment of the matter is the detailed working-out of the conception in terms of the hypothesis of mental causality. I have also set forth somewhat elaborately the scientific and metaphysical premises on which it rests.

Perhaps owing to the brevity with which it has been presented, this explanation has thus far attracted little attention. Most philosophical writers seem not to have grasped it. They are accustomed to treat the connection of mind and body as inexplicable. So settled have they become in the belief that it cannot be explained, that they have almost ceased to regard it as a fact needing explanation.

That the panpsychist explanation is clear to the bottom and altogether free from difficulties, I should be the last to pretend. But it rests on sound metaphysical principles; it enables us, as no other hypothesis does, to construe the facts; and its difficulties are of the nature of obscurities, not of contradictions. Hence I think panpsychists are justified in maintaining that with their principles they are able to explain the connection of mind and body. I have chosen my title with the object of putting this panpsychist pretension distinctly on record.

(2) A further merit of the explanation is that it enables us to settle the controversy between the interactionists and the parallelists in a way satisfactory to both parties. Parallelism is commonly supposed to deny the efficiency of mind; and this is felt to be the great objection to it. The proposition that, so far from denying efficiency, parallelism involves and implies it, may even seem to the reader a contradiction in terms. Yet this is a proposition which the panpsychist theory permits us to justify. Here again I am happy to find myself in agreement with Dr. Stout, who in the chapter of his *Manual* already referred to provides a basis for reconciliation between parallelists and interactionists identical with that proposed here.

In his article "Are We Automata?" in *Mind* for 1879 (vol. iv., pp. 1–22), Professor James made the prediction that, if the 'automaton theory' should ever prove to be the truth, it would be in a translated form in which our common-sense belief in the efficiency of mind would be recognized as essentially accurate. In Dr. Stout's theory and mine this prophecy finds its fulfilment.

It only remains for me to express my obligations to the friends who have assisted me in the preparation of the book. I owe most to my father, Rev. A. H. Strong, D.D., of the Rochester Theological Seminary. My thanks are due to Professor James, to Mr. Henry Rutgers Marshall, and to my colleague Professor Cattell, who read all or parts of the book in manuscript and helped me with their criticisms and suggestions. I have also received some valuable hints from my friends Professor George Santayana and Dr. Dickinson S. Miller. Finally, I should feel that something essential had been omitted if I did not gratefully acknowledge my immense indebtedness to the philosophical writings of Professor Paulsen and to Professor James's *Principles of Psychology*, on which I have nourished myself for years and which have been the main influences in shaping my thought.

LAKEWOOD, N. J.
April, 1903.

CONTENTS

	PAGE
INTRODUCTION	1

PART I

EMPIRICAL

BOOK I
THE FACTS

CHAPTER	
I. GENERAL SURVEY	19
II. THE IMMEDIATE CORRELATE OF CONSCIOUSNESS . .	39
III. EXTENT OF THE CORRELATION ON THE MENTAL SIDE	51

BOOK II
THE QUESTION OF CAUSAL RELATIONS

IV. DEFINITION OF THEORIES	67
V. THE ARGUMENTS FOR AUTOMATISM	87
VI. THE ARGUMENTS FOR INTERACTIONISM	103
VII. THE ARGUMENTS FOR PARALLELISM	126

PART II

METAPHYSICAL

BOOK III
METAPHYSICAL PRINCIPLES

VIII. THE PHYSICAL WORLD	163
IX. CONSCIOUSNESS	194
X. THINGS-IN-THEMSELVES: THEIR POSSIBILITY . . .	211
XI. THINGS-IN-THEMSELVES: PROOFS OF THEIR EXISTENCE	251
XII. THINGS-IN-THEMSELVES: THEIR NATURE	275

BOOK IV

APPLICATION OF THE FOREGOING PRINCIPLES TO THE PROBLEM — CRITICISM OF THEORIES

Chapter	Page
XIII. Interactionist Theories	296
XIV. Automatist Theories	316
XV. Parallelist Theories	330
Conclusion	349

WHY THE MIND HAS A BODY

INTRODUCTION

THE problem of the relation of mind and body takes, for contemporary thought, the form of the issue between interactionism and automatism. Interactionism regards the brain as an instrument employed by the mind in its dealings with the world of objects. It accordingly asserts in sensation an action of the body on the mind, in volition an action of the mind on the body. Automatism conceives the brain-process as the physical basis or condition of consciousness. It therefore holds that consciousness merely accompanies the brain-process, without exerting any influence upon it.

But the term 'automatism,' when thus defined, covers two widely different theories. These are the 'conscious automaton theory' of Huxley and the 'parallelism' of Clifford. Huxley regards consciousness as an *effect* of brain-action, an effect which does not in its turn become a cause and react on the brain, and which is therefore wholly without efficiency. He thus retains still a one-sided causal relation between body and mind. Clifford holds that consciousness and the brain-process merely flow along side by side, the brain being no more responsible for consciousness than consciousness for what happens in the brain. He wholly denies causal relations between body and mind.

This last theory seems alone entitled to the name of parallelism. For, although on Huxley's theory also the stream of consciousness flows along beside the brain-process, yet the corresponding points of the two are not directly opposite, the mental states being always a little later than the brain-events which cause them. Moreover, the idea meant to be conveyed by the spatial figure of parallelism is that of the absence of causal relations, of mere concomitance. On the other hand, both theories are in strictness of speech automatist, since both hold that the brain gets along by itself, without the help of the mind. In the ordinary conception of automatism, however, there lies, in addition to this, some thought of a dependence of consciousness on the brain, some notion of the brain as the primary thing and of consciousness as "somehow superadded"; and I think it therefore allowable to employ the term 'automatism' for Huxley's theory only, which needs a name, and for which it is difficult to find an exactly appropriate one.

There are thus three distinct theories as to causal relations between mind and body: interactionism, asserting that the causal influence runs in both directions — in sensation from the body to the mind, in volition from the mind to the body; automatism, maintaining that it runs in one direction only — always from the body to the mind; and parallelism, denying all causal influence and holding the relation to be of a different nature. Between these theories the contest is fairly triangular: for a theory which asserts causal relations in one direction only is at least as distinct from a theory which denies causal relations as from one that asserts them in both directions.

From causal theories we must distinguish sharply what may be called ultimate theories of the relation of mind and body: theories, that is, which seek to explain and make intelligible to us why mind and body are connected at all. The 'double aspect theory,' with its assertion of one reality manifesting itself under two diverse forms, is an example of such a theory. Whatever we may think of the example, to some such theory we must sooner or later come, if we would solve the problem completely. We cannot rest satisfied with mere determination of the causal issue. For suppose interactionism to be proved true, we should be as far as ever from understanding why two such interacting things are juxtaposed. Or, if parallelism were demonstrated, we should have still to learn how this parallel march of nervous and mental events was brought about. On the other hand, all ultimate theories would appear to rest upon and be varieties of the three causal theories already mentioned.

Philosophers are at present pretty exclusively occupied with the causal issue; and it certainly seems as if they were right in attacking it first. The three causal theories, when compared with each other, show peculiar points of agreement and difference.

If automatism and parallelism alike deny the action of mind upon body, automatism and interactionism agree with each other and differ from parallelism in asserting causal relations of some sort between body and mind; and it is a question which is the deeper gulf. I believe the deeper gulf by far is that between parallelism and its rivals. The great question is not in which direction the causal influence runs, but whether the relation of mind and body is such as to permit of causal relations at all.

Let us stop for a moment, before going further, to consider the consequences to a series of sciences which would result from asserting or denying causal relations between body and mind.

And, first of all, to the most general of the natural sciences, physics. Here the issue at stake is the universal validity of the principle of the conservation of energy. Is this principle, as Helmholtz declared it, "a universal law of all natural phenomena,"[1] or only, as a recent interactionist writer would have us believe, "a useful and valid working-hypothesis applicable to certain classes of physical fact"? Interactionism stands committed to the latter view, automatism and parallelism support the former.

Next, this is a vital question for biology. Sooner or later the biologist must come to close quarters with the question of the place of consciousness in evolutionary theory. Hitherto two tendencies in biology have disputed the field: the thorough-going

[1] Helmholtz, *Vorträge und Reden*, p. 151.

Darwinian, presupposing the mechanical theory of life, and ignoring the possibility that the mind is a factor in bodily evolution; and the Lamarckian, entertaining and building upon that possibility. Many biologists at the present day believe fortuitous variation and natural selection inadequate to account for the actual phenomena of evolution. They suspect the presence of an additional factor, whose nature remains to be determined. The study of instinct brings them close upon the confines of intelligence; instinct seems to involve feeling, and feeling thus to be a factor no less efficient than bodily organs in determining survival. Perplexed to account by physical causes alone for the origin of favorable variations and for their preservation while as yet insufficient in amount to affect survival, what wonder if they have thought to find the needed additional factor in consciousness?[1]

Whether this interactionist tendency in biology be significant or ephemeral, we need not inquire. That it is a creationist hypothesis on a small scale, attributing to the animal mind an intervention in physical affairs which biologists have latterly denied to the divine, is perhaps no conclusive argument against it. It has been plausibly urged, in proof of such intervention, that if consciousness did not contribute to survival by acting upon the body it would never have been evolved. We may reserve this argument for later consideration, merely noting at

[1] See Cope, *Primary Factors of Organic Evolution*, pp. 13, 14 and 495–517.

present that it must make the greatest difference to biology whether it is legitimate thus to appeal to consciousness as a factor in physical evolution.

Next, brain-physiology and mental pathology would be affected. The physiologist, agreeably to that materialism of his which forms so excellent a principle of method but so dubious a philosophy, is accustomed to trace all cerebral events to bodily causes, such as stimulating nerve-currents, nutrition, oxygenation. From Griesinger's enunciation of the principle that insanity is brain-disease the alienist dates the birth of modern psychiatry. Must the physiologist give up his rule of method, and the alienist his fundamental axiom?

When we turn from the natural to the philosophical sciences, we find that the consequences would be no less far-reaching. And, first, to general philosophy or metaphysics. It needs no argument to show that, according as we decide for causal relations or against them, our entire conception of the universe will be a different one. For to reject causal relations is to hold that in the brain none but mechanical causes are at work, that brain-events taken with other physical events form a closed circle; and this is to set the capstone upon the mechanical conception of the universe. Whereas to assert causal relations is to contradict this conception by positing a *hiatus* in the physical series.

Finally, parallelism involves the denial of the physical efficiency of mind, and automatism the denial of its general efficiency. These doctrines thus apparently leave us no longer the authors of our acts! We shall find, when we come to consider the matter, that automatism does this really, since the causal inertness of mind is one of its cardinal principles. Parallelism, on the other hand, which denies only the physical efficiency of mind, may perhaps prove consistent with its possessing some other kind of efficiency, and we must hold our judgment in suspense. But it is plain already how momentous is this issue to ethics and the philosophy of mind.

Thus a whole series of scientific and philosophical conceptions of the first order — the principle of the conservation of energy, the mechanical theory of life, the biological doctrine of evolution, the fundamental postulates of brain-physiology and mental pathology, the philosophical conceptions of mechanism, efficiency, free-will — all converge and come to a focus in the problem of the relation of mind and body. Not only so, but every one of these conceptions is vitally engaged, and will be found to stand or fall or suffer total transformation, according as we espouse interactionism, automatism, or parallelism.

Let us now consider by what means a decision between the three theories might be brought about.

It is evident, to begin with, that the question is partly at least one of fact. When we examine the three theories closely, we find that they are not merely different interpretations of the same admitted facts, but assume differences in the facts themselves. These differences are of three kinds.

(1) Interactionism assumes that for certain physical events, namely, those immediately consequent upon our volitions, no adequate cause is discoverable on the physical side. It assumes, in other words, the non-existence of certain physical facts whose existence is assumed by automatism and parallelism. And the analogous proposition might be worked out for the case of sensation: automatism and parallelism assume that the brain-event which accompanies or immediately precedes a sensation — the sensational brain-event, as we shall find it convenient to call it — goes on to produce all the physical effects which it would have produced had there been no sensation; whereas interactionism assumes (or ought in logic to assume) that the brain-event exhausts itself in producing the sensation, and therefore has no physical effects.

(2) Interactionism would seem to require the assumption that the sensational brain-event happens just previously to the sensation, since the cause must necessarily precede the effect in time, and the volitional brain-event for the same reason just subsequently to the volition. Automatism agrees with interactionism in its account of sensation, but in its account of volition reverses the temporal relation, making the volition come after the volitional brain-event instead of before. Parallelism, finally, assumes that sensational brain-event and sensation, volitional brain-event and volition happen simultaneously.

(3) Automatism and parallelism alike involve the assumption that all mental states — not only sensa-

tions and images, but also judgments, pleasures and pains, desires, volitional decisions, nay, even the consciousness of self — have events corresponding to them in the brain. Interactionism commonly disputes this, holding that the 'higher' mental states are without cerebral correlates.

These differing versions of the psychophysical facts yield a series of empirical problems, investigable presumably by the methods of natural science, quite independently of the views one may hold as to the ultimate nature of physical facts and mental states. Whether mental states are attributes of a Soul, or appearances to a Subject, or contents of a unitary consciousness, or discrete ideas, they exist in some sense; and whether physical events are externally real, just as we see and feel them, or only modifications of the mind, they too exist in some sense: in some sense, therefore, the temporal and other relations between these two kinds of fact must exist, and have validity on any philosophical theory. This being so, no harm can result from ignoring metaphysical difficulties at the outset and seeking by empirical methods to determine these questions of fact. Indeed, it stands to reason that an exact determination of the facts should precede all discussions of theory.

I shall therefore begin with a study of the facts. I shall take up first those primary and indubitable ones which constitute the data of the problem, dividing them into classes and discussing their consistency with each of the three causal theories. I shall then deal briefly with the question, whether consciousness is immediately correlated with the total bodily process, or only with certain parts of it, and, if the latter, with what parts. This done, we may consider the questions referred to above : whether the correlation extends to all mental states, and whether it involves simultaneity or succession. But, without abandoning empirical ground, we may go still further. Having determined the facts, we may proceed to try the issue between interactionism, automatism, and parallelism so far as it is adjudicable by empirical considerations alone; so far, that is to say, as it is a question for physiological psychology as a natural science.

It may seem to the reader that, if this empirical inquiry were satisfactorily concluded, our task would be completed and the problem solved; that physiological psychology, in other words, is in this question the tribunal of last resort. And it must be admitted that the establishment of certain facts would negate or tend to negate each of the three theories. Thus proof that the 'higher' mental states are without cerebral correlates would tend to disprove automatism and parallelism, while evidence of the universality and simultaneity of the correlation would tell strongly against interactionism. If, then, facts could overthrow each theory, could not facts establish each? Cannot physiological psychology, without overstepping the limits of her province, settle the whole question?

To show that this assignment of jurisdiction, even if theoretically correct, is not in practice sufficient for the question's settlement, I need only cite the views actually held by leading writers. There are psychologists who admit the universality of the correlation, yet uphold interactionism. There are physiologists and even philosophers who insist on the universality of the correlation, but see in it a proof of the automatist view that the cerebral correlates produce the mental states. There are others, equally convinced of ₀such universality, who interpret it in the sense of parallelism, and hold that the relation excludes causality. Finally, there are those exceptional parallelists who deny the universality of the correlation. These conflicting interpretations of the same facts sufficiently prove that we cannot be satisfied with mere fact-determination, but must discuss the nature of the causal relation, so as to judge of its applicability between body and mind. Now, the nature of the causal relation has not usually been deemed an empirical question, but a metaphysical one.

But is there not another question, even more clearly metaphysical, which is logically prior? Would it not be well, before debating whether mind can act upon matter, to decide just what we mean by matter, and in what sense we may reasonably conceive it to exist? For if at the present day there is a point on which philosophers show some approach to agreement, it is that matter DOES NOT EXIST, in any such sense as the plain man supposes; that it has no existence independently of mind. But, if matter does not exist independently of mind, it cannot be there for the mind to act upon (or, for that matter, for mental states to run parallel to). One would accordingly think some investigation of the separateness of matter and mind an indispensable preliminary to discussion of their interaction. Yet most interactionists go straight to the causal issue, assuming that we know perfectly well what we mean by matter, that it exists in the universe alongside of mind, and that the only question is whether we will permit mind to act upon it (as a hungry dog might be permitted to attack a bone), or will wickedly forbid such action. In other moods these writers are commonly idealists, but when they discuss the relation of mind and body they forget their idealism and talk like the naïvest of realists.

It is no less indispensable to have a clear idea of what we mean by mind. Despite the apparent testimony of consciousness to its own efficiency, writers of mark are found to declare it exempt from or superior to the causal category, and thus too lofty a thing to soil its fingers with common work. Some, like Kant, resolve it into a series of phenomena no more deserving of the predicate of reality than those of matter. It is therefore as necessary to examine whether consciousness is real and capable of acting as whether matter is real and capable of being acted upon.

For these reasons it is clear that our inquiry must have a metaphysical part, devoted to a critical examination of the conceptions of matter, mind, and causation. But this is equally necessary for a further reason: because without it we should be unable to cope with our problem in its full extent. Of the two questions which together constitute this problem, only the first, as to the causal or non-causal character of the relation, could by any possibility be decided by empirical facts and arguments alone. The second, how two such disparate things come to be associated at all—"ultimate of ultimate problems," in the words of Professor James[1]—is none the less an integral part of our task. The likelihood of any light being thrown upon it in the course of the present inquiry may appear to the reader small. He will at least admit that any treatment of it presupposes definite conclusions regarding the nature of matter and mind. From which it would follow that our problem belongs, not to physiological psychology as a natural science, but to the branch of metaphysics known as the philosophy of mind, whose task it is to deal with the philosophical questions growing out of psychology.

I shall accordingly supplement the empirical inquiry already announced with a metaphysical investigation of the nature of matter and mind, and shall follow this up with renewed discussion of the problem from the vantage-ground of the critical conceptions thus attained. Possibly after this metaphysical clearing of the atmosphere the causal question may appear in a somewhat different light, and even the second and more ultimate of the two questions prove less intractable than it now seems.

I am aware that readers whose metaphysical in-

[1] *Principles of Psychology*, vol. i., p. 177.

vestments have hitherto brought small returns will take a less hopeful view of the issue of our undertaking. Metaphysics is in discredit at the present day, not altogether undeservedly. But metaphysics in this question is inevitable. Is it, or is it not, a real question whether material things exist independently of the mind, or only for the mind? Is it, or is it not, a real question whether the mind itself is real, active, and efficient? Is it, or is it not, indispensable to answer these questions before debating whether the mind can act on the body? To these queries there can be but one answer. We must study the facts, and we must examine the empirical arguments, but when this is done, whatever our misgivings, we must bid farewell to the *terra firma* of experience and embark upon the ocean of metaphysics.

But is this ocean navigable? Can we hope, as the result of our inquiry, to reach any assured and binding conclusions? A widespread notion of metaphysics makes it synonymous with 'speculation' — a discipline whose processes escape rational control, whose results are therefore essentially doubtful. In the natural sciences, we are told, a new theory can be put to the test of experiment and its truth or falsity quickly determined, but in metaphysics this is impossible. I have no desire to undertake the defence of all that passes under the name of metaphysics. But I would point out that our problem, perhaps alone among those with which metaphysics deals, affords an opportunity for something that may be quite accurately described as a metaphysical experiment. In the psychophysical relation mind and matter are somehow associated. We are to investigate the nature of these two things quite irrespectively of their association. We are then to make trial, whether the conceptions at which we have arrived enable us to explain the association. If perchance they should, would not our procedure be like that of the chemist who, suspecting that oxygen and hydrogen together made water, isolated these gases and brought them together and found that in truth they do? A similar success would give to our theory, it seems to me, something like experimental confirmation.

Part I
EMPIRICAL

Book I

THE FACTS

CHAPTER I

GENERAL SURVEY

THE facts which exemplify the relation of mind and body may be divided into three classes, according as they seem to show action of mind on body, or action of body on mind, or dependence of mind on body. I say "seem to show," for if the facts really showed these things, it is evident that the first and second classes would prove interactionism, and the third class automatism. It is therefore an important question for us to discuss, whether the facts necessitate one theory or another, or can be interpreted in terms of all three.

Apparent Action of Mind on Body

The most conspicuous instance of this is of course volition. When I will a bodily movement, and the movement takes place, I may be pardoned for supposing that the mind has acted on the body. But volition is only one case among many. Recent psychologists tell us that *all* mental states are followed by bodily changes — that "all consciousness leads to action." This is true of desires, of emotions, of pleasures and pains, and even of such seemingly non-impulsive states as sensations and ideas. It is true, in a word, of the entire range of our mental life. The bodily effects in question are of course not limited to the voluntary muscles, but consist in large part of less patent changes in the action of heart, lungs, stomach, and other viscera, in the calibre of blood-vessels and the secretion of glands. A few examples will help to make our ideas definite.

Whether the emotions are to be regarded as causes or as reflex manifestations of the bodily changes which constitute their expression, in either case a mental state — on the traditional theory the emotion itself, on the 'back-stroke theory' the idea that arouses it — has been followed by physical changes. And the parallel statement applies to the theories of desire and volitional effort formed on the 'back-stroke' analogy, which explain effort as a feeling of muscular strain, and desire for food, for example, as partly composed of the sensation of the watering of the mouth. On any theory, emotion is accompanied by an overflow of cerebral currents entailing profound and widespread bodily effects. Thus passion breaks forth in physical violence, joy quickens and grief depresses the vital functions, fear leads to a paralysis of movement, anger in a wet-nurse poisons the milk, etc.

The bodily consequences of ideas and states we should describe as cognitive are no less clearly marked. The thought of blushing makes one blush, the sound of others coughing makes one cough. Among these states none is more physically potent than belief, as we see by the phenomena of hypnotic suggestion. Thus the subject's belief that he cannot open his eyes makes opening them impossible, his conviction that a postage-stamp is a mustard-plaster enables it to raise a blister; the hysterical patient's belief that she cannot move her leg or open her hand creates a virtual paralysis or contracture of those parts; and faith or confident expectation may aid in the cure of functional ailments. Indeed, the latest theory of will makes its essence consist in the conviction that the bodily movement is about to take place — a prevision which speedily brings about its own fulfilment.

But why multiply instances, when every instinctive movement, every voluntary act, perhaps even every turn of the attention, is a case in point? The apparent action of mind upon body is one of the most obvious characteristics of our mental life. Let us rather inquire, without further delay, whether the facts necessitate interactionism, or can be formulated in terms of the other two theories.

A moment's reflection shows that the latter is the case. Though the facts seem at first sight to prove interactionism, automatism and parallelism offer alternative interpretations of them which, for anything we can now see, stand an equal chance of being correct.

Let us consider the parallelist interpretation first. The type of this class is the case of volition; and this is the exact reverse of the case of sensation. Now, when a sensory nerve-current seems to cause a sensation, parallelism tells us that it really causes a sensational brain-event, which is merely accompanied by the sensation: and there is nothing in the facts which would permit us to gainsay the account. The sensational brain-event being wholly removed from our knowledge, the assertion of its concomitance with the sensation is as likely to be true as that of their sequence. In the same way, when a volition appears to cause a bodily movement, parallelism tells us that it is accompanied by a volitional brain-event which is the real cause of the movement; and again, there is nothing in the bare facts to contradict such a view.

The analogy of the case of volition holds good for all other cases in which the mind appears to act on the body. Let us take what would be the most impressive, if we could be certain of its truth. We hear of men sick unto death who survive through an effort of will, or recover because of a fixed determination to do so. We read of persons in the last stages of some lingering disease, who continue alive through the strength of some affection. Waiving all doubts as to the facts, let us consider the interpretation which parallelism would put upon them if true. According to the parallelist, the determination to recover, this persistent volitional state, is accompanied by an equally persistent brain-event, which is the real agent in effecting recovery. Similarly, it is not the nurse's anger that poisons the milk, but the agitated brain-state underlying the anger. It is not the hypnotic subject's belief that prevents his opening his eyes, but the inhibitory brain-event corresponding to the belief. What the interactionist, in all these cases, takes for an action of mind on body is in reality, on the purely physical side, an action of the brain upon the rest of the body. Nor can we, at this stage, deny the legitimacy of the parallelist's interpretation, or demonstrate interactionism simply by insisting on the facts. The facts are wholly neutral, and would be exactly what they are on either the interactionist or the parallelist hypothesis.

With a few slight changes the above argument may be made to show that the facts are equally consistent with automatism. This theory, like parallelism, ascribes the physical result — the recovery from illness, the poisoning of the milk, the inability to open the eyes — not to the preceding mental state, but to its attendant brain-event. Automatism differs from parallelism only in holding that the brain-event causes the mental state as well as the physical result. And this, again, is a view which cannot be refuted merely by pointing to the facts, for there is nothing in the facts that contradicts it. I conclude, therefore, that the facts which seem to prove action of mind on body do not really prove it, but can be formulated in terms of each of the three theories.

Apparent Action of Body on Mind

The facts which appear to show such action may be classified according to the mode in which the physical influence takes effect: through the sensory nerves, through the cranial walls and brain-substance, through the blood-supply, or through the working of the psychophysical mechanism itself. They pass over, as we shall see, without a break into the facts which seem to show dependence.

To the first group belong not only ordinary sensations, but also, according to the 'back-stroke theory,' those states of emotion, desire, and effort which this theory explains as due to currents returning from the periphery and thus resolves into sensations. Furthermore, we must include mental images, which are to be conceived as fainter reproduced sensations, called forth by intra-cerebral currents as the sensation is called forth by currents from without.

This whole group due to sensory stimulations represents, as we have seen, the exact converse of the case of volition : as in volition a mental change is followed by a physical, so here a physical change is followed by a mental. It is natural to interpret the sequence as causal; and interactionism and automatism, whose accounts here agree, seem therefore at first sight more harmonious with the facts. But parallelism has its alternative interpretation to offer. It tells us that the sensory nerve-current calls forth a sensational brain-event, which is merely accompanied by the sensation; it tells us that the intra-cerebral current calls forth an ideational brain-event, which is merely accompanied by the idea. Arbitrary as this account of the matter may at present appear to us, determined as we may be to demand some rational explanation of such mere concomitance before accepting it as valid, we cannot deny that it is entirely consistent with the facts.

Apparent Dependence of Mind on Body

From the facts thus far presented it would be natural to infer that mind and body are, in respect of action, on a footing of equality. The interactionist, at this point, might be tempted to set up the claim that every fact showing the influence of body upon mind can be matched with a fact showing the influence of mind upon body, and that by as much as the former demonstrates the mind's dependence the latter demonstrates its power. Even the parallelist might be tempted to subscribe to this claim, after first carefully prefixing 'apparent' to the words 'dependence' and 'power.' Whether this claim can be substantiated — whether the partners to the psychophysical relation enjoy a strict equality in respect of power — we must now consider in the light of further facts.

We saw that, as in volition a mental change is followed by a physical, so in sensation a physical change is followed by a mental. In the great majority of cases the mental effect is limited to the production of a new content, without any change in the vividness or, so to say, illumination of consciousness itself.

From these cases those are to be sharply distinguished in which the physical influence effects, not merely the appearance of a new content, but an alteration in the vividness with which this and all other contents are apprehended. Take, for example, the physical influences that bring about sleep, or the action of chloroform in producing unconsciousness. Whether these cases, like the others, can be interpreted as mere alterations of content, we may better consider after examining the facts.

To recur to our division according to the physical influence at work: sensory stimulations moderate in amount produce mere alterations of content. But as the stimulus becomes excessive, it effects at the same time a change in the degree of consciousness. Thus a smart rap upon the fingers causes pain, which may rouse the subject from a state of listlessness to one of wide-awake consciousness and mental activity: but any moderate sensation of sufficient interest might produce the same result. Suppose the blow to be upon the head, and to be so severe as to cause the subject to 'see stars'; still it might be held that here are only some new entoptic and circulatory sensations superadded to the tactual.

It is when the blow becomes of stunning force, so as to leave the mental faculties benumbed, that we have clearly to do, not with a mere alteration of content, but with a diminution in the amount of consciousness. That this is so, is evident from the fact that a still more violent blow abolishes consciousness altogether. Of course the physical influence has now taken effect, not merely or mainly through the sensory nerves, but through the cranial walls and brain-substance.

Here, then, are facts which seem to show something more than action of body on mind: which prove rather dependence of mind upon body. So, at least, we are in the habit of interpreting them, though we must go on to inquire, as in the case of the other two classes of facts, whether the dependence is more than apparent. It is of the utmost importance that we should appreciate the extent of the relation, whatever it be, which these facts reveal. I propose, therefore, despite their familiarity, to draw up a hasty list of them.

First, there are the effects produced by taking stimulants, intoxicants, and anæsthetics, such as coffee, alcohol, opium and hasheesh, nitrous oxide gas, chloroform and ether. These effects range from slight modifications of consciousness to its total abolition.

If we considered mild alcoholic intoxication by itself, we might perhaps be tempted to explain it by an irruption of strange organic sensations deranging the sequence of consciousness. But drunken stupor and total anæsthesia warn us that not merely the character but the existence of consciousness is concerned. Or, if it be contended that some faint sentiency always remains, the argument may be restricted in scope, and urged with reference to the nine tenths or ninety-nine hundredths of consciousness that have disappeared.

Next, there are the well-known effects of the weather on the mind. The variations of mood which hive-masters notice and allow for in bees, according as the weather is moist or dry, warm or cool, have their parallel in human beings. The Roman is not so much a Roman when a certain wind is blowing.

Curious tales are told of the errors committed by scientific experimenters and observers when the atmosphere was damp or charged with electricity, their minds as well as their bodies being befogged or bewitched. These vicissitudes of thought and feeling are doubtless partly due to the abnormal proportions of oxygen and moisture absorbed into the blood at such times and affecting the nerve-cells.

Next, there are the commonplace but eloquent facts of the necessity for food and sleep. Surely we should not have expected à *priori* that thought would be conditioned on the oft-repeated ingestion of matter, or consciousness on our lying unconscious eight hours out of the twenty-four!

Again, there are those inexplicable conditions of exhilaration and depression, mental efficiency and inefficiency, which seem to depend partly on the weather, partly on the working of other organs than the brain, partly on the brain's own past exertions. The immense differences at different times in the agility and effectiveness of the attention and in the disposable fund of mental energy are probably the mental expression of variations in the permeability of the cerebral nerve-paths, depending partly on the state of the nerve-elements and partly on that of the blood; with corresponding differences psychologically in the number of alternative images or expressions presented for choice and in the ease and success with which selection among them is made.

Coming to conditions distinctly pathological, we may notice first those states of nervous exhaustion and mental enfeeblement which result from excessive intellectual exertion or from long-continued and severe emotional strain. In vigorous health the brain should be as non-existent for consciousness as the stomach; but the nervous sufferer has data inaccessible to his healthy fellow, and is reminded of the psychophysical connection by a thousand distressing sensations. The stream of his consciousness no longer flows steadily forward, but halts and stagnates; the tardiness of his ideas, and the impossibility of accelerating them by effort, beget a sense of mental impotence; his nerveless fancy, stumbling sentences, and general unreadiness make him embarrassed and unhappy in the presence of others; he compares himself to a squeeezed-out sponge, or to a watch whose wheels will not revolve.

In a sicklier soil nervous worry and strain produce emotional instability, with rapid alternations of laughter and tears, as in hysterical patients; or lugubrious brooding over a single painful thought, as in melancholia; or the flow of ideas, instead of being impeded, may be hurried and excited, as in mania. The exact physiological explanation of these morbid conditions is of course not fully known. It will be sufficiently accurate for our purposes if we conceive them as due — heredity apart — to a gradual starvation or poisoning of the cerebral nerve-cells, brought about by over-activity or by toxic influences from other bodily organs.

Different, but hardly less impressive, are the phenomena exhibited when the blood-flow bursts its channels and ruinously submerges the brain-surface, compressing or destroying the underlying tissues; or where a similar result is artificially produced by the surgeon's knife. Here the brain as a whole may continue to operate normally and consciousness be apparently as wide-awake as ever: but among its contents certain sensations, certain memories no longer appear.

Finally, mention may be made of the progressive mental decrepitude which accompanies the decay of the body in extreme old age.

The facts which seem to show dependence are now fully before us, and we can turn to the question of their interpretation.

Surely no one who considers them can doubt that the mind is dependent on the body *in some sense*. Surely every one knows that without normal circulation, respiration, digestion, excretion, healthy mental life is impossible.

Yet idealistic philosophers have a way of speaking of the mind which implies a minimum of such knowledge. If we obtained our notion of it, not from experience, but from perusal of their writings, we should certainly feel no little surprise when informed that this thinking, willing, remembering spirit has its abode in a body. Its punctual habits of eating and sleeping would surely astonish us. They speak of the mind as if it were always wide-awake; as if the contents of consciousness might change, but never its degree or its existence; as if the body were merely one content amongst others; as if eating and sleeping were merely transactions betwixt contents; as if, in short, the mind were a sleepless, immutable eye, and already disembodied.

But if no other fact had impressed us about this content that eats and sleeps but its singular ubiquity, that alone would suffice to differentiate it from all other contents, and give rise to a problem. Very early in life, however, we come upon the track of a relation quite distinct from the cognitive one. By a little use of our eyes we learn that sensations of touch depend upon hands, and sensations of smell on a nose; a little groping, and a little observation of others, teach us that sensations of sight depend upon eyes, and sensations of sound on ears; and muscular sensations we find to be connected with the movements of limbs. These primary observations, supplemented by the more complex ones of which I have given a list above, drive us at last to the conclusion that besides the cognitive relation there is a relation of dependence. And even those to whom experience has not conveyed this instruction may see, by the consequences of taking chloroform or arsenic, that certain transactions between contents have a high importance for the existence of consciousness itself.

These facts necessitate an altered conception of the mind. Seeing "how at the mercy of bodily happenings our spirit is,"[1] we are led to conceive it, not as an ever-seeing supernatural eye, but as a psychical mechanism operating under strict conditions. The

[1] James, *Psychology: Briefer Course*, p. 5.

facts irresistibly suggest the analogy of a delicate machine like a watch, which runs for a time and then has to be wound, and which occasionally gets out of order. So the necessity for food and sleep, the uses of stimulants and narcotics, the occasional need of holidays and vacations, though we commonly shift all responsibility for them upon the brain, yet represent limitations of the mind which ought to be taken up into our conception of it.

If, summing up the results of our survey, we compare the influence of mind on body with the influence of body on mind, we cannot help recognizing a difference in the extent of the two favorable to the latter. The body seems, in this alliance, to have somewhat the advantage of the mind. For, while it is true that every case in which a physical event produces a mental state can be matched by a case in which a mental state produces a physical event, the third class of cases, in which a physical event affects the degree or even the existence of consciousness, is without an analogue in the contrary direction. Mind, so far as we can see, can never do more than change the position of matter; whereas matter can apparently diminish or destroy the existence of mind.[1]

Let us now consider whether the facts really prove dependence — by which we may understand, pro-

---

[1] How would it strike us if a moderate volition produced a moderate bodily movement, a more vigorous volition a more vigorous movement, and a very vigorous volition indeed — the abrupt disappearance of the entire bodily machine?

visionally at least, the causal relation asserted by automatism — or can be formulated in terms of all three theories.

The theory which has most difficulty in construing them is interactionism. Interactionism seems almost to necessitate two juxtaposed realities exchanging influences, and thus to imply a metaphysical dualism. For to conceive the brain as acting on the mind is to conceive the mind as existing prior to such action and as undergoing modification — to conceive them, in short, as separate existents. But, if brain and mind are separate existents and mind dependent on brain only for stimulation, how is it possible that excessive stimulation should destroy the existence of mind?

An easy recourse would be to distinguish between mind and consciousness, and hold that excessive stimulation abolishes consciousness but leaves mind intact. Few interactionists, however, will care to maintain their doctrine at cost of such a distinction. For contemporary psychology, mind equals consciousness, and it is meaningless to assert the existence of mind after consciousness has ceased.

But cautious interactionists will disclaim the apparently implied dualism, and affirm their theory to be simply a statement of observed facts: namely, that moderate stimulation is followed by a new content, excessive stimulation by the disappearance of consciousness; and will then contend that the facts are best expressed by the assumption that the relation is in both cases causal. Doubtless this is the attitude of most clear-headed interactionists.

But there is an inference which these thinkers neglect to draw. If moderate stimulation is followed by consciousness, and destructive stimulation by no consciousness, what does this signify but that moderate stimulation — or rather the brain-activity which is its result — is a necessary condition of consciousness: that consciousness depends on brain-activity, not only for its character, but for its very existence? Consciousness, that is to say, is not something which exists independently of the brain, beholden to it merely for those stimulations which give rise to sensations, but able to evolve all other forms of mental state out of itself: even on the interactionist theory, it is something that cannot exist for a moment without the kindly co-operation of the brain. Nor is this a doubtful theoretical proposition: it is a simple statement of fact. If it be a correct statement — and I do not see how its correctness can be questioned — it follows that the relation of mind and body is a somewhat more intimate one than that of two interacting realities.

This must not be understood as a refutation of interactionism. I have merely shown that a certain form of interactionism — that which conceives mind and brain as separate realities — is out of accord with the facts. The theory may presumably adapt itself to these, perhaps by taking on a phenomenalistic form, but in any case only on condition of frankly admitting that consciousness never occurs except in connection with a brain-process. Yet I think it apparent that interactionism is not a theory originally formed to deal with these facts, but only with the ordinary give and take of influence between mind and body.

Automatism and parallelism are theories devised for this express purpose. The facts showing the intimacy of the connection of mind and body are what originally suggested them both. Do these facts prove dependence as distinguished from concomitance?

(1) Let us ask this question, first, with reference to the two things immediately conjoined: consciousness and the brain-process. Do the facts prove consciousness to be dependent on the brain-process? If by dependence a one-sided relation be meant, such that consciousness depends on the brain-process but not the brain-process on consciousness, our answer must be in the negative. For, if it is true that we never find consciousness in the absence of the brain-process, it is equally true that we never find the brain-process — that is, the particular kind of brain-activity with which consciousness is correlated — in the absence of consciousness. The bare fact is that the two are always found together; there is nothing to indicate that one precedes or one-sidedly conditions the other.

Perhaps it will be urged that such conditioning furnishes the only intelligible explanation of their connection; that the brain is permanent and consciousness evanescent, and that consciousness must therefore be adjectivally attached to the brain; that the physical influence, in most of the above cases, starts upon the bodily side, and must therefore reach the brain before it reaches the mind. I reply that each of these points represents a theoretical gloss on the facts, not the bare statement of what is contained in them. Theoretical explanations are to occupy us later. At present we can only admit that dependence as distinguished from concomitance — or, if the reader prefer, one-sided dependence as distinguished from reciprocal dependence — is not an immediate deliverance of the facts.

In short, here as in the case of the first two classes of facts parallelism presents an alternative interpretation which stands an equal chance of being correct. If consciousness, instead of being the effect of brain-action, were simply its uniform concomitant, in such wise that the two always necessarily co-existed, the same appearance of dependence would arise as if the relation were causal.

(2) We have been considering the relation between consciousness and the brain-process. If, now, we turn to that between consciousness and the body at large, our answer must be somewhat different. The delicate molecular events composing the brain-process obviously presuppose a vast assemblage of material conditions: the nerve-cells must be bathed in arterial blood, and moderately stimulated through the sensory nerves; for their behoof the organs of circulation, respiration, digestion, excretion must discharge their functions aright. Now, these functions are possible without the brain-process, but the brain-process is not possible without them; the brain-process is therefore one-sidedly dependent on the activity of the non-cerebral organs. It follows that consciousness, its

inseparable concomitant, is *indirectly* dependent on the activity of those organs. But mark the sense in which this direct dependence of the brain-process, and indirect dependence of consciousness, on the non-cerebral organs is now admitted. In the first place, the dependence is not *wholly* one-sided, since the brain-process directly, and consciousness therefore indirectly, may react upon and modify the activity of those organs. In the second place, this is no metaphysical relation of something less real or permanent to something more real or permanent, but, in the case of the brain-process, an interaction of two coequal bodily functions; in the case of consciousness, such an indirect relation as is involved in its concomitance with one of them. Nowhere do we find the slightest trace of that one-sided and absolute dependence which is supposed to be the most obvious lesson of the facts.

To sum up: our study of the facts has lent no support to any particular causal theory. But it has brought to light a psychophysical principle of fundamental importance which has to be admitted by all theories alike: that consciousness is inseparably bound up with the brain-process, and cannot take place in its absence. This has sometimes been called the 'principle of parallelism,' with the result of an unfortunate confusion with the theory which denies causal relations; or the 'principle of concomitance,' a word too easily misunderstood to mean *mere* concomitance. It is really an empirical law, on the same level as that of Weber. I propose that we call it *the law of psychophysical correlation* — a name which expresses the fact of intimate connection without any causal or metaphysical implications. This law, then, sums up all that is unquestionably contained in the three classes of facts.

CHAPTER II

THE IMMEDIATE CORRELATE OF CONSCIOUSNESS

WE saw in the last chapter that consciousness is closely connected with certain physical processes, to which its exact empirical relation is one of concomitance or uniform co-existence : this being true on any theory, and whether the temporal relation be one of simultaneity or of succession. In the next two chapters we must study this connection somewhat more in detail, with the aim of determining its scope and limits on each side.

Let us begin with the physical side. Here the question is : Where in the body do the events take place with which consciousness is immediately correlated — the events which on the interactionist theory are the last antecedents and first consequents of mental states, on the automatist their last antecedents, on the parallelist their immediate concomitants?

The reader will probably answer without hesitation : *In the brain.* And in so answering he will have the support of the best contemporary psychologists. Professor James considers this view "so universally admitted nowadays"[1] as hardly to require discussion; Dr. Stout says that we may assume it "without serious inaccuracy."[2] On the other hand,

[1] *Principles of Psychology*, vol. i., p. 4; cf. pp. 65–67.
[2] *Manual of Psychology*, p. 36.

so judicious a thinker as Professor Paulsen devotes a section to proving that consciousness is correlated with the sum-total of bodily processes.[1] The question lies somewhat aside from the main line of our inquiry, and we need not consider it at great length. We cannot wholly neglect it, since in discussing the relation of mind and body it is important to know what parts of the body and what parts of the mind are, so to speak, in immediate apposition. Moreover, the question has metaphysical bearings which will show themselves later.[2]

The knowledge that the brain has anything to do with thought is a late scientific acquisition. Aristotle fancied it a sponge-like reservoir for the cooling of the blood: which would seem to show that there is nothing in our every-day experiences pointing to it unmistakably as the psychophysical organ. The plain man conceives the mind as pervading the entire bodily mass, and as manifesting itself by turns at different points of that mass. His notion is that the mind is "wherever it feels and acts": in the eye when we see, in the finger-tip when we feel, in the brain when we think, in the limbs when we voluntarily move. He assumes, in short, that the physical event underlying a sensation takes place at the point where the sensation is felt, and would be greatly

---

[1] *Einleitung in die Philosophie* (1892), pp. 133–149.
[2] The most important discussions of this question are Fechner, *Elemente der Psychophysik* (2d ed., 1889), vol. ii., pp. 381–428; Lotze, *System der Philosophie* (2d ed., 1884), vol. ii., pp. 574–602; and the passage of Paulsen above referred to.

surprised to learn that the correlate, say, of an itch in the great toe of his right foot takes place, not at that point, but in the opposite side of his head.

Yet this is the conception to which modern nerve-physiology since Descartes has accustomed us. The mind, which once manned the ramparts of the body round their whole circumference, has been driven back from its outer defences and shut up within its citadel, the brain. In the brain, and in the brain alone, the events are assumed to take place with which consciousness is immediately correlated. The assumption may be said to be this, that in the body two different kinds of events go on, describable respectively as primary and secondary: the primary events being those with which consciousness is immediately correlated, and they happen only in the brain; while the secondary events are those processes, partly in the brain, partly in non-cerebral organs, which have psychophysical value only so far as they are necessary to keep the primary events going.

If this distinction be valid, we may look forward to the eventual performance of an experiment which would constitute the cerebral parallel to Professor Newell Martin's famous isolation of the mammalian heart. Some future physiologist may in like manner find means to isolate the brain and keep it artificially alive, and then, connecting his instruments with the stumps of the cerebral nerves, impart to them impulses so like those they have been accustomed to receive from the eye, the ear, and the skin, that the brain's possessor — I mean its natural possessor, not the physiologist — will see, hear, and feel like a normal person, and never know what has happened to him! Such, at least, is the prevision which follows from the doctrine of the physiologists. Whereas, according to the opposite view, the subject's consciousness, if it still existed, would be impoverished to the extent of the feelings corresponding to non-cerebral events. Which, now, of these doctrines is true?

The Telegraph-Wire Conception

Facts like the presence of insensitive areas between the temperature, pressure, and pain spots which physiologists have supposed themselves to find; or the possibility of mutilating the viscera, when in healthy condition, without causing pain; or the anæsthesia produced by severing a nerve in its course; or the sensations frequently felt in lost limbs — facts like these have led to the conception that the function of the peripheral nerves resembles that of telegraph wires. The nerves are assumed to be merely conductors, engaged in the mechanical task of transmitting impulses from the sense-organs to the brain and from the brain to the muscles, and as completely unaware of their inner commotion as a telegraph wire of the messages it transmits. The brain, on the other hand, is conceived as a sort of central telegraphic exchange, where the reports of the nerves are received, read, meditated, and answered.

This view derives seeming confirmation from the doctrine of cerebral localization. The fact that destruction of limited areas deprives the mind of particular sets of sensations or images is thought to prove, not simply that events there occurring form an indispensable *part* of the correlate of those mental states, but that they form their entire correlate. Consciousness is held to reside solely in the thin crust of cortex enfolding the hemispheres, and all the rest of the body, despite its vastly greater bulk, to be psychophysically secondary.

Well-established as this conception appears, it nevertheless has somewhat the air of a paradox, and we think with amazement of the mind, which seems to fill the whole body and even transcend its limits, being in truth correlated with processes happening within so small a space. The paradox, however, would not trouble us, were it not that the line of reasoning which led to it can apparently be followed out farther. There are the fibres forming the internal white matter of the hemispheres, and there are those which enter into the composition of the cortex itself. Without these fibres to connect its different parts, the cortex could not operate for a moment. But the argument that led to the exclusion of the peripheral nerves would apparently require that also of the fibres within the brain. The psychophysical organ would shrink to an assemblage of cells, and consciousness be correlated, not with a continuous process, but with an aggregate of cell-activities.

Inconsistent as this might appear with what is commonly called the unity of consciousness, it was yet the universal assumption prior to the recent discoveries of nerve-histology. These render it doubtful whether the cells have the predominant importance in neural activity with which we have been accustomed to credit them. By showing that the fibre, notwithstanding its length, is an outgrowth or process of the cell, constituting with it a structural unit called the neurone, and that the nervous system is entirely composed of neurones built upon each other's shoulders in multitudinous ways, they exhibit that system as essentially a system of paths, thus exalting the fibre at the expense of the cell. But if the nervous system is essentially a system of paths, the current in the fibre would appear to be the typical neural event.

Consider, then, the nemesis that awaits him who argues that the nerves are merely conductors. The entire nervous system is resolved into a system of conductors, and he is left without so much as a pineal gland in which to locate the mind.

The Wider View

If, moved by this unexpected recoil of the argument, we reconsider the reasonings that led to the adoption of the telegraph-wire view, we find that the facts do not prove that the correlate of sensation is confined to the centres. Both the facts about the peripheral nerves and the facts of localization might be just what they are if central events only formed an indispensable *part* of that correlate, while peripheral events formed another perhaps less indispensable part. On the other hand, we shall have to admit that central events form the more important part, and indeed a part altogether disproportionate in importance to that formed by peripheral events. By no possibility can we return to the plain man's view, that the peripheral event by itself is the true and sufficient basis of sensation.

This will be clear from the instance of vision. When we consider how vision takes us outside ourselves and brings us face to face with remote objects — until, thanks to this wonderful sense, we actually live more outside our bodies than in them — we might be tempted to assume a power of the mind to issue from the body. But, if the mind possessed such a power, what would be the need of the light-rays passing from the object to the eye? We ought to be able to see just as well in the dark. This possibility dismissed, it might next occur to us that the immediate object of vision is the hitherward end of the light-rays, or the image they cast on the retina. But, unfortunately, the retinal image differs in three respects from the object we see. In the first place, there are *two* retinal images. In the second, each of them is upside-down. In the third, each is turned about from right to left, so that the left side of the object is seen with the right side of the eye, and *vice versa*. It is an old psychological puzzle how, with images thus disposed, we can see the object single and erect; but the fact that we do shows at least how small a part peripheral events and how large a part central events play in the immediate correlate of consciousness.

The same conclusion follows from the time-relations of peripheral events and central events. If consciousness corresponds to the total bodily process, peripheral events must affect it and give rise to feelings in advance of inward conduction. Now, if these feelings had any individual mental existence, it would seem that reaction to them might take place at once. We might begin, for example, to react to a painful burn the instant the hot object touched the skin: which would be better because prompter than the present arrangement. Such a suggestion is of course anatomically absurd; but it serves to bring out the extremely tenuous and shadowy character of the feelings corresponding to peripheral events.

In any case, we must distinguish sharply between the feelings corresponding to peripheral events *as such*, and the feelings to which these same events give rise through cortical projection. What we know as sensations, though localized at the periphery or beyond it, belong not to the former but to the latter class: their correlates are brain-events. The feelings corresponding to peripheral events as such must be too slight to attract the attention and warn of danger, or to provoke reaction. If they exist at all, they can have no separate mental identity, but must be swallowed up and lost to view in that vague sensible total which fills the background of consciousness and constitutes the sense of our bodily existence.

If this view be correct, consciousness is correlated, strictly speaking, with a process occupying the entire sensory-motor arc and extending from the sense-organs to the muscles. Feeling begins the moment this process begins, but it has at the first no separate mental existence. It attains to its maximum, it becomes capable of attracting the attention and provoking to action, only when the process reaches the centres. And, as the process recedes towards the muscles, it tapers off again in the same manner that it tapered on. May it be that the capacious background of consciousness contains correlates not only for peripheral but also for non-nervous events, and that those visceral slicings and tearings which we saw provoked no definite sensation nevertheless gave rise to an obscure malaise, a vague prophecy of evil to come? It cannot greatly matter to us, as practical beings, whether it be so or not.

Alternative Possibilities

But the considerations that might incline us to look with favor on an immediate correlate for peripheral events are inconclusive, owing to a couple of alternative possibilities which have not perhaps been sufficiently considered by philosophers.

In the first place, the fact that reactions gradually become unconscious through habit may have a bearing on the matter. We possess also a multitude of reflex and automatic activities which represent the phylogenetic equivalent of habit. It is generally agreed that the spinal cord and lower brain-centres are wholly, and that the cortex is partly, given over to such reflex and automatic activities. Now, if habit really involves a decrease of consciousness, then all events in the nervous system which take place habitually or automatically must *eo ipso* be external to the immediate correlate of consciousness. And why may not the events in the peripheral nerves be among the number, the nerves being conceived as organs that work automatically? On the other hand, it cannot be denied that the feelings corresponding to automatic events may be among those which are fused and lost to view in the background of consciousness. When a mental state is at once so vague and so all-embracing as the sense of our bodily existence, who can say what constituents it may or may not contain?

In the second place, there is the possibility — perhaps only another aspect of the foregoing — that the feelings corresponding to extra-cerebral events may be existent enough, but, as the phrase is, 'split off' from our upper and personal consciousness, and external to it as other minds are external. The assumption of a plurality of souls in a single body may perhaps appear venturesome in the present state of psychology; but we are not obliged to go so far. We need not suppose that these supernumerary feelings are gathered together into a secondary soul or a number of secondary souls; we may ascribe to them the species of existence assigned to psychical dispositions by those who conceive them as metaphysically real. Thus thinkers who are dissatisfied with the purely physiological account of extra-cerebral events have an alternative hypothesis at their command, and are not compelled to attribute to their correlates an equivocal existence in the background of consciousness.

Now, so long as these alternative possibilities remain open, it cannot be argued with cogency that consciousness must needs correspond to the total bodily process. There is no à *priori* necessity that the line between the psychophysical process and other processes should coincide with the superficies of the body. If extra-bodily events can be external to the immediate correlate of consciousness, some intra-bodily events may be external to it also. Moreover, the brain is by general agreement the psychophysical organ *par excellence*, and it is a little difficult to construe its pre-eminence on the theory that non-cerebral events are represented in consciousness directly. Why should brain-consciousness be so vastly more luminous than heart-consciousness or liver-consciousness, if each organ is equally close to the mind? The facts seem more consistent with the view that such cardiac and hepatic feelings as we experience are due to cortical projection.

In this state of things, my practical determination is this. Since we know certainly that the psychophysical process includes brain-events, but do not know certainly that it includes events in other organs, and since brain-events form in any case by far its most important constituents, I propose to speak henceforth as if the brain-process and the psychophysical process were identical, and to use the term 'brain-process' in this special sense. My usage will accordingly be subject to a double or triple correction, in so far as (1) extra-cerebral events may form part of the psychophysical process, (2) not all cerebral events may form part of it, or (3) both of these possibilities may be realized at once. But I think this use of the term will prove sufficiently accurate for our purposes.

CHAPTER III

EXTENT OF THE CORRELATION ON THE MENTAL SIDE

PASSING now to the mental side of the correlation, the question to be answered is: To what extent are our mental states physically conditioned or accompanied? This question includes two: (1) Does the conditioning apply only to consciousness as a whole, or also to the elements of which it is made up? (2) Does it apply to all mental states without exception, or only to certain kinds? Have judgments, pleasures and pains, volitional decisions their cerebral correlates, or have only sensations and images?

The first of these questions is soon answered. The facts of cerebral localization imply not only that consciousness as a whole is physically conditioned, but that certain at least of its elements, namely, sensations and images so far as they have yet been localized, are correlated with events in particular cortical areas. For, after destruction of such an area, while consciousness as a whole may still continue, some special class of sensations or images no longer appears in the mind. The law of psychophysical correlation therefore applies not merely *en gros*, to the relation between the mind as a whole and the brain-process as a whole, but also *en détail*, to the relation between particular brain-events and those mental states which are sensations and images.

The main question of this chapter is whether the law of correlation applies to all mental states without exception. Opinion on the point is divided. Some writers hold that the law applies universally, others restrict it to sensations and images.[1] In general, automatists and parallelists take the former view, interactionists the latter; though there are notable exceptions to this rule. I think there is of late years a tendency observable, among writers of all schools, to admit the extreme intimacy of the connection of mind and brain, to acknowledge that "the relation to the physical realm pervades our entire mental life."[2] Nevertheless, some are still found to exempt what they call the 'higher' mental states from the operation of the law. The states exempted are usually the consciousness of relation, non-sensational pleasure and pain, and the volitional *fiat* or active attentive effort. The grounds on which exemption is based are partly the inconceivability of a physical correlate for states so intelligent and spontaneous, partly the view that these states are 'subjective' in origin and nature, special manifestations of the activity of the Ego: two ideas that easily fuse into one.

Full discussion of the question would involve, first, psychological analysis of the exempted states, to determine whether a physical correlate for them is

[1] For the latter view see Wundt, *Philosophische Studien*, Band x., art.: "Über psychische Causalität und das Princip des psychophysischen Parallelismus," esp. pp. 43, 44 ; Ladd, *Elements of Physiological Psychology*, pp. 592–596.

[2] Stumpf, in *Dritter Internationaler Congress für Psychologie in München* 1896, p. 7.

thinkable; secondly, examination of the physiological and pathological evidence, to ascertain whether such a correlate exists and, if so, what is its nature. But a chapter conceived on these lines would amount too nearly to a complete treatise on physiological psychology. The present discussion must be much more summary. I cannot attempt to show by analysis that these states may be so conceived that a 'psychophysical representation' for them is thinkable, but must content myself with pointing out that the work of the empirical school represents a steady advance in this direction — recent theories of emotion, pleasure and pain, volition, even of relational consciousness and the consciousness of self, being increasingly psychophysical. Nor can I discuss the nature of their cerebral correlates, a matter difficult of approach except from the mental side and not yet ripe for treatment. Without, however, going into either of these questions, I think it will be possible to establish the existence of such correlates, if we show that the states in question are affected, either in the direction of exaggeration or in that of suppression, by physical influences. At least the reader is invited to weigh the evidence, and ask himself whether it admits of any other interpretation.

Proof from the Effects of Physical Influences

Physical influences acting on the brain should affect only those states which have cerebral correlates. A mode, therefore, of determining whether a given state has a cerebral correlate will be to examine whether that state is affected by stimulants and narcotics, food and fasting, sleep and the loss of it, etc. Let us take up, one after another, the states for which correlates are doubted, and see how they respond to this test.

We may begin with pleasure and pain. The facts are sufficiently familiar. Other things being equal, to be well-nourished is to be physically comfortable, to enjoy good spirits, to live with zest; while to be underfed or hungry is to be weak, irritable, and despondent. In the one case all experiences have a coloring of pleasure, in the other all have a coloring of pain. Sleep, by enabling the brain to rid itself of the accumulation of waste products, promotes happiness and well-being; whereas every stimulus may be painful after a sleepless night. The different forms of intoxication involve profound alterations of the feelings, from the glow of happiness or the massive sense of physical well-being to the lowest depths of despair. In certain forms of insanity these states become permanent, and we have the chronic exaltation of mania or the chronic depression of melancholia. Is it conceivable that states so profoundly affected by physical influences are without cerebral correlates?

The upholder of a limited correlation may reply by distinguishing between pleasure and pain as organic sensations and pleasure and pain as mental attitudes, and maintaining that the former only are affected, directly at least. But this is a doctrine which hardly accords with the facts. If we face these frankly, we cannot fail to perceive that physical influences have produced a strong tendency to a certain mental attitude — in insanity a perfectly irresistible tendency. The only way to save the theory of a limited correlation is to hold that the physical influences first affect the organic sensations, and that these then determine the mental attitude with which they shall be regarded — to admit, in other words, an indirect conditioning as absolute as the direct conditioning from which it is sought to escape.

Let us next inquire whether physical influences affect the attention. The ease and success with which we attend are a variable quantity, prominent among whose factors are food and sleep. If hunger is at first not unfavorable to mental effort, it is because the blood is free for cerebral use while still sufficiently well-nourished; when the hunger of the stomach becomes a hunger of the blood and nerves, the attention begins to flag. Whether the drowsiness that ushers in sleep be due to such hunger, or to thirst, or to the toxic action of waste materials, in any case we have a physical influence affecting the attention. Consider, again, the effects of stimulants: how coffee widens the 'span' of consciousness, heightens the power of concentration, and lends to the faculties just that edge which is necessary for their finest operation; how alcohol at first promotes the flow of soul but then impedes it, narrowing the 'span' of consciousness, weakening the mental grasp, and inhibiting all complex thought. Finally, we may note the alterations of the faculty of attention characterizing insanity, from the maniac's rush of ideas to the painful monoïdeism of the melancholiac.

Turning to the consciousness of relation, it may be pointed out that attention largely serves for the perception of relations. A stimulant which, like coffee, heightens the power of attention thereby enables us to perceive relations that would otherwise have gone unnoticed. Insanity is in part a disease of the judgment, which depends on the perception of relations. Alienists may be wrong in regarding all insanity as brain-disease; but, if they are right, there must be a cerebral correlate for judgments.

To sum up: if there are mental functions which coffee does not stimulate or alcohol benumb, which remain unaffected by fasting and insomnia, and which suffer no alteration in insanity, they may be admitted to be without physical correlate. But since it is precisely the highest functions which these influences affect, this proves that what is higher, instead of being without correlate, is simply correlated with more refined mechanism.

Indeed, if these functions were without physical correlate, why should they be brought to a standstill by the administration of chloroform? Why should not a person under chloroform still continue to judge, to feel pleasure and pain, and to attend? If, on the other hand, chloroform abolishes not merely sensations and images but the 'higher' states as well, does not this prove that all states without exception are physically conditioned?

It will be replied that, if by 'physically conditioned' we mean having a correlate distinct from that of sensations and images, this does not necessarily follow, since the facts can be equally well explained by supposing the conditioning to be indirect, through the sensations and images. The upholders of a limited correlation make a sharp distinction between two sides of the mind: its sensational elements, and the 'higher' states and processes into which these enter. They maintain that the sensational elements alone are cerebrally conditioned, and hold that, if consciousness ceases when the brain-process is brought to a standstill, this is merely because the supply of sensory materials is cut off out of which the mind is obliged to build up its 'higher' states. They think that this explains the effects of coffee, alcohol, and chloroform as well as the other hypothesis.

Those who quiet their minds with this convenient distinction can hardly be aware of the consequences to which they are committing themselves. They suppose themselves to have secured for the nobler parts of the mind an immunity from physical conditioning highly advantageous to the spiritualistic cause; but this immunity will be found to be more shadowy than real.

For, while their distinction relieves the 'higher' states of cerebral *correlates*, it by no means exempts them from cerebral *conditioning*. Indirect conditioning is still conditioning. If the 'higher' states are conditioned on sensations and the sensations on brain-events, then the 'higher' states too are conditioned on brain-events, and cannot take place in their absence.

This, indeed, is inevitable on any theory, being a simple transcript of the facts. The only difference is that the 'higher' states, instead of being conditioned on brain-events of their own, are conditioned on the brain-events corresponding to sensations — which does not seem a very great gain from the spiritualistic point of view. Since the 'higher' states cannot arise unless the brain-events take place, this hypothesis merely denies a category of brain-events without thereby lessening the cerebral dependence of the 'higher' states. The mind remains powerless to think, feel, or will except as the brain supplies it with the materials out of which thoughts, feelings, and volitions are manufactured. It is therefore the brain which has the say whether there shall be consciousness or no, not the mind.

But we shall be told that, while this is so, the exemption of the 'higher' states is a great gain in another way: by providing for their indeterminism. If they had correlates, they would be fatally determined to resemble those correlates, and the kind of thoughts, feelings, and volitions with which we react would be determined by the brain, and not by the mind. Whereas, as a matter of fact, the same identical sensations may excite very different thoughts, feelings, and volitions at different times, the mind's reactions being free.

Let us see how far this is so. And, first, as regards the time-rate of consciousness. Since the mind cannot think without sensory materials, and since these are supplied by the machine-like operation of the brain, the stream of consciousness necessarily flows at the exact rate set by the brain, and cannot move either faster or slower. If the brain gets out of order and runs down with a whir, the mind must keep it company in its mad career; if the brain halts and stagnates, the mind must do the like; if the brain persistently resuscitates a single insane idea, about that idea and no other the mind must continually think. Such are the consequences of being tied Mazeppa-like to a soulless machine.

But hold! some critic will say, the mind has a limited power of reacting on the brain, and arresting or hastening its course. Does the mind exert this power, I ask, without consciousness, or only by thinking beforehand of the desired result? Evidently the latter. But this thought, like all others, is subject to the rule that it cannot occur unless the sensory materials for it are furnished by the brain. That the maniac, by an intense effort of will, may preserve a calm exterior for a time, is a well-known fact; but he does so only through the brain having consented to furnish him with the sensory materials for this volition. What the critic takes, then, for a reaction of the mind on the brain is in reality a reaction of the brain upon itself.

The critic's idea is that the same sensations may give rise, according to circumstances, to very different thoughts: thus two sensations may be thought of as alike, or as near together, or as co-existent; they may be felt as pleasant or as painful; they may be attended to singly, or jointly, or not at all — in short, that the mind is not controlled by its materials, but can deal with them in a variety of ways, at its pleasure. Taken in one sense, this is an indubitable introspective fact : of course the mind is relatively independent of the objects about which it thinks, feels, and wills. It is another question whether its thoughts, feelings, and volitions about those objects are themselves free from sensational elements having cerebral correlates. The profound influence of food and sleep, coffee and alcohol upon our mental attitudes strongly suggests that these attitudes contain sensational elements, quite apart from the objects towards which they are taken up. If this view be accepted, I have nothing further to say : the attitudes as total states are acknowledged to have cerebral correlates. If it be rejected, I can only reply that the alternative required by the facts is to suppose that the attitudes have correlates of their own.

Proofs from Fatigue and from Habit

Another mode of determining whether pleasure and pain, attention, and relational consciousness have physical correlates would be to examine whether these functions are subject to fatigue. For we may assume that fatigue is possible only to functions having physical correlates.

That the attention is subject to fatigue, is the most obvious of facts. Nor does this merely mean that its exercise gradually breeds sensations of weariness and disgust, but rather that the power itself is progressively lamed by its exercise. The power of perceiving relations seems to pass through analogous stages. Even the faculty of pleasure, as in listening to music, may be fresh or dull; our enjoyment is apt to be keener at the beginning of a long programme than towards its close. The fatigue may conceivably be due, in both of these cases, simply to the weakening grasp of attention; but for that faculty, in any event, the argument holds.

A somewhat similar argument may be based on the phenomena of habit. Habit, by universal admission, rests on a physiological basis, being correlated with the increased permeability of the nerve-paths; and memory is to be conceived as a species of habit. It follows that any mental function which can be remembered, or can become habitual, or can be perfected by practice, must from the very outset have been physically conditioned; and, conversely, that mental states and activities without physical correlates cannot be retained, or be perfected by practice, or become habitual.

But retention and habit cover the entire field of our mental life. Whatever we can experience we can remember; whatever we can do at all we can do better with practice. We can remember past pleasures and pains; and if we find it difficult to revive their exact value for sense, we find it equally difficult to revive sensations of taste and smell. We can remember relations; not merely the shapes and sizes of objects, but their positions, distances, similarities, differences, temporal and causal relations remain in the memory with perfect exactitude. Control of the attention, again, is pre-eminently matter of habit: the young student is *distrait*, and must struggle painfully to concentrate his mind; only at length does he attain to an easy command of his powers. Finally, the same law holds of the passions: repeated resistance to impulse builds up a habit of self-control, repeated yielding a habit of self-indulgence; if the law of habit did not apply to the highest manifestations of will, there would be no such thing as character.

Either, then, we must have a new non-physiological theory of habit, or all mental states must be acknowledged to have cerebral correlates

Taking the arguments from fatigue and from habit in connection with the argument from the effects of physical influences, I think a pretty strong case has been made out for the universality of the law of psychophysical correlation.

Are the Correlates Successive or Simultaneous?

We have now determined as fully as the plan of this book permits the scope and limits of the psychophysical correlation on each side, and our study of the facts would be complete but for a single point. This is the question whether the correlates are successive or simultaneous.

This question seems as purely empirical, as much one for natural science to settle, as whether two physical events are successive or simultaneous. Yet, despite its theoretical importance, it has not been distinctly raised by physiological psychologists; and philosophers have been free to assume one alternative or the other, as the spirit moved or the interests of theory required. Without raising it, physiological psychologists have commonly assumed the two events to be simultaneous; and interactionists have often unreflectingly copied the assumption, though its consistency with their theory is more than doubtful.

When we ask ourselves how the question might be settled, an apparently insuperable obstacle presents itself to its determination by experiment. For experimental psychology measures the time-relations of mental events, not directly, but only through the intermediary of the physical events by which they are accompanied. Even the cerebral correlate of a mental state it cannot get at and measure directly, but must content itself with measuring the stimulus, or the motor effects, or the relation between the two. Much less can it get at and measure directly the mental state itself, apart from its cerebral correlate. So that experimental determination of the question seems not only impossible but even inconceivable.

In this state of things, we might be tempted to leap to the conclusion that mental events in themselves, apart from their cerebral correlates, are not subject to the temporal category. But this would be at once a *non sequitur* and contrary to fact. A feeling of pain, or a memory, is as clearly in time as any physical event. Indeed, since physical events, on idealistic principles, exist only as mental states, if mental states were not in time physical events could not be. Suppose I hear a clock strike and at nearly the same moment experience a flash of pain : I am able, roughly and subjectively, to estimate their temporal relation, judging them to be either successive or simultaneous; but this wavering and fallible subjective judgment implies that a certain definite temporal relation is objectively true — in other words, that the mental state equally with the physical event is in time. No valid objection to the asking of the question can be taken on this ground.

Objection might, however, be taken on the ground that the question itself is not perfectly clear and unambiguous. We ask to know the temporal relation between two events — say, sensation and sensational brain-event — but the identity of one of them, namely, the sensational brain-event, is not clear. The question implies that we already know which particular brain-event is correlated with the sensation and entitled to the name of the sensational brain-event, and that it only remains for us to learn whether the two are simultaneous or successive; whereas, in truth, we only know which *is* the sensational brain-event by the fact of its being either simultaneous with or immediately prior to the sensation, according to our theory. We select the event, that is to say, from out of a continuous brain-process, taking the phase just prior to the sensation if we are interactionists or automatists, the phase simultaneous with it if we are parallelists.

We may grant that the conception of the sensational brain-event is to some extent a different one on the three theories. On the theories of automatism and parallelism, the sensational brain-event is not only necessary to the occurrence of the sensation, but always accompanied or followed by it; whereas, on the theory of interactionism, this last statement is not true, but the brain-event might very well occur without the sensation. Nevertheless, since all three theories make the brain-event indispensable to the occurrence of the sensation, this sufficiently fixes the former's identity, independently of the temporal question. On all three theories, the sensational brain-event is that brain-event — and there is but one — which is indispensable to (and, we may add, under ordinary circumstances sufficient for) the occurrence of the sensation.

The question, then, is both legitimate and unambiguous; one thing or the other must be true; the facts appear to admit of either interpretation: yet it seems futile to hope that experimental investigation will ever decide the matter. Certainly, whatever light is thrown upon it in this book will have to come from abstract theoretical considerations. Instead of determining the temporal relation first, and using it then as a means of determining the causal, we shall have to look upon the temporal question as merely an aspect of the causal, and let our decision of the latter determine our view of the former. Possibly both questions will appear in a different light from the vantage-ground of metaphysical criticism. In any case, we must enter upon our discussion of the causal question without having decided whether the correlates are successive or simultaneous.

We have now reached the end of our study of the facts. In the course of this study, nothing has been established to the advantage or detriment of any particular causal theory. We carry away from it a single positive result: the law of psychophysical correlation. This law includes two propositions: first, that consciousness as a whole never occurs except in connection with a brain-process; secondly, that particular mental states never occur except in connection with particular brain-events. But this correlation of mental with physical in great and in small may, so far as we can yet see, be interpreted either in the sense of simultaneity or in that of succession, either in the sense of causal relations or in that of a non-causal concomitance.

Book II

THE QUESTION OF CAUSAL RELATIONS

CHAPTER IV

DEFINITION OF THEORIES

HAVING completed our study of the facts, we are now ready to consider the arguments that may be urged from the empirical point of view in favor of interactionism, automatism, and parallelism respectively. Perhaps it may be thought, after what has been said about the importance of critical conceptions, that our investigation of the nature of matter and mind should come first. But it is desirable that we should acquaint ourselves with the problem in the form in which it presents itself in current debate; and we shall better appreciate the strength and weakness of each theory, the considerations that commend it to its supporters, the objectionable implications it has for its opponents, and, finally, the difficulty or impossibility of reaching a decision on empirical grounds, if we postpone metaphysical criticism till later. Besides this, there are arguments in favor of each of the three theories which are entirely independent of metaphysical distinctions, being founded on empirical facts and principles alone, and they can either be refuted at once, or must hold good on any ulterior theory. For these reasons, it seems best to proceed with the empirical arguments at once. But, before doing so, we must have a more precise definition of the three theories than was possible in the introductory chapter.

Interactionism

This is doctrine of common-sense. It is formed to explain the most familiar of the facts about the relation of mind and body: the facts of sensation, the facts of voluntary action. Its original and proper basis is the assumption of the coequal reality of mind and matter. On this assumption, the only natural construction of those facts is that which says that the mind acts on the body, the body on the mind. The doctrine may still be retained after its common-sense basis has been overthrown: but this is a matter we have agreed to reserve.

The only other point that requires fixing is the temporal relation between brain-event and mental state which the theory involves. This is quickly done. Since the causal relation necessarily implies sequence, sensational brain-event and sensation, volition and volitional brain-event must needs be successive. And the same statement, I may add, holds good for automatism, except that the relation between volition and volitional brain-event must here be reversed. If it be argued that causes pass over into their effects by insensible gradations, and that the difference of time can therefore at most be infinitesimal, the reply is that priority, even though infinitesimal, is not the same thing as simultaneity, and that if the two events were simultaneous they could not be causally related.

Parallelism, on the other hand — to finish at once with this matter of the temporal relation — which is often expressed by saying that brain-event and mental state are opposite sides of the same real fact, seems bound to conceive them as simultaneous. The correspondence which is essential to the theory has its temporal aspect, and implies that the two events begin at the same instant and continue for the same length of time, the first thousandth-of-a-second of the one being synchronous with the first thousandth-of-a-second of the other, the second thousandth with the second thousandth, and so on.

Automatism

This theory arises under the impression of those less familiar facts which seem to prove the dependence of mind on body — the facts which show "how at the mercy of material happenings our spirit is." It follows irrefragably from these facts that brain-action is in some way necessary to the existence of mind. In what way? The most natural idea to suggest itself is that of a causal relation. Brain-action is necessary to consciousness because it is the agency for its production. This view is encouraged by the fact that the brain is a relatively permanent thing, while consciousness is evanescent; and by the further fact that in sensation the peripheral stimulus obviously precedes the mental state, from which it is argued — as we shall see, illogically — that the brain-event also precedes it. The relation thus established for the case of sensation is then transferred — since volitions are impossible without brain-action, quite as much as sensations — without too much ado to the case of volition, and the principle proclaimed as universal that mental states are in all cases preceded and conditioned by brain-events.

The doctrine thus reached is variously expressed by saying that brain-action 'causes,' 'generates,' 'manufactures,' or 'calls into existence' states of consciousness; that consciousness is 'dependent on' the brain; that consciousness is a 'function' of the brain. All these expressions I take from the writings of Professor Huxley.[1]

Here, then, is a doctrine one half of which is identical with interactionism, while the other half is interactionism turned about. From this point of view we might characterize it as a one-sided materialistic interactionism. On the other hand, it agrees with parallelism in denying the physical action of mind and in making the physical world a closed circle; and we might therefore judge it equidistant between interactionism and parallelism. But, once again, it belongs to the same order of ideas as interac-

---

[1] *Collected Essays* (1894), vol. i., essays "On Descartes' Discourse" and "On the Hypothesis that Animals are Automata"; and vol. ix., essay "Science and Morals."

tionism in that it assumes causal relations of some sort between body and mind; and this, after all, is the deepest point of view. There remains, however, this important difference to be noted, that the one-sidedness of the causation results in the brain appearing not so much to determine the character of consciousness by its impact, as rather to *create* consciousness — a materialistic notion. Indeed, the theory is often called materialism.

If I hesitate to apply to it so harsh and metaphysical a name, it is partly because other doctrines than automatism lead also to philosophical materialism, as, for instance, that form of interactionism which makes consciousness part of the energy of the universe and subject to the principle of conservation; partly because I think that the causal thesis, regarded simply as one account of the order of facts, is separable from the metaphysical and creationist thesis to which it undeniably has a strong tendency to lead. Thus it might be said that the sequence of states of consciousness upon brain-events happens in virtue of a law of the universe, is an ultimate fact of nature, rather than something we can in any way understand. The more enlightened automatists have never been backward in confessing the impassableness of the gulf that separates mind from matter. Professor Huxley was even an idealist. He was not the less convinced that the brain, as a matter of empirical fact, 'generates,' 'manufactures,' or 'calls into existence' states of consciousness.

Parallelism

This is a proposition which the parallelist finds it difficult or impossible to accept. He compares the two things conjoined in respect of their nature — surely a natural and even scientific thing to do — and finds them to be totally and profoundly unlike. Nor does the assertion that one generates the other appear to him more credible when qualified by the admission that between cerebral cause and mental effect there is a chasm for thought, that we are not and never shall be able to understand *how* brain-action produces consciousness. The impossibility of understanding how brain-action produces consciousness amounts rather, in his view, to an impossibility of believing that it does or can. Since interactionism appears to him little congruous with the facts that seem to show dependence, he sees himself driven to formulate the connection in some other way than by means of a causal relation. He surmises vaguely that perhaps mind and body are aspects or opposite sides of the same thing. Thus parallelism is the doctrine which first dimly discerns the metaphysical possibilities of the situation and reaches after light, whereas interactionism and automatism represent the smug contentment and self-sufficiency of the non-metaphysical mind.

The parallelist takes his departure from the minute correspondence between mind and brain. Of this correspondence it cannot be denied that automatism furnished a perfectly natural explanation: if each mental state is engendered by a brain-event, no wonder if the brain-event corresponds minutely to the mental state it engenders. But this explanation is now barred by the metaphysical difficulty. It might be thought that interactionism can explain the correspondence: thus, that between sensational brain-event and sensation might be due to the brain, so to speak, imprinting itself on the mind, that between volition and volitional brain-event to the mind imprinting itself on the brain. But a difficulty arises regarding the latter half of this, when we consider that the relation is not merely one of correspondence but also one of correlation; that, just as the brain-process as a whole is necessary to the existence of consciousness as a whole, so the volitional brain-event is necessary to the existence of the volition; since otherwise the volition, at the first moment of its existence at least, would be without a correlate. Now, this is consistent with the brain-event preceding the mental state or with its accompanying it, but not with its following it: since, in the last case, the volition would exist and be efficient in advance and independently of its brain-event.

I do not insist on the absolute logical cogency of this, for I am not now defending parallelism, but merely retracing the steps by which it is reached. But it is obvious what follows from this dismissal of both causal theories: first, that the relation is non-causal, and, secondly — since there is no longer any reason for assuming the brain-event's priority — that the two events are simultaneous.

Parallelism is usually represented as a deduction from the principle of the conservation of energy, or, as a recent writer puts it, from "the postulates of the mechanical theory" of the universe. I think there are other sources co-operating which might of themselves suffice to suggest it. A consideration that carries great weight is the difficulty of causal relations between mental and physical. But its primary source is the minute correspondence and correlation which the facts establish. Let me explain this point. The conception of the physical world as a closed circle would imply an exact 'psychophysical representation' for all mental states, to account for their apparent action. But if, without thinking of the mechanical theory, we *come upon* this exact representation — as we do in fact — it might of itself suggest that the mental states act only through their representatives.

The interactionist may endeavor to adapt himself to the facts of correlation by admitting the simultaneity of volition and volitional brain-event, but may then insist that we have every reason to acknowledge the two events *joint* causes of the next physical event, the motor discharge.[1] This is not interactionism in the ordinary sense, which is the doctrine that the volition, acting alone and not in conjunction with anything else, causes the volitional

---

[1] I assume throughout that the volitional brain-event is followed, and the motor nerve-current preceded, by a 'motor discharge' in cells of the brain which are 'insentient.'

brain-event. It is rather an amalgam of interactionism and parallelism. But let us consider the conception on its merits.

Here two events happen simultaneously, the volition and the volitional brain-event. Between them there is a minute correspondence, the volition being mirrored in all its details — not merely its elements but its character as a whole, its activity and spontaneity, being mockingly reproduced by the brain-event. They happen simultaneously, and are followed the next instant by the motor discharge. Now, it is impossible to consider the case without perceiving a certain rivalry between them for the credit of causing the latter. Both are spontaneously active, and each by itself seems adequate to produce the motor discharge.

Our natural feeling ascribes all the causality to the volition. A volition seems the very type of a cause, and nowise in need of assistance in producing its effects. But what, in that case, is the rôle of the volitional brain-event? Why, in particular, should it ape and parody the volition with such exactness? We seem to have two duplicate causes brought in to produce a single effect, where one alone would suffice. Thus, if we follow our natural tendency and impute the deed to the volition, the volitional brain-event remains on our hands as an anomalous fact, difficult or impossible to construe. There ought, on this theory, to *be* no volitional brain-event: the unaccompanied volition should be the sole antecedent of the motor discharge. But, unfortunately, there *is* a volitional brain-event, which by its mere existence contests the claim of the volition to be the movement's exclusive cause. Hence the revised interactionist account, according to which the two events co-operate, and between them produce an effect the volition would be incompetent to produce alone. But now, this view seems negatived by the very fact of their minute correspondence. If they differed, and were mutual complements, the one might help the other out. But, being duplicates, they cannot but be rivals: it must be *either* the volition *or* the brain-event, it cannot be the two acting conjointly.

Thus, to avoid ignoring the brain-event and getting it left on our hands, we seem forced to regard *it*, and not the volition, as the movement's cause. For, if we make the volition the cause, we shall not know what to do with the brain-event: it will remain on our hands as an unaccountable and altogether superfluous fact. Whereas the view that the brain-event is the cause, and the volition its mere concomitant, seems to fit all the facts into their places.

A similar line of reasoning applies to the case of sensation. Here the incoming nerve-current is followed by two simultaneous events: the sensational brain-event and the sensation. Which of these is the nerve-current's effect? We incline to say, Both; for the wish to give exclusive power to the mental state is not here operative. But did any part of the nerve-current's energy go to the producing of the sensation? Did not the nerve-current produce exactly the same physical effects, in the way of cell-explosions, association-currents, and so on, that it would have produced had there been no sensation? If so, is it not more accurate, more exactly true to the facts, to limit the nerve-current's proper effects to these physical changes, and to conceive the sensation as their mere concomitant?

Finally, what holds of sensations and volitions would hold likewise of the ideational processes intermediate between them: these too would be merely concomitant with brain-events exactly representing them, which latter would alone be operative in determining our physical history.

Thus arises parallelism, with its thesis that our bodily life is a closed circle, in which nervous processes run their course between sense-organs and muscles without consciousness from beginning to end having anything to do with the matter. The detailed correspondence from which we set out has served to make possible a purely mechanical view of the physical world: a view of that world as a self-contained whole, into which mental causality never intrudes, but where every physical event is completely explained by physical causes. The fact still remains that certain physical events — namely, the processes in the higher nerve-centres — are passively accompanied by states of consciousness. Why this should be so — why these processes, of all others, should be thus privileged, why any physical process should be thus privileged at all — parallelism makes no attempt to explain, but contents itself with registering the fact. This facile contentment, this want of complete perspicuity in the conception of concomitance, mark the limitations of the theory, its purely empirical character and need of metaphysical revision and interpretation.

Parallelism and Automatism

Since parallelism and automatism are frequently confused, under the joint name of 'automaton theory' or 'psychophysical parallelism,' I am anxious to make the difference of their theses unmistakably clear. Perhaps I cannot do so better than by pointing out that not one of the expressions quoted above as descriptive of automatism can be properly employed by the parallelist. It goes without saying that on the parallelist theory brain-activity does not 'generate,' 'call into existence,' or 'manufacture' consciousness, any more than consciousness generates, manufactures, or calls into existence brain-activity. Enough has been said in Chapter I to show that parallelism does not make consciousness 'dependent' on the brain, any more than it makes the brain dependent on consciousness. Hence the parallelist cannot speak of the brain as the 'physical basis' of consciousness. He can speak of it as the 'physical condition' of consciousness only in that literal sense of the word 'condition'—as signifying something uniformly given with another thing—in which it is equally true that consciousness is the condition of the brain-process. Finally, the parallelist cannot describe consciousness as a 'function of the brain.' For the word 'function,' in this phrase, is of course to be understood in the physiological sense; and parallelism does not, like automatism, make consciousness a product of brain-action. On the other hand, parallelism does — in virtue of the minute correspondence it involves — make consciousness a function of the brain in the mathematical sense: but an expression so ambiguous is better avoided.

Parallelism is the total and consistent denial of causal relations between mind and body, the view that the relation is of a different nature. The assumption of any responsibility of one for the other, of any dependence of one on the other, not only contradicts its anti-causal essence, but is inconsistent with the thorough-going correspondence it involves. This correspondence applies not merely to the elements on each side but also to their relations and arrangement. <u>The brain-process becomes a sort of translation of consciousness into physical terms, the relation between the two being comparable to that between a sentence in Greek and its translation into English</u>. The correspondence implies, in other words, that the mental element has the same place and function in the mental series that the physical element has in the physical series. If, then, the cerebral correlate of a mental state is a cause, the mental state must be one likewise, and cannot be a pure effect; and if two cerebral correlates are causally related, so also must be the corresponding mental states, and they cannot be mere accidentally sequent side-effects of the correlates as causes. In a word, the parallelism extends to causal relations.

I offer no proof of this conception at present: I simply present it as the logical development of the parallelistic idea, as the view which results from following out that idea with perfect consistency. I think it will be admitted that a view which makes the correspondence extend to causal relations is more justly entitled to the name of parallelism than one which merely assumes a brain-event for every mental state.

The Question of Efficiency

The point just made has an evident bearing on the question of the attitude of parallelism towards the efficiency of consciousness. We come here to a misconception of parallelism very widespread, and due partly to its confusion with automatism; a misconception which can be set right only by bearing in mind and following out consistently the fundamental idea of parallelism, that of a thorough-going correspondence.

Friends and foes alike assume parallelism to involve denial of the efficiency of consciousness. The latter is held to become, on this theory, an 'inert and passive spectator' of physical events, powerless to interfere and alter their course; or, in the consecrated phrase, a 'mere epiphenomenon.' How does epiphenomenalism arise? By immediate inference from the fundamental thesis of parallelism, the denial of causal relations between mental and physical. If the volition is not the cause of its movement, then consciousness is inefficient. If the physical world is a closed circle, then the mind is a 'mere epiphenomenon,' on the roof of things but looking helplessly down. Everything goes on exactly as if it were not present. It is therefore, so to speak, a potential absentee. If it were an actual absentee, the world would be no different.

Such a view evidently makes the position and very existence of consciousness unintelligible. Why should consciousness exist at all, if it has nothing to do? What is worse, it flatly contradicts our sense of volitional efficiency. If there is one thing more than another which seems to the plain man self-evident, it is that his will counts for something in determining the course of events. Epiphenomenalism makes this belief an illusion. And it might be plausibly urged that, if mankind should ever become convinced of its truth, they would inevitably adopt an entirely different practical attitude from that founded on the notion of their being the responsible authors of their acts — supposing it to be consistent with the theory that they should adopt an attitude.

The epiphenomenalist will disavow all such deductions, and insist that his theory in no wise alters the facts of life. It is not, he will observe, as though we were now for the first time deprived of an efficiency which we formerly possessed. Since we always possessed as little and as much as we possess now, our practical attitude need undergo no alteration. The convert to epiphenomenalism who should forbear to act would be like the idealist who should throw himself over a precipice, or the fatalist who should refuse to call in a doctor.

It is perfectly true, the epiphenomenalist will add, that parallelism denies the efficiency of the will. But, though the will, on this theory, is not itself efficient, it is efficient by proxy. For every volition is accompanied by a volitional brain-event which knows its wishes with the utmost exactness, and which *is* efficient. Thus consciousness is not at all in the position of a prisoner, obliged to look on with manacled hands and see his dearest wishes thwarted; but rather in that of a business-man with a confidential clerk, who knows his employer's mind so fully that the latter needs only to think his commands in order to have them executed. The volitional brain-event is the volition's authorized representative in the physical world, and no agent could be better equipped to serve a principal. But, if the brain-event sees to it that the movement regularly follows in conformity with the volition, the will is at least *virtually* efficient in spite of epiphenomenalism.

A precisely similar apology may be made for the inefficiency which is an even more conspicuous feature of automatism. Though the brain-event here precedes the volition instead of accompanying it, the correspondence between the two is not on that account the less complete. And since we can never have a volition which has not been preceded by a brain-event exactly corresponding to it, and which goes on to produce exactly the movement which the volition would produce if it had efficiency, ere too the will is virtually efficient, and the doctrine need make no difference to our practical life.

An instinctive sense of this virtual efficiency is what reconciles the epiphenomenalist to a conception so bizarre. The perception of the actual and literal *in*efficiency is what makes the interactionist declare the theory "in the strictest sense incredible." In passing judgment on it we must distinguish. Since it provides that our volitions shall be regularly followed by corresponding movements, we may admit that the virtual efficiency retained suffices for the purposes of every-day life, and that the theory neither necessitates nor warrants any change in our behavior. On the other hand, it may be doubted whether epiphenomenalism establishes a *nexus* between volition and act sufficient for the purposes of ethics. It may fairly be held that the literal *in*efficiency it involves sacrifices the basis for responsibility left intact even by determinism. Determinism, though it established a rule of necessity, left us still the authors of our acts. It is not enough for the exigencies of ethics that the will should be virtually efficient: it must be actually so. If the true author of the act is the volitional brain-event, the responsibility for the act is shifted upon the brain-event, and away from the volition. So long as the brain-event appears (as from the empirical point of view it must appear) something distinct from and equally real with the volition, the latter's disclaimer of responsibility will have to be allowed, since it cannot be held responsible for an act which it did not perform. Nor will it avail to remind the volition that it knew perfectly well the act would happen. It may retort that it is not even responsible for being what it is, since the laws of the universe fatally determine it to resemble the volitional brain-event.

Thus arises that illusion of mental impotence, that vision of a mind shrunk to ghostly insignificance by contrast with a brain-process holding all the power, which is supposed to be the authentic conception of the parallelists. Such a notion of the mind and its agency recalls the notion of matter usually carried away by the novice in idealism. Idealism, when but partly digested, seems to deprive matter of solidity, of empirical reality, and to leave us shuddering in the presence of a ghostly world. It is supposed to spare matter's visual qualities but abolish its tangible ones, so that inference of the latter from the former becomes no longer secure. Only when we recognize that idealism in no way suppresses or alters the facts of experience, but merely re-edits their nature, does the world become again a world of flesh and blood. In the same way, parallelism seems at first sight to have designs upon the efficiency of consciousness. It seems to tell us that our acts, which we have always supposed to have their spring and source in consciousness, are in reality the product of a material clockwork behind it, and that we err when we ascribe them to ourselves. So inevitable is this inference, that perhaps every parallelist has to serve a shorter or longer apprenticeship in the school of epiphenomenalism.

DEFINITION OF THEORIES

The inference is inevitable, yet is fallacious. Parallelism does not necessarily involve epiphenomenalism. The current notion that it does is due wholly to failure to carry through the parallelistic conception with perfect consistency. Parallelism, so far from involving the passivity of mind, excludes it, and the activity of mind is a necessary inference from parallelism itself.

This becomes evident the moment we consider that the correspondence extends to causal relations. Since brain-events are active things, we must ascribe a corresponding activity to the accompanying mental states, otherwise the parallelism would be incomplete.

This holds, to begin with, of sensations. If the sensational brain-event is an active thing, and cause or part-cause of the ideational brain-event that follows, it is implied in parallelism itself that the sensation must be an active thing, and cause or part-cause of the idea it evokes or suggests. Similarly, if the ideational brain-event is cause or part-cause of the volitional brain-event, then on parallelist principles the idea must be cause or part-cause of the volition.

When we come to the causality of the volition, a difficulty arises: we seem to have reached the end of the mental series, and there appears to be no consequent of mental order for the volition to act upon, or to be its effect. The physical series is continuous, it goes on from volitional brain-event to motor discharge, from that to motor nerve-current, from that to external movement. The mental series appears discontinuous, it contains no members corresponding to the last three physical events. And yet, since the volitional brain-event is an active thing, it follows from parallelism that the volition must be active too: only its activity seems without an object, seems to discharge itself, as it were, into vacancy.

This is one of those difficulties which show, to my mind, the futility of discussing this problem without the aid of metaphysics. <u>I cannot attempt to resolve it here; I am solely concerned to show that parallelism does not exclude, but rather implies, the efficiency of consciousness.</u> This has been successfully shown not only for the case of sensations and ideas, but also for that of volitions; except that the latter have not been provided with an object upon which to act. How the metaphysical theory to be later developed will fill out this *lacuna*, it is impossible at present to explain. But, if such an object could be provided, it is evident that the will would possess not merely virtual efficiency, but that actual and literal efficiency which common-sense assumes and which ethics requires.

CHAPTER V

THE ARGUMENTS FOR AUTOMATISM

AUTOMATISM is our name for the doctrine that mental states are in all cases effects of brain-events, and do not in their turn become causes. We have seen that this does not lie upon the face of the facts considered simply as such. Nevertheless, it is one possible explanation of them, an explanation not without plausibility. Let us consider the arguments that may be urged in its favor.

Professor Huxley's Arguments

Professor Huxley, who first brought the 'automaton theory' to general notice, does not hesitate to describe consciousness as a 'function of the brain.'

While disclaiming materialism, he is "not aware that there is any one who doubts that, in the proper physiological sense of the word 'function,' consciousness, in certain forms at any rate, is a cerebral function." [1] And he argues that, if it is proper to speak of the movement which is brought about by stimulating a motor nerve as a function of muscle, it must be proper to speak of the sensation which arises when the current travels in the opposite direction as a function of nerve. The fact that the one event is physi-

[1] *Collected Essays*, vol. ix., essay "Science and Morals," p. 135.

cal, while the other is mental, suggests no doubts to his mind as to the exactness of the analogy.

Now, if it can be shown that mental states are always effects of brain-events, we shall of course have to accept this description as accurate. But it may be pointed out, first, that in all other cases the function of an organ is physical like the organ itself; secondly, that, whether the brain has this function of 'generating' consciousness or not, it has at all events — and I refer here only to that part of the brain which is immediately correlated with consciousness — another distinct function expressible entirely in physical terms.

What is the function of the spinal cord? It is one entirely expressible in physical terms: that of adjusting the relations of the organism to its environment. Now, the brain has a similar function, only the environment to which it adjusts the relations of the organism is a wider and more complex one, including the past and the future as well as the present. Since in this adjustment the past and the future are represented by present images having brain-events corresponding, the function is still one completely expressible in physical terms. But, if the brain has this purely physical function, it cannot but be doubtful whether it possesses at the same time the totally disparate function of 'generating' or 'manufacturing' states of consciousness. I fully admit that, before this reply can have cogency, some explanation must be offered of the fact that states of consciousness arise in connection with brain-activity, more satisfactory than the ill-understood relation of mere concomitance.

But let us come closer to the exact thesis of automatism. Professor Huxley speaks of " changes in the brain . . . *giving rise* to the feeling or consciousness of redness,"[1] and declares that " we have as much reason for regarding the mode of motion of the nervous system as the *cause* of the state of consciousness as we have for regarding any event as the cause of another."[2] This is a statement which will have the approval not merely of automatists but of interactionists. We have seen that the two doctrines agree in their account of the case of sensation. It is interesting now to observe that they agree also in supporting this account by appeal to the fact — for such is the precise fact — that sensory stimulation is uniformly followed by sensation. In interpreting this fact, both doctrines are glad to avail themselves of the support of common-sense.

But when this fact is interpreted in the sense of the joint thesis of interactionism and automatism, it is altered and perverted. The exact fact is that sensory stimulation — that is, an event at the periphery of the body — is uniformly followed by sensation. It is not a fact, and there is no warrant in the facts for assuming, that — not the peripheral event, but — the cortical event, the sensational brain-event, precedes

---

[1] *Collected Essays* (1894), vol. i. : essay " On Descartes' Discourse," p. 173 (italics mine).

[2] *Ibid.*, essay " On the Hypothesis that Animals are Automata," pp. 238, 239 (italics mine).

and is the cause of the sensation. This is pure assumption.

It may be replied that the process begins upon the physical side, and must therefore affect the brain before it affects the mind. This again is pure assumption. It simply rules out the alternative theory, that of parallelism, which tells us that, though the peripheral event precedes the sensation, the cortical event does not precede but accompanies it. This hypothesis would equally well explain the facts. The only legitimate criticism on it is that such concomitance itself requires explanation — that he who maintains it is bound to tell us why the two events are simultaneous. *Subject to this legitimate demand*, the parallelist account must be admitted to equal standing with the other. And the absolute gulf which all authorities admit between cortical event and sensation, the utter impossibility of understanding how the one produces the other, shows that the unintelligibility is not all on one side. But, if the parallelist account be admitted to standing, it cannot be argued with cogency that in this exceptional case " we have as much ground for assuming a causal relation" as where both events are physical.

Let us nevertheless suppose, for argument's sake, that the automatist account of the case of sensation has been made good, and let us next consider the extension of the principle to all mental states. If automatism was glad, in the case of sensation, to shelter itself under the wing of common-sense, it shows no similar disposition here. There is undeniable piquancy in a theory which admits a causal relation between incoming nerve-current and sensation, but declines to recognize one in the opposite direction between volition and motor discharge. If parallelism by its denial of the latter seems to do scant justice to our sense of volitional efficiency, what shall we say of a doctrine which reverses the apparent relation, and makes the volitional brain-event cause the volition?

I will not deny that, *if* it were satisfactorily shown — of course by other arguments than those discussed above — that the sensational brain-event causes the sensation, a case might be made out for inferring that the volitional brain-event causes the volition, on the ground that a brain-event is necessary to the existence of each mental state. But when the causal relation between sensational brain-event and sensation has been established purely by appeal to the common-sense observation that sensory stimulation is uniformly followed by sensation, it becomes the height of inconsequence to deny an equal validity to the common-sense observation that volition is uniformly followed by movement. If the facts of sensation prove an action of body on mind, then the facts of volition prove with equal evidence an action of mind on body. These two apparent actions stand on the same footing, and must be accepted or rejected together.

Thus neither the automatist account of the case of sensation nor its extension to other mental states has at all been made good. It is difficult to see anything but loose reasoning and assumption in Professor Huxley's arguments — inspired though they are by a just sense of the necessity of brain-action to consciousness — for the view that the brain 'generates,' 'manufactures,' or 'calls into existence' states of mind. And the expressions he allows himself to use have a crudity disappointing to meet with in a thinker of his calibre and very genuine metaphysical powers. The truth is that, though he rejects dogmatic materialism and holds that "there is a third thing [besides matter and motion] in the universe, to wit, consciousness,"[1] he has but half thought himself free from materialistic trammels, and still conceives — or asserts — that this third thing arises out of the other two. But, if consciousness is really a third thing, how can the brain 'call it into existence'? One would think that an organ entirely composed of material atoms might call a long time before anything so disparate from it as a state of consciousness would begin to exist.

Mr. Shadworth Hodgson's Arguments

Mr. Shadworth Hodgson has given such a vigorous and telling presentation of the arguments for automatism as opposed to parallelism — or, as he puts it, of the arguments for dependence as opposed to mere concomitance — a piece of reasoning so apparently unanswerable, until one takes account of an alternative possibility which he has not considered, that

---

[1] *Collected Essays*, vol. ix., essay "Science and Morals," p. 130.

I think we shall find his exposition of the theory highly instructive.[1]

He starts with the proposition that concomitance, or mere simultaneity, is not an adequate scientific conception. The simultaneity, if it be not purely accidental, must be traceable to a relation of dependence or 'real conditioning,' which is the fundamental conception of science. This is the same thing as "what is commonly called causality." Between mere simultaneity and dependence there is a difference analogous to that between mere sequence and causation. "To science the fact of mere simultaneity is always an *explicandum*, not an *explicatio*."

This initial proposition may be admitted without reserve. Certainly, when two physical events are discovered to be simultaneous and the simultaneity is not accidental, our curiosity is excited rather than gratified. And analogy would point to the conclusion that, even between mind and body, the fact of simultaneity is a thing requiring explanation, a thing that needs to be traced to some deeper and more perspicuous relation.

This relation, according to Mr. Hodgson, is that of dependence or 'real conditioning.' Consciousness does not merely accompany the brain-process, but the latter is its 'real condition' or cause.

By dependence Mr. Hodgson means nothing mythological. To Professor Flournoy's objection that the causal bond is incomprehensible and that we

[1] *Brain*, vol. xvii. (1894), review of Flournoy's *Métaphysique et Psychologie*, pp. 103 ff.

must therefore be satisfied with asserting concomitance, he replies that, to establish the fact of dependence between phenomena, it is "not necessary to have a knowledge of what constitutes a bond or *lien* between them," this idea having long since been given up in the physical sciences; but it suffices, as between physical phenomena, to have evidence that the two are in fact dependent. In what, then, does such dependence consist? " Dependence means a relation such that, given the conditioning phenomenon, the dependent phenomenon invariably occurs, and, in the absence of the conditioning phenomenon, the phenomenon called dependent invariably makes default." In short, it is simply a name for "the real order of their occurrence, both in co-existence and in sequence, expressed as subject to constant laws."

What evidence have we that consciousness is thus dependent on the brain? The evidence is supplied, according to Mr. Hodgson, by the facts themselves. Those who limit the relation to mere concomitance are guilty of "a departure from the simple truth of observed facts." " In point of fact, the very same observations which show the concomitance of the two series of events, physiological and psychical, show also the dependence of the psychical on the physiological, in respect of their coming into and continuing in existence." Sensations are "dependent upon, as well as concomitant with, neural processes "; and what is true of sensations is true of all other mental states.

Let us hear Mr. Hodgson's justification of this.

THE ARGUMENTS FOR AUTOMATISM

"We never find sensations setting up the neural processes which are concomitant with them. Take away the neural process, and there is no sensation. Take away the sensation — it cannot be done, save by taking away the neural process. There is therefore dependence of the sensation on the concomitant neural process, but not *vice versa*." We may state the point in somewhat different language by saying that, while we can cause the cessation of a mental state by putting a stop to the accompanying brain-event, there is no analogous way of causing the cessation of a brain-event by putting a stop to the accompanying mental state. "The same reasoning must be taken to hold good also of intra-cerebral processes and their concomitant psychical events or states of consciousness, I mean such as association, thought, volition, and emotion. . . . " So that "all the ascertainable facts indicate dependence (as well as concomitance) of psychical on physiological phenomena, without a trace of any reaction of the psychical on the physiological."

A round assertion, surely; but scarcely a judicious one. Even admitting the correctness of the reasoning for the case of sensation, its extension to all mental states is by no means so obviously in accord with facts. Take volitions, for instance. If we "never find sensations setting up the neural processes that are concomitant with them," we certainly do seem to find volitions doing so — on the assumption, that is, that physical events and mental states ever set each other up at all. If the facts of sensation indicate an action of the physical on the mental, then those of volition indicate with equal clearness an action of the mental on the physical, and the latter is as much an "ascertained fact" as the former. The case of volition is the exact converse of the case of sensation, and by as much as the one set of facts proves the dependence of mind on body, the other set proves that of body on mind. If, on the other hand, the facts of volition do not prove that the mental state sets up the neural process, then those of sensation do not prove that the neural process sets up the mental state. To admit the evidence for causation in the one case, but reject it in the other, is to have two weights and two measures.

But at least in the case of sensations and ideas, it will be said, while we can cause the cessation of the mental state by putting a stop to the brain-event, there is no analogous way of causing the cessation of the brain-event by putting a stop to the mental state. This is an assertion only less infelicitous than the former. In truth nothing is easier or commoner, in the case of sensations and ideas as in that of volitions, than precisely to cause the cessation of a brain-event by putting a stop to the corresponding mental state. Suppose that, while thinking, I come within sight of some painful memory or inconvenient thought, and turn deliberately away, saying, No, I must not think of that: surely, by so doing I cause the cessation of the corresponding brain-event, as effectually as if I went at the cortex with a knife. It is as easy to turn the attention away from an idea as to turn the eyes away from an object. Nay more, it is as easy to turn the attention away from a sensation. To make a visual sensation lapse from consciousness, it is not necessary to look away, but only to think away. So that even for the case of sensation it is not true that we can put a stop to the mental state only by putting a stop to the accompanying brain-event.

In short, whatever evidence can be adduced to show that brain-events set up or abolish mental states can be balanced by opposite cases in which mental states as evidently set up or abolish brain-events. This way of interpreting the facts simply leads to ordinary interactionism. If, on the other hand, we doubt these apparent causal relations in any case, we must in consistency do so in all, and the result is parallelism. Interactionism and parallelism are the two natural interpretations in the premises. Automatism is a theory which maintains itself only by flattering one set of facts and flouting another.

It will be retorted that there are still other sets of facts which justify and even necessitate the automatist account. Can any one consider the relations of consciousness to nutrition and blood-supply, as exemplified by the effects of drugs, or the necessity for food and air; the results of circumscribed cortical lesions in depriving us of special groups of memories; the unconsciousness that results from serious brain-injury; finally, the discontinuity and fragmentariness of the mental series as compared with the continuity and completeness of the physical — can any one consider these facts without recognizing that consciousness depends on the bodily processes in a way in which these processes do not depend upon consciousness? And, if it is so abundantly evident that consciousness is dependent on the bodily processes as a whole, are we not justified in concluding that it is directly dependent on the brain-process?

I reply that we must distinguish between the immediate correlate of consciousness and the rest of the bodily processes. The fact that a whiff of chloroform annihilates consciousness proves clearly that consciousness is dependent — but, on any theory, only indirectly dependent — on our breathing air and not chloroform. It does *not* prove that consciousness is dependent on the brain-process. The sequence of loss of consciousness upon breathing chloroform is observed fact. The sequence of loss of consciousness upon cessation of the brain-process is not only *not* observed fact, but it is wholly unfounded inference, for which not a single valid reason can be alleged.

But it may be asked: Is not the effect of taking chloroform to interrupt the brain-process? The answer is: Doubtless; but from that it does not follow that the brain-process and consciousness are successive, and related as cause and effect. Exactly the same phenomena would be observed if their relation were one of simultaneity and uniform concomitance. I am not asserting that this *is* so: the arguments for parallelism have yet to be presented. I am only urging that the automatist cannot prove that it is *not* so; that his theory, consequently, as opposed to parallelism, rests on pure assumption.

Mr. Hodgson's initial proposition still remains, that mere simultaneity is not a self-explanatory or scientifically adequate conception, but requires to be traced to some deeper relation that *is* so. This I fully acknowledge. But I submit that there are other alternatives than to accept the causal relation asserted by automatism. For instance, the mental state might be the cause of the brain-event, instead of *vice versa*. This may seem to the automatist an absurd suggestion; but he will have to admit that, *if* the suggestion could be made good, such an inverse causal relation would satisfy Mr. Hodgson's scientific scruples as completely as the direct one.

The fact is, that the automatist has thus far presented no single solid proof that the brain-event is prior to the mental state, rather than simultaneous with or subsequent to it. Abstractly speaking, any one of these three relations is possible. It is therefore perfectly arbitrary to single out one of the two correlated events and say to it: You are dependent, and the other event is your condition. Since we cannot discover their temporal relation, we have, from the point of view of natural science, absolutely no means of knowing which event is the conditioning and which the conditioned; and any selection between them is purely arbitrary. For consciousness disappears no more quickly than the brain-process, in case of physical accident: they make their entrance and their exit together. Mr. Hodgson's remark above quoted should therefore read: "In point of fact, the very same observations which show the concomitance of the two series show also some sort of dependence between them, in respect of their coming into and continuing in existence." That is, their concomitance is no accident, but the result of a deeper relation. But what that relation is — whether a causation of the mental by the physical, or a causation of the physical by the mental, or a causation of both by some third thing — natural science cannot tell us, and we must look for light on the subject to metaphysics.

To sum up the results of this discussion: no satisfactory reasons have been produced for conceiving the relation between consciousness and the brain as a causal one, in which the brain is antecedent and consciousness consequent.

And our doubts as to the validity of this conception must increase when we consider certain further points.

(1) Such a causal relation, if admitted, would have a peculiar and unique character differentiating it from all others of which we know. Where both cause and effect are physical, the effect is never merely such, is never a pure effect, but always in its turn becomes a cause. Each event is an effect when considered with reference to previous events, but a cause as related to those that follow. An event which it takes previous

events to produce, but which is itself unable to produce anything further, is something unheard of in the physical realm. We are asked, therefore, to interpret the connection of mind and body, not by the aid of a relation with which we are already familiar in other spheres, but by the aid of one so altered as to be essentially new; we are asked, practically, to invent for this case a relation of which we have no example elsewhere. And this is asked of us, not because we have conclusive evidence that mental states are impotent as compared with physical events, but in the face of the fact that our volitions *appear* as capable of effecting physical results as any mass of matter.

(2) Considerations regarding the nature of the causal relation may increase our doubts still further. Perhaps causation is something more than uniform sequence; if so, that something more may conceivably connect brain-events with mental states, but not mental states with anything further. But, if causality is nothing but uniform sequence (I do not say that it is), then why is there not just as much a uniform sequence between volition and movement as between stimulus and sensation? These are both points to which we shall later return, when we come to discuss the nature of causality.

(3) The impossibility of understanding how a brain-event could create, or even ensure itself being followed by, a mental state, is evidence, to say the least, that all is not luminous and self-evident in the automatist conception.

Nevertheless, notwithstanding these doubts, we have no right as yet to deny finally that automatism may be the truth, and the key to the connection of mind and body. All we can say is that it has not been established from the empirical point of view. It still remains thinkable that metaphysics may establish it, and show us in "that matter which we have hitherto covered with opprobrium" the deepest fact of the universe, and the source of what we call mind.

CHAPTER VI

THE ARGUMENTS FOR INTERACTIONISM

I WILL single out for consideration what I take to be the three strongest, or rather most plausible, arguments for interactionism — arguments which, in one form or another, constantly recur in interactionist writings. The first is based on the apparent facts of voluntary action, the second on the intelligent character marking those of our movements which we call acts, and the third on certain fundamental principles of biology.

Argument from the Apparent Facts of Voluntary Action

This is an argument which makes a great impression on the uncritical, and may be urged with effect before popular audiences; but it turns out, on examination, to rest upon an error as to fact.

It runs as follows. When I will to move my arm, and the movement takes place, I am distinctly conscious that the volition was the movement's cause. Not only so, but the causal connection between volition and movement is directly perceived. It is an integral part of the experience that the volition is the thing, and the only thing, that is responsible for the occurrence of the movement. Any theory, therefore, which denies this causal connection is in conflict with experienced facts.

It is customary to add that the experience of voluntary movement is the original source from which our conception of causality is derived, and that if we deny a causal connection here, where it is directly experienced, we shall have to deny it in all other cases, where it is only inferred, thus reducing all causality to mere sequence.

In stating this argument, I have laid upon the assumption that the causal relation is directly perceived a weight which may not be welcome to interactionist readers. They would perhaps prefer to leave it doubtful just how the causal relation comes to our knowledge, and emphasize our moral certainty of its existence. But this would be more convenient than analytic. There are just two possibilities : either the causal relation is inferred, in which case all that is directly perceived is a uniform sequence, and the argument then holds, as before, that parallelism and even automatism provide for as much ; or, if the interactionist is to profit by this argument, he must hold that the causal relation is *not* inferred, but directly perceived. Readers who dissent from this are requested to consider that they have in mind a different argument from the one I am discussing.[1]

Let us begin by asking the interactionist what, in his view, is necessary to the direct perception of a

---

[1] I will not undertake to determine how far the present argument is that of Bradley, *Appearance and Reality*, p. 324, and of Ward, *Naturalism and Agnosticism*, vol. i., preface, p. ix.

causal sequence. Suppose we have a causal chain consisting of five successive events. Is it possible to perceive directly the causal connection between the first and the fifth, or only between the first and the second, the second and the third, the third and the fourth, the fourth and the fifth? I think there can be no doubt as to the answer. All will admit that a causal connection can be directly perceived (if at all) only between adjacent events. If, for instance, I stand five bricks on end, and overturn the first, and the motion runs along the line, I can see the first brick throw down the second, the second the third, and so on, and I can *infer* that the fall of the first brick is the remote cause of the fall of the fifth, but I cannot be said *directly to perceive* their connection.

This, however, is not the precise admission I desire to extract from the interactionist. The latter might maintain that the causal connection, being directly perceived between the pairs of adjacent events, is *eo ipso* perceived between the events at the ends. He will at least admit that, if the second, third, and fourth events were concealed from view — if, for instance, a screen covered the three middle bricks and prevented our seeing them fall — direct perception of the causal relation between the first event and the fifth would be impossible. For the fall of the fifth brick might, for anything we know, be due to some different cause, such as a spring or a dexterously inserted hand, operating beneath the screen. Consideration of the attendant circumstances might permit us with high probability to exclude such alternative causes, yet only as a matter of inference: so long as the three intermediate events were concealed from view, we could not be said directly to perceive the causal connection between the first event and the fifth.

The reader must be requested to pardon the elaboration of so obvious a point, in view of the promptness with which it permits us to dispose of the argument under consideration. *For between volition and movement there are immediate events which are wholly concealed from view.* These are the motor discharge, the motor nerve-current, and the events which happen in the muscles during what is called the 'latent period.' Of these intermediate events, which are not the less real and indispensable because they occupy but a fraction of a second, the ordinary man knows nothing, and even the interactionist philosopher may perhaps have been momentarily oblivious. Yet their presence between volition and movement effectually disposes of the view that a causal connection between these two events is directly perceived.

Not only so, but when we scrutinize the experience, we find that the causal connection to which it appears to testify is not the same as that asserted by interactionism. The point of application of the volition is different in the two cases. In the experience, the volition appears to act directly on the muscles, and there is nothing to indicate the presence of indispensable intermediate events. On the interactionist theory, the point of application of the volition is to the brain. I need hardly insist on the futility of attempting to prove that the volition acts on the brain,

THE ARGUMENTS FOR INTERACTIONISM

by appealing to an experience in which it appears to act on the muscles!

What, then, is the correct account of the experience, and how does the illusion of a directly perceived causal connection arise? It is plain that all we really perceive between volition and movement is a uniform sequence. What leads us to transform this sequence into a causal connection? We shall be helped in answering this question if we recall that voluntary movement is not the only case in which the interactionist assumes action of mind on body; that he assumes such action equally where an emotional object causes trembling and beating of the heart, where the fear of stammering makes one stammer, where the thought of food produces watering of the mouth, etc. Now, in these latter cases, though on the interactionist theory the causal relation exists just as truly, we have no apparently immediate perception of it. Why the difference? Why do we transform the sequence into a directly perceived causal action in the case of will, but not in that of thought, emotion, and desire?

The reason lies in a peculiar quality of the antecedent in the former case: that will is an active-feeling state, while thought, emotion, and desire are not. Wherein this active quality consists psychologically — whether it be an immediate consciousness of mental activity, or a reflex awareness of muscular strain — is irrelevant to the point. Whatever its analysis, it is an unquestionable fact of consciousness, and that which explains the illusion of a directly perceived causal connection. This illusion arises through misinterpreting as a feeling of the connection between volition and movement that sense of activity which is in truth only a quality of the volition. This account of the case is corroborated by the fact that the paralytic may have to the full the sense of activity without any movement actually taking place.

Thus the first argument for interactionism turns out to rest on an error as to fact: it assumes the perception of a causal connection, where all that is perceived is a uniform sequence. But, if all that is perceived is a uniform sequence, the experience cannot be invoked as an argument for interactionism; since just such a sequence would be observed if the other two theories were true. I conclude (as I concluded in Chapter I) that there is nothing in the experience of voluntary action which tells against automatism and parallelism or in favor of interactionism, but any one of the three theories would account for the facts. On all three, the volition is an active-feeling state, and is regularly followed by the movement. On the other hand, this disproof of a directly perceived causal connection must not be mistaken for a disproof of interactionism. There may *be* a causal connection, although none is directly perceived.

Philosophical critics may feel dissatisfaction with my treatment of this first argument on two grounds.

(1) They may find fault with the very notion of a causal relation being directly perceived. The causal relation, they may say, is never a thing given to the

eye, as a material object is given to the eye, but always something supplied or superadded by the mind on occasion of sense-experiences. On this I observe that, if not directly perceived, it is at least always superimposed by the mind on the strength of something which unmistakably calls for it and which *is* directly perceived. There is the clearest difference between sequences where it is right to think a causal relation and sequences where it is not; and the justification must lie in something directly perceived. Let it be supposed, then, that when I speak of the causal relation being directly perceived, what I refer to is the justification for it.

(2) Interactionists may persist, in spite of this discussion, in thinking that the volition has something to do with the production of the movement, and that the experience informs us of the fact.

Here I can only agree with them. Indeed, I hope, before finishing, to have established this view on what seems to me the only solid basis. But our duty at present is to try each argument on its merits and stick to our conclusions at the risk of paradox.

Argument from the Intelligent Character of our Acts

The second argument is based, not on the mere fact that a mental state is followed by and appears to cause a movement, but on something in the character of the movement which seems to imply that the mental state was concerned in its production. This is its adaptiveness, its teleological fitness in view of the conditions, its seeming intelligence.

When, for example, we hold fast a pleasant stimulus or recoil from a painful one, we cannot — so the argument runs — explain the adaptiveness of the reaction without assuming that the pleasure or pain had some share in evoking it. Similarly, drinking implies the action of thirst, weeping and wringing the hands that of grief, crouching and quivering that of fear, etc. Not only are the acts adaptive in the sense of being suited to the general purposes of the organism, but they have an obvious reference to the feelings, an appropriateness in view of them, in some cases also a retro-active function of prolonging or stopping them, only to be explained on the hypothesis that the feelings were partly or wholly their causes.

The foregoing are examples of instinctive acts. The argument holds with equal if not greater force for acts of volition and purpose. When I conceive and then execute a movement, it is impossible — it is argued — not to believe conception and execution to be causally related. It is true that the relation between movement and mental state is now a slightly different one from what it was before, in that the movement, instead of being merely adjusted to the mental state, is now its outward expression, its physical realization. But the argument holds good just the same. Whence does the movement get its intelligence if not from the mental state, and must not the latter therefore be its cause?

To this argument the law of psychophysical correlation is evidently alone a sufficient reply. If each mental state is accompanied by a brain-event which exactly mimics all its details, and which is, as we have seen, its physical translation, this brain-event may be the source from which the movement gets its adaptiveness. In the case of instinctive acts, the movement may be indirectly adjusted to the feeling by being directly adjusted to the brain-event; in the case of voluntary acts, the movement may appear a translation of the mental state because it is a translation (into non-cerebral terms) of the brain-event. Unless the law of correlation be rejected, this reply must be admitted to be sufficient and final.

But let us look into the argument somewhat further, considering separately the case of instinctive and that of voluntary acts. As an instance of the former, we may take the movement of recoil from a painful stimulus. It is evident that, even granting the pain to be the cause of the movement, this would not explain the movement's adaptive character. The movement is preceded by a mental state, but not by a mental state capable of explaining its adaptiveness. We are apt to trick ourselves by imagining, over and above the pain, some further consciousness that foreshadows and intends the movement. But, if such consciousness existed, it and not the pain would be the movement's cause; and originally it does not exist, but the movement is a purely instinctive response to the feeling as stimulus. Now, if such are the facts, how does it help our understanding of the movement's adaptiveness to know that it was evoked by the pain? The pain does not contain, as part of its analysis, any indication of the movement that would stop it. Still less is it the latter's conscious author; it is at most its mere blind, helpless antecedent. Whatever action it has must be due, so to speak, to its weight — to its physique, not to its intelligence; for intelligence it has none.

Thus, even granting the causal relation, the pain can at most be the movement's stimulus, and deserves none of the credit for the latter's adaptiveness. All the adaptiveness is external to the feeling, and lies in the association with it of the appropriate movement, an association determined by the connections of nerve-paths in the nervous system. The adaptiveness is consequently the work, not of consciousness, but of nature — that is, of natural selection, which fashioned that system.

These remarks hold good, even conceding the appropriateness of movement to feeling on which the argument is based. But that appropriateness is far from being an ultimate fact. The more we compare pain and movement, the more clearly do we see that they are wholly different things and simply juxtaposed, and that no rational connection between them is discernible. If it seems a matter of course that we should welcome what is pleasant and avoid what is painful, that is not because we perceive in pleasure or pain any special power of evoking those movements or in the movements any native appropriateness to pleasure and pain, but simply because custom makes the actual sequences appear the only possible

VI.] THE ARGUMENTS FOR INTERACTIONISM 113

ones. Grant, besides the feelings, the desire to enjoy the one and escape the other, and the conjunction becomes intelligible; but these desires are no part of the analysis of the feelings, and might equally well go out toward their opposites. Taking pleasure and pain in themselves, we can see no reason why pain should not elicit movements of welcome, and pleasure movements of recoil.

When, on the other hand, we turn from the feelings to the physiological processes underlying them, the case is altered. We find that pain is the sign of processes injurious to the organism, and pleasure of processes beneficial; and, in the light of the principles of natural selection, it at once becomes intelligible why we should hold fast to pleasure and recoil from pain. Similarly, eating and drinking, which might seem designed to gratify the feelings of hunger and thirst, serve in reality to supply the needs of the organism. Thus the supposed appropriateness of the reactions to the feelings proves to be really and primarily an appropriateness of the reactions to the bodily states of which the feelings are the signs; and the argument, instead of proving that the movements are caused by the feelings, proves rather that they are caused by the latter's cerebral correlates. In other words, it faces right about, and from an argument for interactionism becomes one for automatism or parallelism.

That the adaptiveness of movements does not necessarily prove them the work of intelligence, is allowed in the admission of a distinct class of reflex actions, which by general consent take place wholly without consciousness. It was the observation of their adaptiveness, it is true, which led Pflüger and Lewes to their hypothesis of a 'spinal soul.' The reason why this hypothesis fell to the ground, and is now a bygone episode of physiology, was not because it was incorrect or susceptible of refutation, but because it was put forward for the purpose of explaining the movements' adaptiveness. Physiologists, confident of the possibility of explaining the latter mechanically, consequently judged it wrong in method and physiologically idle. Nor has this judgment ever been reversed. On the contrary, the ability of the nervous system, within certain limits at least, to " work the work of intelligence" is now universally recognized.

The experience of Pflüger and Lewes should serve as a warning to those biologists and philosophers who, though they admit that reflex actions take place without consciousness now, think that consciousness was concerned with producing them at an earlier period: namely, at the time when the nerve-paths now so stereotyped were in process of formation. This view forms an essential element of the Lamarckian hypothesis, referred to in the introductory chapter. The question is one so momentous to biology, that I may be pardoned for discussing it at some length.[1]

The Lamarckians hold, then, that originally all reflex as well as instinctive actions were consciously

---

[1] For an exposition of this phase of Lamarckism, see Cope's *Primary Factors of Organic Evolution*, pp. 13, 14 and 495–517.

performed; that their present unconscious performance is to be construed after the analogy of automatic accomplishments like piano-playing, which had once to be painfully learned; that these actions, in a word, are to be conceived as ancestral habits. This is known as the theory of 'lapsed' or 'fossilized intelligence.'

This theory evidently differs from the account of the origin of instincts given by Darwin, who considered them in large part at least the work of natural selection, and therefore at no period consciously purposive. Moreover, it presupposes the transmission of acquired characters, and would fall to the ground if that hypothesis should be finally disproved. It is not, however, from the biological point of view that we are called upon to consider it. The question for us is whether it is psychologically and philosophically justifiable.

To answer this question, we must know in exactly what manner consciousness is supposed to have assisted at the genesis of our reflex and instinctive activities. It may have assisted in three different ways: (1) it may have intelligently contrived them; (2) it may have been an unintelligent factor in generating them; (3) it may have assisted in the French sense, being present as the earliest movement's passive accompaniment but taking no active part. This last mode of assistance would be parallelist or automatist, the first two would be interactionist in their implications. Let us see which of these modes the Lamarckians mean.

Is it conceivable that all reflex actions down to the lowest were actively contrived by consciousness? Take the reflexes of digestion, for instance: is it conceivable that consciousness once presided over this function, and found it useful to agitate the digestive tube in a rhythmic manner, or to inject into it a certain juice? The suggestion is absurd. It is no less absurd to suppose that consciousness deliberately contrived the protective reflexes of the spinal cord. Plainly, a consciousness capable of contriving even the simplest adaptive movement already presupposes an organism in a high stage of development, equipped with a great number of reflexes which cannot have originated in this manner. The whole notion of explaining our primary reactions as in this sense the work of consciousness would be such a monstrous *hysteron-proteron*, that we cannot suppose that this is what the Lamarckians mean.

The consciousness, then, that assisted at the birth of the earliest reflexes cannot have been a high contriving intelligence like the human, but must have been a very rudimentary affair, a dim form of feeling. If so, we must apparently choose between the second and the third modes of assistance, and suppose that this dim form of feeling was either an unintelligent factor in generating the earliest reaction or else that reaction's passive accompaniment. We might then argue, as before, that this dim form of feeling cannot be appealed to in explanation of the reaction's adaptiveness; that the adaptiveness lies in the conjunction of the appropriate movement with the feeling; and

VI.] THE ARGUMENTS FOR INTERACTIONISM 117

that this conjunction is the work of nature, not of consciousness.

But it will be replied that this mode of refutation involves a gross caricature of the view refuted; that the kind of assistance intended is the first, not the second, the theory being one of 'fossilized *intelligence*'; and that a form of the first is thinkable having none of the absurdity that marks the caricature. Because we do not assume — it will be said — a consciousness as intelligent as the human, we need not fly to the opposite extreme and assume one wholly without intelligence. The idea is rather that a lowly mind, conscious of pain and dimly striving to escape it, stumbled by accident upon the movement that gave relief; that it remembered this movement and associated it with the pain, and on future occasions utilized the discovery, till in process of time the reaction became automatic. Without intelligent association and retention, it will be said, the durable acquisition of the reaction would be inexplicable. If learning involves intelligence, the Lamarckian view must be admitted; for the case supposed was as truly an act of learning as where the human adult has a disagreeable experience and resolves not to repeat it.

There is no denying that the theory, thus interpreted, is a conceivable one psychologically. Although many instincts must have originated through natural selection, others may (apart from biological arguments to the contrary) have arisen in this manner. But the question that interests us is whether, granting the theory to be psychologically possible, the intelligent character of the reactions thus acquired implies an action of mind upon body.

If such an action occurred, it must have been either on the occasion of the first performance of the movement, or else in connection with the functions of association and retention by which the latter was made permanent. Let us take up the second alternative first, considering the matter from the point of view of physiological psychology. The feeling of pain has a brain-event corresponding, and when the adaptive movement takes place, nerve-currents from muscles, joints, and skin call forth besides a kinæsthetic brain-event, to which the consciousness of the movement corresponds. Between these brain-events a contiguous association is struck up. Now, there is no mental function more universally acknowledged to be physiologically intelligible than contiguous association; unless it be retention, which is the other of the two functions concerned. So that we have not the slightest excuse for assuming an action of mind on body here.

But it is not here that the Lamarckian theory assumes such action. It is on the occasion of the first performance of the movement. The pain, as a mental state, is conceived to be the agency which secures that first performance. By its steady pressure, it keeps the animal reacting until the appropriate movement is hit upon.

Though such an account of the matter is perfectly intelligible, it may be doubted whether it is in any way necessitated by the facts. If consciousness struck off creatively the first idea of the movement, or if it arranged the cells and fibres in the form of the nerve-paths needed for its execution, the Lamarckian account would be necessitated. But the pain admittedly deserves no credit for the adaptiveness of the movement; the latter originates in the material world as the result of happy accident. And, since the pain's only rôle is to spur the animal to action until the right movement is hit upon, I do not see why an importunate brain-event would not do as well. Ah! but the animal knows, some one may say, when the right movement has come, and that is why it stops reacting. Not at all, I reply; it stops reacting because the right movement removes the painful stimulus. But, at least, it may be rejoined, it lays the right movement away in its memory. It does so, I answer, because association and retention are automatic functions of its mind.

In short, nothing could be more misguided than the notion that biology in distress may turn for aid and succor to psychology. To explain an adaptive movement by the operation of feeling is only to double and deepen the mystery. The adaptiveness has still to be accounted for in a manner wholly physical, and the feeling remains on our hands as a supernumerary and, for the biologist, entirely superfluous problem. What wisdom or intelligence, what special mechanical talent do the lowest forms of feeling possess, that they are called in to solve the most difficult biological problems? Do biologists understand so clearly how feeling can direct and influence motion? They may be requested to enlighten the philosophers. The Lamarckian theory, in this form, is a conception that will have to be abandoned.

It would be an entire mistake to suppose that these strictures touch the essence of the Lamarckian theory. That essence is defined by the theory's opposition to Darwinism: Darwinism assumes that all adaptations originated by natural selection acting on the germ, Lamarckism explains them by ancestral experience and hereditary transmission. What the Lamarckians really mean (or ought to mean) is that all our reflex and instinctive activities were once consciously performed, *whether interactionism, parallelism, or automatism be the true theory of such conscious performance.*

Even this, however, is a proposition difficult to admit, for a number of reasons. In the first place, when we reconsider the account of the origin of instincts given above, we find that it presupposes throughout an innate tendency of the organism to continue reacting to a stimulus until the appropriate movement is hit upon. Thus the acquisition of definite movements in the manner assumed is possible only on the basis of an original tendency to *in*definite movements implanted by nature, or natural selection. But such indefinite movements are, in their measure, as much adaptive reactions as the definite ones into which they are developed by education. It is therefore impossible to extend the theory to *all* reactions; it can account for some only by presup-

THE ARGUMENTS FOR INTERACTIONISM

posing others which have to be accounted for by natural selection.

In the second place, I do not see how it is possible to exclude natural selection from a large share, at least, in the production of all such activities. For, whether or no they were once consciously performed, they are at all events performed *un*consciously now. Nor are they a whit the less adaptive because thus performed. Even the Lamarckians expressly admit that intelligent adjustments may *become* automatic, and that without losing any of their adaptiveness. It is admitted on all hands, then, that intelligent adjustments may be carried out by mere mechanism, that the nervous system can "work the work of intelligence." On the other hand, no one can deny that natural selection is capable of producing organs that operate adaptively.

But, if intelligence *can* be fossilized and natural selection *can* produce adaptive organs, there is room for the hypothesis that some or even all of these activities have been thus produced. Natural selection appears as a rival to consciousness, and can be denied some share in their production only on the impossible theory that it has had no action on the nervous system. Natural selection is a *vera causa;* it must have acted on the nervous system; and it would be strange if it had not produced tendencies to action of precisely this character. If we consider that the adaptiveness of these activities is not an isolated fact, but is entirely analogous to the adaptiveness of the non-nervous functions, functions which are not accompanied by consciousness and which have to be explained by natural selection wholly; if we consider, furthermore, that consciousness has to attain to a considerable development under the fostering care of the earliest adaptations before it can have any hand in the creation of new ones, we shall realize what an inversion of the true order of things is involved in a theory which would trace all adaptation to consciousness.

The preceding discussion has already refuted, by implication, the claim that voluntary action implies an influence of mind on body in so far as the movement is a physical translation of the mental state. We have seen that at the beginning the mental state is not the source of the movement, but the movement occurring accidentally precedes and is the source of the mental state; that the movement, with all its seeming intelligence, thus originates in the physical world. Now, even on the interactionist theory, the movement calls forth the mental state only by first calling forth a brain-event, and its seeming intelligence has to be communicated to the brain-event as a condition of being communicated to the mental state. This seeming intelligence, then, which the brain-event receives from the movement, it may give out again into a new movement, without any assistance from the mental state. Whereas the seeming intelligence of the mental state may be due simply to its necessary correspondence with the brain-event which calls it forth.

THE ARGUMENTS FOR INTERACTIONISM

Thus the argument from the intelligent character of voluntary acts collapses, like that from the intelligent character of instinctive.

Argument from Certain Principles of Biology

We come, last of all, to an argument far superior in logical force to those we have been considering, and indeed quite unanswerable from the empirical point of view; though metaphysical considerations suggest the doubt whether the thesis it proves be really that of interactionism.

Speaking of parallelism, Professor James declares: "This 'concomitance,' in the midst of 'absolute separateness,' is an utterly irrational notion. It is to my mind quite inconceivable that consciousness should have 'nothing to do with' a business which it so faithfully attends. And the question, 'What has it to do?' is one which psychology has no right to 'surmount,' for it is her plain duty to consider it."[1]

The conviction that consciousness *must have something to do* becomes more than ever urgent when we consider it in connection with the process of evolution. On Darwinian principles, no organ or function is ever evolved except because of its utility. Natural selection produces no organs *gratis;* they must pay their way by ministering to the body's survival. Now, consciousness is a thing evolved; indeed, on no other function does nature seem to have lavished such tender care. The conclusion is inevitable that consciousness must be of use. And, when we consider the

[1] *Principles of Psychology*, vol. i., p. 136.

various things which we do with our minds, we cannot ignore that a majority of them are of use. But, for consciousness to be of use, it must act on the body. Theories, therefore, which like parallelism and automatism make the bodily organism sufficient unto itself, and tell us that it would run on exactly as well without consciousness as with it, are inconsistent with evolutionary principles and biologically absurd.[1]

This must be admitted to be, for anything we can now see, a valid and conclusive argument. It does not, like its predecessors, contain errors of reasoning or false assumptions as to fact. It certainly seems successfully to prove the interactionist thesis. We cannot reply, as we could to its predecessors, that consciousness is accompanied by a brain-process which exactly mimics all its details, and which can render as well the biological services demanded of consciousness. The existence of consciousness as a fact additional to the brain-process is the whole point of the argument. Since consciousness appears to be an evolutionary product, we cannot demur to the application to it of evolutionary principles, and the interactionist conclusion seems to follow.

Nevertheless, even from our present point of view we can see that all is not well with this conception, but that it is afflicted with a fatal weakness. For, although on evolutionary principles the physical world would contract to produce a consciousness on

---

[1] For this argument, see James, art.: "Are We Automata?" in *Mind*, vol. iv. (1879), pp. 3, 4; Bradley, art.: "On the Supposed Uselessness of the Soul," in *Mind*, N. S., vol. iv. (1895), p. 176; Ward, *Naturalism and Agnosticism*, vol. ii., pp. 38, 39.

condition of the latter being of use, yet this is a contract which the physical world would be powerless to perform, for the simple reason that the physical world is physical, and consciousness, unfortunately, mental. Bodies and brain-processes the physical world can produce, they are but collocations of atoms: but thoughts and feelings are beyond its capacity. Yet it is only on the assumption that the physical world has, as a matter of fact, succeeded in this impossible attempt that the argument we are considering has validity!

Here, once again, we reach the boundary-line which separates empirical science from metaphysics. It must rest with metaphysics to decide whether the biological argument has a core of soundness, or is to be rejected as altogether worthless.

CHAPTER VII

THE ARGUMENTS FOR PARALLELISM

THERE can be no question what are the two arguments most commonly appealed to by parallelists in support of their doctrine. The one is based on the principle of the conservation of energy, the other has to do with the nature of the causal relation.

Argument from the Principle of the Conservation of Energy

This is, of all arguments for parallelism, the one most frequently heard, and indeed — taken in conjunction with the facts showing the intimacy of the connection of mind and body — the original source of conviction of most parallelists. Judgments as to its validity are various.

Physicists tell us that, if we consider any material system in isolation from others, the amount of energy, potential as well as kinetic, contained in it is a constant quantity, and is neither increased nor diminished by any transactions between the parts of that system. It is but a step to the deduction that the same must hold true of the sum of all material systems, the physical world as a whole. And we found as great a physicist as Helmholtz confidently describing the principle of the conservation as "a universal law of all natural phenomena."

This principle implies that the amount of energy contained in all the effects in the universe at a given moment is exactly equal to the amount contained the moment before in all the causes. But, if so, the physical action of mind is excluded. For to explain the cause of any event is to trace the energy contained in it to its source, and this source must be some preceding physical fact possessing the exact amount of energy now contained in the effect, since otherwise the total sum of energy would not be constant. But, to just the degree that an event was due to the action of mind, its energy would not be traceable to physical sources, but would be a contribution made by mind and an increment to the common store; and the principle of conservation would be infringed.[1]

The effect of this principle is thus to make of the physical world a 'locked system,' into which non-physical causes never intrude, but where all physical events are fully explained by physical causes. This purely physical explicability of all physical events must apply to the brain, as much as to the rest of the physical world; and it follows — to pass at once to the most interesting case — that the volitional brain-event must be completely explicable as the result of the stored-up energy of the nerve-cells, the influences exerted through the blood, the currents from the periphery and from other centres, without any help from the volition.

---

[1] For this argument, see Wundt, *Physiologische Psychologie*, 3rd ed., vol. ii., p. 544, 4th ed., vol. ii., p. 639; Höffding, *Outlines of Psychology*, p. 55; Münsterberg, *Willenshandlung*, p. 7.

This methodological tendency in physiology is evidently the exact counterpart of the procedure introduced into biology by the doctrine of evolution. Biologists were formerly in the habit of explaining the origin of new species or the first appearance of living things by creation, that is, by miracle: the doctrine of evolution rules out supernatural interferences, and explains all events by natural causes. So parallelism denies the minor miracle of interference with the organism by the finite mind, thus applying to the microcosm a principle already applied by biology to the macrocosm.

How may the interactionist meet this argument from the principle of conservation?

His most obvious course would be to impugn the major premise — the universal validity of the principle. This, however, is a course from which the interactionist commonly shrinks. He is accustomed to hear this principle acclaimed as the greatest achievement of modern physics. He cherishes a wholesome respect for the generalizations of science, and is by no means averse on general grounds to recognizing in the physical world a reign of universal law. Hence his first impulse is to seek to patch up an accommodation between the principle of conservation and the physical efficiency of mind.

Such an attempt certainly seems foredoomed to failure. Energy is defined as " the capacity of doing work," and work is said to be done whenever a mass or a molecule is made to move or has its previous motion arrested. "If feelings are causes," says Professor James, "of course their effects must be furtherings and checkings of internal cerebral motions."[1] What is this but to do work, and by doing it increase or diminish the amount of energy in the brain? When by the action of an external agent, says Clerk Maxwell, the configuration of a system is changed, the external agent is said to do work, and the energy of the system is increased in proportion to the amount of work done.[2] Is not the brain such a system, and the mind exactly in the position of an external agent? If so, how can the mind influence the brain without violating the principle of conservation?

Incompatible as this principle appears with the physical efficiency of mind, ingenious attempts have been made to reconcile them, the merits of which it now befalls us to consider.

(1) The first of these goes back to Descartes, who had a principle of the conservation of *motion* which was the forerunner of our modern principle of the conservation of energy. Descartes saw that the mind cannot bring forth a new motion in the brain if the total sum of motion is to remain constant. But he thought that it might alter the *direction* of an already existing motion without altering its quantity. This is an idea that often recurs at the present day; indeed, it is the favorite device of the reconcilers. They think that the mind, without increasing or

[1] *Principles of Psychology*, vol. i., p. 137.
[2] *Matter and Motion*, p. 60.

diminishing the energy of the brain-molecules, may produce a little change in their direction, and so exert an influence upon the brain-process without infringing the principle of conservation.

The first thing that strikes one, in considering this idea, is that it attributes to the mind a rôle often played by physical objects; but that, when physical objects produce changes in each other's direction, they never do so without the expenditure of energy. Thus a moving billiard-ball might, by an adroit stroke of the cue, be made to move at a different angle with exactly the same velocity as before : but only by the cue striking it with a certain amount of force. Or the same result might be accomplished by means of a perfectly elastic cushion : but only by the ball losing its energy to the cushion and receiving it again. In each instance, the result comes clearly under the head of those changes in the configuration of a system which, according to Clerk Maxwell, cannot be effected without the expenditure of energy. This appears if we consider that, for the cue to impart to the ball its old velocity, a greater expenditure of energy is requisite than if the ball were simply arrested; one part of the energy going to arrest the ball, and the other part to produce the new motion. Thus the original velocity, instead of being a help, is a hindrance, in exact proportion to its amount and to the amount of change of direction effected. But, if physical objects can change the direction of other objects only by expending energy, must not the same be true of the mind?

It will be replied that, since the velocity of the billiard-ball is the same after as before, there has been no alteration of the total sum of energy, and consequently no infringement of the principle of conservation. But consider how this result has been attained. The ball has first given up all its energy to the cushion or cue, and has then received an equal amount in return. Without such a double transfer of energy, no change in its direction could have been effected. Now, the cue or cushion to which it gives up its energy is still part of the physical world; hence the energy thus given up remains part of the total sum, and that total sum is conserved. But when for the cue or cushion we substitute the mind, this no longer holds true. The mind, not being a part of the physical world, is unable to harbor that energy even for the infinitesimal instant needed to make the transfer; and the result is that the energy has been momentarily annihilated. In short, the hypothesis comes to this: that the mind, instead of simply creating energy, has first annihilated it and then recreated it in equal amount. But such an hypothesis, so far from being consistent with the principle of conservation, violates it twice.

Even assuming the reception and recommunication of the energy to be instantaneous, and the total sum therefore at no time actually reduced, it is the letter of the law, not its spirit, that has been observed. Suppose the mind could subtract from the energy of one molecule, and simultaneously add an equal amount to that of another at a distant point of space:

would such a transaction be consistent with the principle of conservation? As little as the annihilation of a particle in one place and its recreation in another would be consistent with the principle of the indestructibility of matter. It would be a translocation of energy, not a transformation of it in the sense of the principle. For the latter applies, originally and primarily, to the connection between particular causes and effects, and only secondarily and by consequence to the connection between the sum of all the causes and the sum of all the effects. It therefore implies a certain continuity between the cause and the effect whose energy it asserts to be equal.

Now, in such a translocation of energy to distant points the breach of continuity, the physical *hiatus*, is only quantitatively greater than where the mind is assumed to alter the direction of a molecule. The altered motion is not the immediate effect of the original motion, in such wise that the same amount of energy appears at every point of the process, but between the two a mental state is interposed which is the medium of transference and source of the alteration. There is therefore no such smooth transformation as the spirit of the principle requires, but a physical *hiatus* and consequent breach of the principle, as truly as in the supposed translocation of energy to distant points. Of course, if the mental state could be conceived as an embodiment of energy analogous to the cue or cushion whose place it takes, there would be no breach, but the total sum of energy in brain and mental state together would be conserved.

But this is a materialistic way of conceiving the mind from which most interactionists will recoil; moreover, it constitutes a method of reconciliation quite distinct from the one we are considering.

A different yet analogous suggestion is made by Professor Wundt, not as an argument for interactionism, but to support his later view that parallelism should not be put forward as a deduction from the principle of the conservation of energy.[1]

Professor Wundt holds that the mind might act on the brain without violation of this principle, by preventing the passage of potential energy into actual. If, for example, a stone, on being raised by physical means to a certain height above the ground, could be held suspended there by miracle or by effort of will, this would involve no breach of the principle of conservation, since the potential energy in the stone would simply be prevented from becoming actual.

On this suggestion the same line of comment is appropriate as before. Again the mind is intrusted with a task ordinarily undertaken by physical objects; and again we are justified in demanding that its action should be judged by the same principles. Suppose a stone to be thrown vertically into the air; on reaching the limit of its course, it remains for an instant suspended, in virtue of the equilibrium of the forces acting on it; but at the next instant the pull of gravity makes itself felt, and the stone must fall,

---

[1] *Philosophische Studien*, Band x., art. : " Über psychische Causalität und das Princip des psychophysischen Parallelismus," pp. 30, 31.

unless some countervailing force prevents. This may be represented by a roof or wall. Now, it is clear that the roof or wall resists the tendency of the stone to fall, opposing an equal and opposite action to action of the stone. Then a similar action is demanded of the mind by the hypothesis that it prevents the passage of potential energy into actual. And the proposition holds good, as before, that such action can be reconciled with the principle of conservation only on the hypothesis that the mind is itself an embodiment of energy.

We may now generalize this proposition, and affirm that any view which ascribes physical action to the mind, no matter what the nature of that action, can be reconciled with the principle of conservation only on the hypothesis that the mind is itself a form of energy. For when by the action of an external agent the configuration of a system is changed, the external agent does work, and the energy of the system is increased in proportion to the amount of work done.

Entirely different from the foregoing is the attempt at reconciliation made by Professor Stumpf in his presidential address before the Congress of Psychologists at Munich.[1] Instead of looking for loopholes in the principle of conservation, he seeks to accomplish his end by means of certain quasi-metaphysical hypotheses as to the relation of mind and

[1] *Dritter Internationaler Congress für Psychologie in München* 1896, pp. 3–16.

matter. He suggests two such hypotheses, and leaves us to take our choice.

(1) The first is the hypothesis to which the analogy of the action of mind to that of a cue or cushion, a roof or wall seems to invite us: that consciousness is a form of energy, and thus one member, along with other members not mental but physical, of the total system to which the principle of conservation applies. This, it may be noted, is the view of Mr. Herbert Spencer, who regards consciousness as "only the occasional result of the 'transformation' of a certain amount of 'physical force' to which it is 'equivalent'"[1]; and apparently also of Professor Huxley, who holds out the hope that we may yet determine the mechanical equivalent of consciousness, as we have determined that of heat.[2]

To dispose of this suggestion, it is not sufficient, at the present stage of our inquiry, to affirm that, as a matter of fact, consciousness is *not* a form of energy. For, while it is plain that thoughts and feelings are not, like masses and motions, visible and tangible facts, and that consciousness therefore cannot without absurdity be conceived as a form of *motion*, yet it is entirely conceivable that, whenever consciousness arises, a certain quantity of motion has to disappear, being expended in its production; that consciousness therefore, though not itself physical, fills, so to speak, a gap or pocket in the physical world. At least

[1] The words are Professor James's — see *Principles of Psychology*, vol. i., p. 154, note.
[2] *Collected Essays* (1894), vol. i., essay "On Descartes' Discourse," p. 191.

this view must be admitted to be a possible one until metaphysical criticism shall have shown its untenableness.

Nevertheless, it involves, we can see even now, a difficulty well-nigh insurmountable. The difficulty is the same that threatens automatism, to which this theory is in one aspect closely allied. It concerns the transition between the motion and the consciousness, the apparent origin of the one out of the other. Whether consciousness be conceived as a pure effect or as an effect which in its turn becomes a cause, this difficulty remains just the same. The two things being disparate in nature, what we have is not properly a transformation but rather a transmutation, the annihilation of one kind of existence and the creation of another in its place. Only in case we understand by energy, not what physicists understand by it, namely, either present motion or else position as betokening the possibility of future motion, but an unseen reality of which motion is the phenomenal sign, does the hypothesis of its transformation into consciousness begin to be conceivable; and, even then, only on the assumption that this reality has a nature sufficiently like that of consciousness to permit the evolution of consciousness out of it. But this is an illegitimate use of the term. Energy properly means either present motion or the future possibility thereof; and neither of these things is in any way fitted to give birth to consciousness.

(2) For the benefit of thinkers who on philosophi-

cal grounds object to conceiving consciousness as a form of energy, Professor Stumpf suggests the alternative hypothesis that mental states are causes and effects of physical events in a way that involves no expenditure or creation of physical energy. That is, the incoming nerve-current gives rise to two things: a sensational brain-event to which it transmits all its energy, and a simultaneous sensation to produce which no energy is required; and, in the same way, two things call forth the motor discharge: a volitional brain-event which contributes all the energy, and a simultaneous volition which, though contributing none, is nevertheless its cause.

This view makes the physical world a 'locked system' from the point of view of energy, but not from that of causation; causation being distinguished from the transference of energy as something wider. Though exact quantitative relations connect incoming nerve-current with sensational brain-event and volitional brain-event with motor discharge, it is held that this does not prevent the sensation from being part-effect of the nerve-current, the volition from being part-cause of the motor discharge. The sensation, so it is argued, follows upon the nerve-current, and must be the effect of something, and there is nothing else for it to be the effect of but the nerve-current; the volition precedes the motor discharge, and intends it, and has every title to be esteemed its cause. The nerve-current is the 'indispensable precondition' of the sensation, the volition the 'indispensable precondition' of the motor discharge: and 'indispensable precondition' is held to be the same thing as cause.

An ingenious attempt at reconciliation, surely. The only trouble is that interactionism, when thus interpreted, becomes indistinguishable from parallelism. For the only *nexus* now claimed between incoming nerve-current and sensation, between volition and motor discharge, is one of uniform sequence: but parallelism asserts as much. Parallelism has no difficulty in admitting that the former of each of these pairs is the 'indispensable precondition' of the latter. Or does the interactionist perchance conceive that the volition in some inscrutable way *co-operates* in producing the motor discharge? A 'real tie' being a superstition, and quantitative relations connecting the motor discharge only with the brain-event, he may be invited to explain wherein such co-operation differs from uniform antecedence.

The truth is that this is a sham kind of causation, which retains the name after sacrificing the thing, and is in reality indistinguishable from complete inefficiency. For it is admitted that the motor discharge is connected with preceding physical events by equations which account for all its energy, and that it is as fully explained by those preceding physical events as one physical event is ever explained by another; so that, if this event happened outside the body, the explanation would be deemed entirely sufficient, and further explanation superfluous. It is admitted, in other words, that the physical events succeed each other exactly as if they were unaccompanied by consciousness. But this is precisely the contention of the parallelists. So that Professor Stumpf's second hypothesis may be said to be nothing more nor less than an unintentional surrender to the parallelists.

To sum up: we are confronted by the following dilemma. Either in the production of a sensation a certain quantity of energy is used up, in which case we have a *lacuna* in the physical world, a *lacuna* filled out with consciousness, and consciousness must therefore be looked upon as a form of energy; or else *no* energy is expended in producing the sensation, the latter is not properly the effect of the preceding physical events at all but only their uniform consequent, it is therefore the uniform concomitant of the sensational brain-event, and the theory that results is parallelism. I conclude that the only way to reconcile interactionism with the principle of conservation is to conceive consciousness as a form of energy.

This is a conception to which, despite the recommendations of so able an advocate, few interactionists will feel themselves drawn. The difficulties inseparable from a materialistic account of the origin of consciousness will prevent its acceptance by circumspect thinkers. The interactionist has therefore no alternative left but to attack the universal validity of the principle of conservation. Considering the authority of this principle's promulgators and the high consideration it enjoys, this is a course requiring courage; but the interactionist who conceives that the efficiency of consciousness is at stake will be found equal to the task. He will boldly describe the principle as " only a valid and useful working-hypothesis applicable to certain classes of physical phenomena."

Let us consider the reasons that might be advanced in support of such a contention. In the first place, it might be pointed out that the application of the principle of conservation to the brain presupposes the truth of the mechanical theory of life; and the universality of the principle might then be assailed by way of this premise. Such a course, however, would be at once unwise, unnecessary, and ineffective as an argument. Unwise, because an assumption which has been the working-hypothesis of physiology since there was such a science, and under whose inspiration all its greatest discoveries have been made, stands too good a chance of being true. Unnecessary, because the same laws may apply to the brain as to inorganic matter, but the principle of conservation be no universal law. Ineffective as an argument, because a clear conception like the mechanical theory is to be preferred to an obscure one like vitalism, with its anti-scientific postulate of the non-resolvability of vital into simpler mechanical processes. In view of the past history and present methods of physiology, it may fairly be held that, at the very least, the burden of proof rests on him who calls the mechanical theory in question. Hence no valid objection to the extension of the principle of conservation to the brain can be taken on this ground.

The interactionist who shrinks from making consciousness a form of energy has, therefore, a single course left: to attack the universality of the principle of conservation directly. He must affirm that this principle is not a necessary law of thought in physical matters, but merely an induction from experience, which as such can lay claim only to probable truth. He must point out that it has been arrived at solely from the study of inorganic phenomena, and that it involves illegitimate generalization to extend it without further ado to organic. He must brand it as a glaring instance of *petitio principii* to take a principle provisionally established for a part of the physical world from which mind is absent, to apply it to a part of that world where mind is present, and to draw the startling inference that mind is physically inefficient.

The premise of this reasoning — the merely inductive value of the principle of conservation — though it would be denied by some parallelists, is freely admitted by others. The reasoning is certainly plausible, and may seem to the convinced interactionist to justify him in rejecting the parallelist's argument as unwarrantable and even impertinent. The parallelist himself must admit that, so long as the relations of mind and matter are conceived in ordinary dualistic terms, his argument remains inconclusive. If the principle of conservation is an induction from experience, based solely on the study of physical events which are unaccompanied by consciousness, it cannot be argued without fallacy that where physical events are accompanied by consciousness it must hold good just the same. And I think even the working physicist is usually a little taken aback by the use which the parallelist makes of his principle.

Either, then, the parallelist must show this principle to be a necessary law of thought in physical matters, which is an undertaking attended with difficulty; or else, by means of metaphysical criticism, he must exhibit the relations of mind and matter in such a light that the interactionist will withdraw his objections. Certain it is that, so long as consciousness and the brain appear separate but connected realities which conceivably *might* influence each other, no appeal to this principle in proof that they do not will soften the hard heart of the interactionist or pass muster in the court of logic.

It is relevant, nevertheless, to consider that what hardens the interactionist's heart is his conviction that the efficiency of consciousness is at stake. Otherwise he would be only too glad to recognize in the principle of conservation a universal law and master-generalization of science. It is the fear of epiphenomenalism that makes him adopt those obstructionist tactics and contest the physicist's demonstration inch by inch.[1] But what if this fear were illusory? What if parallelism makes as ample and sounder provision for the efficiency of mind? The interactionist who recognized this would be condemned to an about-face like that of theologians with reference to the doctrine of evolution. It would be

[1] See the first volume of Ward's *Naturalism and Agnosticism*.

too clear that, when we apply the principle of conservation to the brain, we exercise as legitimate a function of thought as when we assume the law of gravitation to hold true in the most distant regions of space.

Argument from the Nature of the Causal Relation

The second argument for parallelism, and the last we shall consider, holds that the causal relation is of such a nature that it cannot connect physical events with mental or mental events with physical, but only events of the same order — either two physical or (possibly) two mental events.[1]

This contention is clearly a piece of metaphysics. Indeed, it is pretty much the only piece to be met with in current discussions of the relation of mind and body, which otherwise abstain from metaphysical criticism successfully. It is a little curious that the feeling of the metaphysical incongruity of interaction (an incongruity to be explained in our metaphysical part) should express itself in this form. It would seem so much more natural to say, Matter is not the sort of thing upon which mind can act, than to say, Causality is not the sort of relation that can connect mind with matter. But we must take philosophers as we find them.

Since the argument is metaphysical in its nature, its discussion might seem to belong in our second part. And, unquestionably, its full force and value will appear only after metaphysical criticism of the

[1] For this argument, see Wundt, in *Philosophische Studien*, Band vi., art.: "Zur Lehre von den Gemüthsbewegungen," p. 353.

conceptions of matter and mind. But we planned, before undertaking such criticism, to study the issue between the three theories as it appears in current debate; and as this argument cuts a considerable figure there, our study would be incomplete without it. Moreover, it is commonly urged quite without reference to critical conceptions of matter and mind, and we may consider and criticize it as commonly urged. Finally, the relation of cause and effect has its empirical side: the work of physical science consists largely in the discovery of causal relations; and if we consider the nature and elements of the causal relations there discovered, this may help us to decide whether similar relations are possible between mental and physical.

Let us inquire, then, first of all, as to the nature of the causal relation where both cause and effect are physical. Let us take a simple case of causal action — say, that of one billiard-ball communicating its motion to another — and ask wherein the causal bond consists.

Here the cause is the motion of the first ball up to the moment of impact, and the effect the motion of the second ball from that moment onward. So far, we have simply a sequence of phenomena. Is the sequence of phenomena all, or is there more? Naïve thought vigorously insists that there is more: otherwise, it is argued, there would be no difference between a causal sequence and an accidental one. In what, then, does this *more* consist? It consists, for naïve thought, in a certain power or influence proceeding from the cause and manifesting itself in the effect. It consists in a sort of constraint put by the cause upon the effect, necessitating the latter to happen. This power or influence is not the less real or efficacious because unseen. It is what transforms the world from a ghostly phantasmagoria into a scene of real activity. This it is which connects cause and effect in a way in which accidental sequents are not connected, constituting a 'real tie' between them.

Such an unseen influence or 'real tie' the great philosophers since Hume regard as a superstition. For all that we can perceive through the senses is a sequence of visual and tactile phenomena; yet it is through the senses alone that our knowledge of physical events and their causal or accidental connections is obtained. Even between mental states — as, for instance, where a volition helps in the recall of a forgotten name — we perceive no influence or 'real tie,' but merely a phenomenal continuity. The notion of such a 'tie' therefore appears fictitious.

It will not do, however, to brand a notion as fictitious unless one is prepared to explain how it arises. For such notions are never inventions out of the whole cloth. Hume's explanation is, that frequent experience of a sequence begets in us a confident expectation of the effect, and that we project this strong expectation into the cause in the form of influence or power. We shall be more likely to feel the adequacy of this account if we consider certain further facts about the relation which explain, as it seems to me, why we regard power as an *unseen* property of the cause.

Consider how the word 'power' and its equivalents are used in ordinary speech. These words often have a purely phenomenal signification. When, for instance, an express train thunders by, or a strong wind slams a door, we speak of the occurrences as exhibitions of force or power; meaning simply that a phenomenal thing has produced intense effects, likewise phenomenal, in the way of motion and sensation. To maintain that, even here, 'power' signifies, not a phenomenal cause producing phenomenal effects, but a non-phenomenal something in the cause which enables it to produce these effects, seems less a plain statement of the common notion than a scholastic gloss upon it.

In other cases, the qualities that adapt a thing to produce its effects are less completely revealed to the eye. To account for the latter, we have to consider other facts about the cause, such as its mass or the potential energy stored up in it. Only when to its apparent qualities we add these hidden ones are we in a position to account completely for the effects. Yet these hidden qualities are still essentially phenomenal. When physicists speak of mass or potential energy, they mean nothing non-phenomenal or metaphysical. Mass signifies simply the number of molecules crowded together within a given space; potential energy means actual position as betokening the possibility of future motion; both belong to the category of essentially visible facts.

THE ARGUMENTS FOR PARALLELISM

Now, may it not be that the vulgar notion of cause as something additional to the phenomena immediately presented to the eye has its source in an instinctive sense of these supernumerary factors of physical action? If so, must we not admit that this notion has more foundation in reason than philosophers have been wont to allow? Of course these supernumerary factors would not constitute a tie *between* cause and effect, but only an amplification of the cause as at first presented, more completely adapting it to produce the effect. The metaphysical notion would then arise — as so many metaphysical notions do arise — by misrepresentation and distortion of the phenomenal fact in which the vulgar notion has its source.

Hume deserves great credit for pointing out the fictitious character of the metaphysical notion. But his criticism is directed, at one and the same time, against two conceptions of the causal relation which are far from identical: the notion of a 'real tie,' and that of a rational connection. He is quite as concerned to prove that no rational connection is discernible between cause and effect as to disprove a 'real tie.'

What is meant by a rational connection? A rational connection is something in the cause which enables us to infer the effect, and foresee it in advance of actual experience. Since this is assumed to be possible only so far as cause and effect are alike, it means that we can "discover the effect in the cause." The idea is that, by contemplating the cause, we can see in it a reason why this particular effect should follow rather than another, an appropriateness of this particular effect to this particular cause. Is Hume equally successful in refuting this notion?

He denies such a rational connection in the most unequivocal terms. "The effect is totally different from the cause, and consequently can never be discovered in it." We cannot predict in advance of experience what effect will follow from any cause. "When I see, for instance, a billiard-ball moving in a straight line towards another; even suppose motion in the second ball should by accident be suggested to me as the result of their contact or impulse; may I not conceive that a hundred different events might as well follow from that cause? May not both these balls remain at absolute rest? May not the first ball return in a straight line, or leap off from the second in any line or direction? All these suppositions are consistent and conceivable." "In a word, then, every effect is a distinct event from its cause. It could not, therefore, be discovered in the cause." "All events seem entirely loose and separate. One event follows another, but we never can observe any tie between them. They seem *conjoined*, but never *connected*."[1]

In short, what events follow from particular causes we can learn, according to Hume, only from experience, and cannot discover by reflection on the

---

[1] *Inquiry Concerning Human Understanding*, in Green and Grose's ed. of the *Essays*, vol. ii., pp. 26, 27, 61.

nature of the causes. We can see no reason in the events themselves why any cause should not be conjoined with any effect. What, in Hume's view, prevents anarchy in nature is simply the uniformity with which the same effects and the same causes are as a matter of fact associated. Is Hume right? Is it true that we must content ourselves with this bare juxtaposition of different things, and can never discern between cause and effect any rational bond which may make it intelligible why one should be followed by the other?

On this point Hume was certainly wrong. Though we follow him in rejecting a 'real tie' and in holding that all we have to do with is a continuous tissue of phenomena, yet this causal empiricism by no means implies that the relation is absolutely opaque and impenetrable to thought, in such wise that any cause might conceivably be joined with any effect. For the progress of science has brought to light certain phenomenal relations which go far towards helping us to understand why this particular cause produces this particular effect and not another. I refer to the qualitative and quantitative relations between cause and effect which it has become more and more the business of physical science to demonstrate.

The great example of such demonstration is the modern doctrine of the correlation of forces, according to which such apparently disparate facts as heat, light, and electricity are in reality modes of motion. This reduction of heterogeneous phenomena to a single fundamental kind is already a distinct advance towards making the causal relation intelligible. When, for example, molar motion is transformed into heat, this seems at first sight a juxtaposition of two totally different things; but when we learn that heat, in itself, is a motion of particles, the unlikeness disappears, the transformation becomes partly intelligible, we begin to "see the effect in the cause."

Still more does this happen when cause and effect are shown to be quantitatively alike. The idea of a certain proportionality between them is not merely an esoteric doctrine of science, but a familiar fact of every-day life. Every boy knows that it requires a greater expenditure of force to throw a ball a hundred yards than to throw it fifty, to lift a weight of twenty pounds than to lift one of ten; that a strong wind produces greater effects than a breeze; that the havoc wrought by a collision depends on the mass and the velocity of the colliding bodies. And, long before the discovery of the principle of the conservation of energy, we find the same proportionality recognized in Newton's laws of motion, where they assert the equality between the force which acts and the motion which results, as when one billiard-ball communicates its motion to another. In the practice of contemporary physics, this principle leads to the construction of causal equations. To illustrate by the instance just cited: when molar motion is transformed into heat, there is found to be a proportionality between the amount of heat evolved and the amount of molar motion that disappears. The equivalences demonstrated in this and analogous cases form the experimental basis of the principle of the conservation of energy.

Now, these qualitative and quantitative relations constitute a phenomenal bond between cause and effect which remains entirely unaffected by the criticism of Hume. Their demonstration gives us a far more perfect understanding of the connection between two events than the mere knowledge that these are causally related. We have gone a long way towards "discovering the effect in the cause." These relations make it appear to a certain extent rational that one should be succeeded by the other, to a certain extent irrational that any cause should be followed by any effect.

To a certain extent rational: for, even granting all this, the causal connection is still far from being so rational that the effects of all causes can be predicted in advance of experience. We understand as little as ever why a billiard-ball imparts its motion to another, instead of " returning in a straight line " or "leaping off from it in any line or direction." Not even the law of inertia possesses the character of rational necessity : we can without difficulty conceive a world in which the laws of motion should be different, because even the present laws do not at first sight appear to be obeyed. Nevertheless, these qualitative and quantitative relations are at least an element of rationality, in the midst of non-rational elements that have to be learned from experience. And they appear an essential constituent of the causal relation where both cause and effect are physical.

From causal relations between physical events, let us turn now to causal relations (if such there be) between physical and mental events, and ask how far the latter can conform to the type established for the former. The demonstration of causal relations between physical events may be said to have three stages: (1) the determination, through the criterion of uniformity, of the cause corresponding to a given effect; (2) the construction of a continuous phenomenal series reaching from the cause to the effect; (3) the demonstration of qualitative and quantitative relations. All three stages seem essential to the complete demonstration of causality where both cause and effect are physical. How far is it possible to carry out this programme where one is physical and the other mental?

It is plain, to begin with, that the demonstration of qualitative and quantitative relations is here impossible. There can be no equivalence between sensational brain-event and sensation, between volition and volitional brain-event, since mental and physical facts are incommensurable. Mental states not being a form of energy, their quantity cannot be estimated in terms of physical units. There might be a certain proportional variation between the two, like that expressed in Weber's law, but there could be no causal equality, as in physical science. If, then, a causal relation exists, it must be non-quantitative in its nature. Furthermore, it can involve no such qualitative similarity between cause and effect as is implied in the conception of heat, light, and electricity as modes of motion, but must be a mere juxtaposition of totally different things.

This being so, it is evident, in the second place, that there can be no construction of a continuous series reaching from cause to effect, but must be a sharp demarcation and absolute break at the point where the physical ends and the mental begins, or *vice versa*. We cannot, as in purely physical causation, picture to ourselves the cause passing over into the effect or giving birth to it by transformation, since the two belong to different orders of existence.

Hence the only kind of explanation here possible would consist in barely *pointing out* the cause corresponding to a particular effect — *digito monstrare*. After all was said, the connection would still remain doubly obscure: first, owing to the breach of continuity, and, secondly, owing to the absence of quantitative and qualitative relations. In a word, the cause of an effect could be indicated, but its connection with the effect could not be explained. *Why* a physical cause should produce, not a physical effect connected with it by quantitative and qualitative relations, as in other cases, but a totally different kind of thing, a mental state, would to the end remain absolutely incomprehensible, and their conjunction would simply have to be accepted as an ultimate fact.

How far, now, do these undeniable peculiarities of causal relations between mental and physical events constitute a reason for denying such causal relations altogether?

The argument appears in a cruder and in a more refined form. In the former, the weight is laid on the inconceivability, or even the unimaginability, of the connection in dispute. Of course, if the mind acts on the brain, it can do so only by uniting or separating the cerebral molecules. But this, according to Dr. Mercier, is inconceivable: "Try to imagine the idea of a beefsteak binding two molecules together"— you fail in the attempt. Or, as Professor James puts it, "we can form no positive image of the *modus operandi*."[1]

This form of the argument must be admitted to be somewhat naïve. Hegel's well-known dictum that "ideas have hands and feet" would, apparently, only have to be literally true to set the objector's mind at rest. Though perhaps even then the difficulty would return, in that we should be unable to understand how the idea moved its hands and feet. The *modus operandi*, in short, would have to be either mental or physical, and in either case the gap would remain, and is indeed essentially unbridgeable. But to urge this inevitable gap seems very like begging the question.

If, on the other hand, the argument be meant in the sense that we are not in the habit of conceiving an idea as capable of moving a molecule, and that when we bring the two things together in thought we

[1] *Principles of Psychology*, vol. i., p. 135.

find difficulty in executing the conception, it may be dealt with even more briefly. The experience of interactionists proves that the difficulty is not insurmountable. If the automatist and the parallelist are not in the habit of thinking of ideas as capable of moving molecules, possibly this is a habit they would do well to form.

The more refined type of the causal argument emphasizes, not so much the inconceivability, as the extremely meagre and limited character which the causal relation would have if it exist. This, of course, counts for nothing with the interactionist, who insists that causation in this limited form is still causation, and that we have as good ground to assume it between mind and body as anywhere else. Professor James even argues that the Humian criticism cuts both ways, dissolving causal relations between successive brain-events as much as between brain-events and mental states. If causation is nowhere anything but uniform sequence, such sequence exists as truly between volition and movement as between volitional brain-event and movement, and we have no right to pretend that the volitional brain-event is and the volition is not the cause.[1] But this, we may reply, is to count without the quantitative and qualitative relations which Hume overlooked, and which

---

[1] *Principles of Psychology*, vol. i., p. 137 : " As in the night all cats are gray, so in the darkness of metaphysical criticism all causes are obscure. But one has no right to pull the pall over the psychic half of the subject only, as the automatists do, and to say that *that* causation is unintelligible, whilst in the same breath one dogmatizes about *material* causation as if Hume, Kant, and Lotze had never been born."

exist where both cause and effect are physical but are impossible where one is physical and the other mental. If these relations help us in any degree to *understand* the connection of physical events, to just that degree causal relations between physical events and mental must be relatively unintelligible.

The causal argument, recast in the light of the foregoing explanations, may accordingly run as follows. The purpose for which causal relations are everywhere assumed is that of explaining events. Suppose the event to be explained is the motor discharge. The alternative presented is to explain it by means of the volition or by means of the simultaneously occurring volitional brain-event. Now, the volition can at most be the uniform antecedent of the motor discharge, and the connection between the two must perforce remain unintelligible. Whereas the volitional brain-event is connected with it by qualitative and quantitative relations which make the transition as intelligible as any transition ever is in the physical world. The question therefore comes to this: whether we will explain the motor discharge in the manner usual for physical events, by connecting it quantitatively and qualitatively with preceding physical events, or will decline to explain it at all. To take the former course is to do no prejudice to the volition, which remains, after as before, the motor discharge's uniform antecedent; while to take the latter is to reject the only explanation of which the nature of the case admits. The volition becomes a sort of dog-in-the-manger, unable to explain the motor discharge itself, and refusing to allow it to be explained by antecedent physical events. The energy contained in the motor discharge has to be assumed to be newly created, though it might so easily have been traced to its source in the volitional brain-event; the violation of the principle of conservation involved is therefore perfectly gratuitous.

When we turn to the relation between incoming nerve-current and sensation, the case is even clearer. Not only are these two incapable of being quantitatively connected, but the genesis of a mental state through the action of purely physical causes is incomprehensible, and has to be set down as a miracle. But what became of the energy embodied in the nerve-current? It cannot have been expended in the production of the sensation, since the latter is not a form of energy. It is impossible to see why it should be debarred from producing all the physical effects which it would have produced had there been no sensation. To these effects it must have transmitted all its energy, and with them it must be connected by qualitative and quantitative relations. But the sensation, in that case, appears not so much the effect of the nerve-current as this brain-event's mere concomitant. In short, only by regarding sensation and volition as forms of energy, and connecting them with antecedent and subsequent brain-events by means of equations, can causal relations between mental and physical events in the proper sense be upheld.

To this the interactionist may reply that it begs

the question, by assuming the existence of sensational and volitional brain-events simultaneous with the sensation and the volition, and connected with the nerve-current and the motor discharge by qualitative and quantitative relations. *If they exist,* they are necessarily causal rivals of the mental states, the principle of conservation must be presumed to apply, and interactionism falls to the ground. But the interactionist contention — he may affirm — is precisely that they *do not exist,* as events simultaneous with the mental states; that the sensational brain-event *precedes* the sensation, the volitional brain-event *follows* the volition, as they must to be in the proper sense their cause and effect; and that, while in these cases cause and effect are not connected by quantitative and qualitative relations, yet causation without these relations is still causation, and there are, in short, these two differing types of it, one more and the other less intelligible.

To which the parallelist may rejoin that, on critical principles, causation *minus* these relations either involves a 'real tie,' or is nothing but uniform sequence. Can it be that the average interactionist hugs to his breast the conception of a mysterious influence proceeding from the volition and taking effect upon the brain, and would not be satisfied with the statement that the volition is merely active in its nature and regularly followed by the motor discharge, a statement which would have the assent of the parallelist? The critical interactionist, in any case, will hasten to admit that the relation is merely one of uniform sequence, but will insist that it is nevertheless causal.

When the interactionist thesis is put in this form, it is doubtful if the argument we are considering can make any headway against it. The issue narrows down to a question of fact: whether sensation and sensational brain-event, volitional brain-event and volition are successive or simultaneous. And this is a question which we have seen the difficulty of answering empirically. If the interactionist would but admit the simultaneity of the pairs of events, the parallelist would have him at his mercy; but, if he persists in holding them to be successive, I do not see how the issue can be decided by any means known to natural science.

The result of our study of the empirical arguments is that they seem insufficient to justify a decision. Several of them have been shown to be fallacious. Of the sound ones, the causal argument proves the parallelist thesis, but its validity is hypothetical, resting on the assumption that mental events are simultaneous with their cerebral correlates. We may therefore dismiss it from consideration. The argument from the principles of biology appears to prove the mind efficient; but it is subject to the difficulty regarding the origin of consciousness. The argument from the principle of the conservation of energy raises a strong presumption, not amounting to demonstrative proof, that the contrary is the case. Thus two great branches of natural science seem arrayed against each other. Physics and biology appear to authorize opposite conclusions concerning the efficiency of mind. And it does not appear who is to be the arbiter between them.

PART II

METAPHYSICAL

Book III

METAPHYSICAL PRINCIPLES

CHAPTER VIII

THE PHYSICAL WORLD

Our empirical inquiry has been somewhat barren of result. Even the causal issue we have not been able to decide except hypothetically. Much less has any light been thrown upon the deeper question, why mind and body are associated at all. Indeed, this question now appears quite beyond the reach of empirical methods of investigation, while as regards the causal issue we have employed those methods in vain.

Under these circumstances, the time seems to have arrived for the metaphysical inquiry announced at the beginning. Hitherto we have been operating with counters whose exact value was left undetermined: we have discussed the relation of mind and matter without knowing exactly what mind and matter are. We must now turn critically upon the conceptions that have answered our purpose thus far, and seek to make them adequate. It may be that an exact knowledge of what mind and matter are will help us to understand their relation.

It is impossible not to recognize that certain metaphysical theories have a direct bearing on the problem. Thus most philosophers maintain that material objects have no existence apart from the mind. But, if the body exists only as a modification of the mind, the question of causal relations between them appears in a new light. Again, assuming that material objects exist as modifications of the mind, philosophers differ as to whether these modifications stand for realities outside. But, if they do, there must be such a reality corresponding to the body; and the problem passes into a fresh phase. Finally, in the issue between the three theories, everything depends on whether the mind itself is real and active.

The capital defect of most discussions of the subject lies in the failure of writers to define the metaphysical premises on which their contentions rest, or even to conceive the problem as necessarily involving metaphysics at all. The result is that they spend their time in discussing the relation of two things of whose nature they have no clear conception. They assert that the mind acts on matter, but they neglect to tell us what they mean by the matter on which they assert that the mind acts. They speak of matter as if the term had a definite unambiguous meaning, or as if any ambiguity in its meaning were irrelevant to the problem. When directly discussing the nature of matter they usually show themselves idealists, but they fail to bring their idealism to bear in discussing the relation of mind and body. As a rule they reject extra-mental realities represented by our perceptions, yet they do not think it incumbent on them to explain how interaction, on such a theory, remains any longer possible. This unsystematic habit of thought may suffice for the purposes of natural science, but in philosophy its only result is to multiply words and retard conclusions.

It is therefore our duty to provide ourselves, without further delay, with a set of definite metaphysical principles, which may enable us to assign to each theory its true and final meaning. Thus only can we hope to decide the causal question or to get light upon the ultimate one.

The problem of the nature of matter includes two distinct questions: (1) whether the objects we immediately see and touch exist independently of our minds, or only as modifications of our minds; (2) assuming the latter to be the case, whether these modifications stand for real existences external to our minds.

A word at the outset regarding this use of 'external.' The adjective is of course not to be understood in the literal spatial sense. For the physical world to be spatially external to the mind, the mind and it would have to be in space, only in different places. But that is absurd. On the one hand, the mind is not in space, for it cannot be conceived as either punctiform or extended. It appears to be in space only because it is existentially connected with something, the body or head, which *is* in space. On the other hand, the alternative of being either independently real or a modification of the mind applies to the physical world with all its characters included, and therefore to space itself. The true meaning of 'external' is accordingly 'apart from,' 'independent of,' 'other than' — *praeter* rather than *extra* consciousness. And this is also the sense in which I shall allow myself to use the word 'extra-mental.'

By 'idealism' I would be understood to mean the Berkeleian doctrine that material objects exist as modifications of the mind, that their *esse* is *percipi*, without any decision of the second question, whether these modifications stand for realities outside; in a word, the critical as distinguished from the constructive side of Berkeley's philosophy. This, I think, is a doctrine all but universally accepted by philosophers. Few who deserve the name imagine that in perceiving material objects we have immediately to do with anything but our own mental states. The divergence of opinion relates rather to the second question, whether the mental states of which alone we are immediately conscious stand for realities outside the mind. Such realities (for reasons to be later explained) I shall call 'things-in-themselves.' Those who deny things-in-themselves may be termed phenomenalists, those who assume them idealistic or critical realists.

Now, the problem of the relation of mind and body will be found to be inseparably bound up with the question of the existence of things-in-themselves.

Indeed, these are in truth but aspects of a single problem, and the possibility of solving the former depends on the answer given to the latter. But, to answer the latter intelligently, we must review from the beginning the steps by which the idealistic theory is reached. And our starting-point must be the plain man's view, of which idealism presents itself as a rectification.

Naïve Realism

In reflecting upon this question, it is important to distinguish *the two times* regarding which the question of the nature of matter is asked: the time of perception, and the intervals between perceptions. It is obvious that, during perception, objects are immediately and intuitively known: since something thus known is what we mean by material objects. They are then found to possess colors and shapes and sizes and other sensible qualities. Now, the plain man believes that, after perception is over, objects continue to exist in exactly the same way, retaining all their sensible qualities. But, if they do, it follows that, even at the moment of perception, they are distinct in existence from the percipient mind. For they existed thus distinctly before perception began, and they can hardly be supposed to have lost their distinctness in the process of becoming perceived. Thus, if the very objects we perceive exist whether we perceive them or not, it follows that even while we perceive them they are distinct in existence from our perceptions. And this implies, finally, that the mind possesses a power of looking outside itself, and being immediately and intuitively conscious of what is out of consciousness. Naïve realism consists essentially in the assertion of such a power.

We may consider this view as made up of two tenets, the first relating to the mode of existence of objects, the second to our powers of knowledge: (1) objects with all their qualities are distinct existences from the mind; (2) they are nevertheless immediately and intuitively known.

As regards the first, the naïve realist holds that the very objects we perceive exist outside our minds in exactly the shape in which we perceive them. They are not first created and brought into existence by our perception of them, nor is anything added to or altered in their qualities by the mere fact of their being perceived. When perception is over, they continue to exist exactly as before, retaining all their qualities intact.

As regards the second tenet, the naïve realist insists on the immediate and intuitive character of the knowledge. Objects are not merely represented or pictured by our perceptions, they are not merely mirrored in a subjective medium, they are directly contemplated: we behold them, as the Scottish philosophers love to say, "face to face." Now, this is a proposition which no one will think of disputing so long as the objects thus known are not expressly declared to be without the mind. If the mode of existence of material objects be left undetermined, it is the plainest of facts that the things to which we give that name are immediately perceived. The only question is, whether what is thus perceived is an extra-mental reality or a modification of consciousness. It is only when the objects referred to are by hypothesis extra-mental realities that the doubt arises whether they can be immediately known.

The whole question therefore comes to this: whether it is possible for us to have immediate and intuitive knowledge of realities distinct from our minds — whether it is possible to be immediately conscious of what is out of consciousness. Idealists do not hesitate to deny the possibility, and to hold that we can have immediate knowledge only of our mental states.

The proofs of idealism embrace two distinct lines of argument, the first based on physiological considerations, the second on metaphysical analysis. The physiological argument takes its departure from the fact that every perception is correlated with a perceptional brain-event, which latter is a fairly remote effect of the action of the perceived object on the senses; and argues from this that it is impossible the knowledge of the extra-bodily object should be immediate. It points, moreover, to the account of the constitution of the object given by physical science, according to which color and other secondary qualities are in the object something entirely different from what they are for the mind. The metaphysical argument is based on the necessary distinctness and separateness of knowledge, as a mental state, from the extra-mental object assumed to be known, and deduces from it the same idealistic conclusion.

These two arguments it will be instructive to compare. It would be curious if two such different processes of thought led logically to the same conclusion. We shall find that, while both disprove naïve realism, the metaphysical argument is consistent with either a realistic or a phenomenalistic interpretation of idealism, while the physiological argument is not.

Physiological Argument for Idealism

Certain of the physiological facts referred to in Chapter II have an evident bearing on the issue between naïve realism and idealism, and constitute a kind of argument for the latter. Nor can we be restrained from considering them on the ground that physiology is irrelevant to philosophy. Rather ought theories about the mind to be viewed with suspicion which ignore the accompanying physiological facts.

For perception is not merely a mental state, it involves a physiological process. Now, this process is apparently of such a nature as to make an immediate relation between the mind and the extra-bodily object impossible. On the other hand, such an immediate relation is apparently one of the plainest facts of consciousness. Hence a seeming contradiction, which it must be our business to resolve.

The philosophers of common-sense used to appeal to the " testimony of consciousness " in an illegitimate way, which threw the mantle of infallibility not only over the facts of introspection but over our instinctive beliefs. But the immediacy of the relation between the object and the mind is not an instinctive belief (like the existence of the object when no longer perceived), it is an introspective fact. When I look at my watch, I feel that there is nothing interposed between my mind and it, and this feeling gives me a comfortable sense of immediate enjoyment and possession. If I were told that between the object and my mind there was a whole train of physical events, distinct from both, occupying an appreciable interval of time, and absolutely necessary to the object's eliciting the perception, I should feel cut off from the object, and should judge this comfortable immediacy of perception an illusion. The object would no longer appear the contemporary and datum of the perception, but at most its antecedent and cause.

Now, the science of optics reveals just such a train of intermediate events. It is essential to vision that light-rays should pass from the object to the eye, and these are events distinct both from the object and from the perception, yet indispensable to the one evoking the other.

Thus vision, physically considered, involves not so much a supersensible cognitive energy issuing from the mind and appropriating the object (as we naïvely imagine), as rather a chain of physical causes and effects enabling the object to act on the brain. If the mind possessed such a space-transcending energy, it would be impossible to understand the rôle of the light-rays: we ought to be able to see just as well in the dark. If, then, the facts of optics have any philosophical validity, it follows that the object of which I am immediately conscious cannot be the object which acts on my senses and calls forth the perceptional brain-event, but can at most be a mental duplicate of that object. In short, naïve realism proves to be in contradiction with certain elementary facts of physical science. And any philosophy — we may note — seems committed by those facts to recognizing some kind of twofold existence of the object.

The naïve realist may seek to accommodate his doctrine to the facts by relinquishing part of his original thesis, and holding that the immediate object of the mind in visual perception is not the actual distant object, but the image on the retina. This, however, would be to abandon the appeal to the "testimony of consciousness," which was the naïve realist's strength, without setting up a doctrine harmonious with science. For consciousness testifies, if it testifies to anything, that we immediately see, not the retinal image or anything else near at hand, but the actual distant object. Furthermore, there are *two* retinal images and they are inverted, whereas the object we see is single and erect. Surely no further argument is needed to prove that what we see is not the retinal image.

Yet a further argument offers itself, in the now admitted fact that visual consciousness is at least mainly correlated, not with the activity of the retina, but with that of the brain. As light-rays must pass from the object to the eye, so nerve-currents must pass from the eye to the brain and excite it to action, otherwise there is no perception. Now, these nerve-currents constitute a second chain of causes and effects, continuing the former chain, and still further interposed between the object and the physical correlate of the perception.

If, then, the naïve realist desires to accommodate his theory to the facts of physiology as well as those of physics, his only course is to hold that the immediate object of the mind in perception is the perceptional brain-event. This would be a still further and monstrous departure from the "testimony of consciousness," which avers that what we perceive is not a brain-event or anything else internal to our bodies, but a world of objects without. If what we immediately perceived were the perceptional brain-event, we might study neurology by the introspective method, which has hitherto been considered the exclusive property of the psychologist; but it does not seem likely that this suggestion will meet with a welcome in physiological circles, or supplant at an early day the use of the scalpel and microscope. In truth, the perceptional brain-event is not the object of the perception, but its physiological correlate. What we perceive is not brain-cells and molecular agitations, but animals and trees and houses.

On the other hand, the perceptional brain-event is the condition of the correspondence between perception and extra-bodily object. Its rôle in this respect may be compared to that of the retinal image. Objects can be seen only so far as images of them are projected on the retina, and the retinal image must contain a detail for every detail of the object that is to be seen. In the same way, objects reveal themselves to perception only so far as they act on the brain and call forth perceptional brain-events, and the perception manages to resemble the object only by first resembling the perceptional brain-event. This brain-event thus constitutes a cerebral image of the object, analogous to the retinal, and has to resemble it in respect of everything that is to be perceived. The evolution of perception, physiologically considered, is the evolution of nerve-centres capable of producing such images. Thus the channel of cognitive communication between perception and object is the chain of physical causes and effects by which the object calls forth the brain-event. But, as surely as this causal chain secures their resemblance, so surely does it cut off the perception from anything like immediate knowledge or intuition of the object.

Nor can it be maintained that the perception, though not contemplating the object and though cut off from it by this causal chain, still penetrates to it by some mysterious cognitive power and knows it as it is. For suppose a pane of yellow glass to be interposed between the object and the eye: the result is to alter the brain-event in the sense of yellowness, without producing any change in the object. Now, under these circumstances the object is seen yellow: which shows that the perception varies with the brain-event, and not with the object. In the second place, the very existence of the object in any given case is a doubtful inference, which not the single perception but only the concordance of many can justify. There is no internal means of distinguishing a hallucination from a normal perception, the validity of the inference depending on the accident of the perceptional brain-event having in this case been evoked *ab extra* in the usual manner.

Primary and Secondary Qualities

To the above reasoning it may be objected that at least in all ordinary cases the inference is valid; and that, when we see an object yellow and *no* pane of yellow glass is interposed, we may confidently conclude that the object truly is yellow. But this brings us to those further facts of physics and physiology which are the basis of the distinction of primary and secondary qualities. It will have to be admitted that this is, from a scientific point of view, a legitimate and valid distinction. There are qualities called secondary which it is possible to explain by the action on the senses of other qualities called primary, the qualities of bodies thus falling into two opposed and irreducible classes. Nor can a phenomenalistic idealism be reached, as is so often attempted, by showing that the argument which proved the subjectivity of the secondary qualities can be extended to the primary also. This would be to destroy the basis on which the argument rests. When we interpret the extra-bodily causes of the secondary qualities in terms of the primary, we imply that the latter are as objective as the former are subjective. But, assuming the distinction to be valid, it may be argued with a show of reason that the primary qualities are resemblances, and that in so far as we apprehend them we do truly penetrate to the object and know it as it is.

It is, I think, by this process of thought that the ordinary scientific view of the physical world is reached — I mean the view ordinarily entertained by scientific men : the view that behind the curtain of colors and sounds presented to our senses there lies a world neither colored nor sonorous, consisting of bodies having no other qualities but shape, size, and impenetrability, and engaged in no other business but motion.

Whether this view be really essential to science, so that to controvert it is to undermine the basis on which science rests, we may consider later. In any case, the notion of such a second world of bodies behind the bodies we see and touch is open to the most serious objections.

Let us ask, in the first place, whether the bodies composing this world are capable of being seen and touched. Evidently not. For they lie *behind* the bodies we see and touch, and are by no means identical with them. Moreover, they have no color, and nothing can be seen which has not color. It is worthy of note that we ordinarily misconceive this world by attributing to the bodies that compose it, not, it is true, such brilliant colors as red or green — that would be too gross a self-contradiction — but the duller colors of black or gray. But black and gray are plainly as much secondary qualities, produced on the visual sense by the comparative absence of light-rays, as the gayer colors of red and green. Evidently, if we would fully live up to the sense of the doctrine, we must cease to try to picture this second world altogether, and be content to think it. And what we must think is something, of course, that has length, breadth, and thickness. But what? Is it perchance the impenetrability? That would be absurd. Then it must be something that *has* the impenetrability. But what, again? The question is not easy to answer.

In any case, it is clear that the bodies composing this world are incapable of being seen and touched. Now, if these bodies (we may suppose them to be atoms or molecules) were capable of being seen through an ordinary microscope, or through an imaginary microscope far more powerful than any we possess (of course they would have to be black or gray to be thus visible, unless they happened to be red or green), they would simply constitute an extension of our ordinary sensible world, and the doctrine in question would still be naïve realism. But the deprivation of color makes them essentially non-perceptible. Hence they lie wholly beyond our faculty of perception, and conform to the definition of things-in-themselves.

As such, knowledge of them is of necessity purely representative. Now, of the two tenets of naïve realism, one was the immediate and intuitive character of our knowledge of objects. But the scientific doctrine, though it holds that the primary qualities are resemblances, by no means holds that we perceive their originals immediately. For, clearly, it would be impossible to divide, in what we immediately perceive, between a part which should be subjective and a part which should be externally real: if color is subjective, the length and breadth which mark the limits of the color must be subjective too. What we immediately perceive is simply the curtain of colors and sounds, and the shape, size, position, and motion which we immediately perceive are simply the characters of the curtain, and entirely distinct from the *real* shape, size, motion, and position which the characters of the curtain symbolize. In short, it would be impossible to admit more unreservedly the idealistic thesis — which is the main contention of this chapter — that the objects we immediately see and touch are modifications of consciousness.

Doubts as to the validity of the scientific view cannot but arise when we recall that matter means, originally and properly, something we immediately see and touch. Is this second thing, then, also matter? If so, the material world appears reduplicated. There are really *two* material worlds, one accessible to touch and vision, and another lying concealed behind it. Or, if atoms are potentially visible, by some such means as those suggested above, then there are *two* worlds of atoms, one perceptible and the other not. It cannot but strike us that worlds have here been multiplied *praeter necessitatem*. We must be the victims of some illusion, by which the world given in perception has been projected outside perception, thus acquiring twofold existence.

When we reflect that our whole knowledge of matter has been gained through perception, that all our observations and experiments, all our weighings and measurings have been performed upon perceived matter, that we never have had any dealings with matter except through this faculty, it becomes evident that, if we have attained to the knowledge of a second matter behind that which is perceived, knowledge has here risen higher than its source. But this would be contrary to all principles of intellectual hydrostatics.

How came we, then, thus to overpass perception and enter a region of things incapable of being perceived? It was through the distinction of primary and secondary qualities — or rather through the assumption on which that distinction, and indeed the entire physiological argument, rest. And it may be objected that all the results of science are capable of statement in terms of perception except precisely this distinction.

The assumption to which I refer is that the perception is accompanied by a perceptional brain-event. As a mere statement of observed fact, this is not only unexceptionable, it is one of the fundamental truths of physiological psychology. But, true though it be, we are almost certain to apprehend it in a sense which makes it metaphysically false. We are almost certain to understand it to mean that *two real events,* one physical, the other mental, happen more or less simultaneously. But to do this is evidently to take for granted at the outset that matter exists independently of consciousness. For, if the brain-event exists independently of the perception, all the rest of the physical world must do so likewise, and therefore also the extra-bodily object which the perception represents. So that, even before entering on our discussion, we have assumed the independent existence of matter. And what we have illicitly introduced into the premises, we naturally find in the conclusion. This, then, is the way in which the physical world acquires a second existence beyond the reach of perception, instead of remaining to the end what alone it properly is, a perceptional datum.

Two difficulties will be felt in this account of the matter. In the first place, it will be asked what becomes of the distinction of primary and secondary qualities. It might be thought that, if matter has no existence apart from perception, both alike become subjective. And so in one sense they do. We have seen the difficulty of conceiving a world of bodies which shall have length, breadth, and thickness, but not color. The more we reflect upon the matter, the more do we see that, while it is easy to think length, breadth, and thickness in terms of the visual sense, as dimensions of color, or in terms of the tactile sense, as dimensions of solidity, or in terms of the muscular sense, as room for movement, yet, when we try to think them without any sensible filling at all, we fail in the attempt. And the conviction will grow upon us that length, breadth, and thickness are as much characters of our sensibility as sound or color. Certainly psychologists are in the habit of so regarding them.

But this by no means implies that the distinction of primary and secondary qualities vanishes altogether. That distinction arose out of observations concerning the sequence of phenomena — such as that the vibrations of bodies are the cause of sensations of sound, or that the conformation of their surfaces determines the color they shall have. It must therefore retain to the end at least this phenomenal value. Whether it possesses also a deeper realistic value, as implying that the primary qualities, while not exactly resemblances, are yet in some way more truly descriptive of reality than the secondary, is a question we cannot discuss at present. The reader must be referred, for light on the subject, to the chapters on things-in-themselves.

The second difficulty has reference to the validity of the physiological argument. Does not this argument, it may be asked, lose all cogency if the correlation between perception and perceptional brain-event be taken, not in a realistic, but in the suggested phenomenalistic sense? I answer, No. For that perception and perceptional brain-event are *in some sense* correlated is an unquestionable fact. Now, when taken in the phenomenalistic sense, this correlation signifies simply that the brain-event is a possible perception whenever the extra-bodily object is an actual perception; our world therefore consists of nothing but actual and possible perceptions, that is, it contains nothing essentially non-phenomenal. Whereas, if the correlation be taken in the realistic sense, it follows that the extra-bodily object exists really, as much as the perceptional brain-event; but the perception varies solely with the latter: it is consequently cut off from the extra-bodily object by the whole intervening chain of causes and effects; and the necessary result is, that we cannot know that object immediately, but only our subjective image of it.

I think, then, that even after all due allowance has been made for the irrelevancy of physiological considerations in metaphysics, we are justified in asserting that naïve realism is irreconcilable with certain physical and physiological facts. This negative statement perhaps most accurately renders the significance of the physiological argument. But, if naïve realism is untenable, we are necessarily thrown back upon an idealistic account of the world immediately perceived.

Metaphysical Argument for Idealism

The following argument, upon which idealists have relied since the days of Berkeley, rests on analysis of what is involved in the fact that our knowledge of matter is intuitive. Its result is to prove that nothing can be intuitively known except modifications of the knowing mind.

The question at issue is, whether material objects exist independently of our minds. The idealist begins by pointing out that, whenever we have to do with material objects, *we* — that is to say, our minds — are always present perceiving them. This is a fact we are prone to overlook: in our preoccupation with the object, we forget the percipient mind. Whenever there are objects, there is always a mind present perceiving them — except when objects are assumed to exist unperceived. But it is precisely then that we have no empirical evidence of their existence. Our knowledge of their existence then (supposing that we possess it) must apparently be derived from some other source than experience, which in the nature of the case can testify only to their existence while perceived. Again, when we imagine objects as existing unperceived, we always imagine ourselves present perceiving them, and cannot completely imagine ourselves away without their vanishing in our grasp. Thus we can think of the absence of matter only in terms of its presence; and, whether absent or present, it seems essentially relative to mind.

The duality of the mind and its object, being a manifest fact of experience, must of course remain in some form on any theory. The question is, whether the naïve realist's interpretation of this duality as that of two distinct but related existences is consistent with that immediacy of the knowledge which is the other half of his thesis. Let us, for argument's sake, assume a duality of existences, and inquire what must be the consequence as respects the immediacy of the knowledge.

Suppose a candle to exist outside a mind. And, at the first moment, let the mind have no perception of the candle. Now, what happens when the perception of the candle arises in the mind?

The naïve realist conceives knowledge as a sort of energy of intuition proceeding from the mind and laying hold of the candle. But how can knowledge lay hold of the candle without passing outside the mind, since the candle is outside? Can knowledge issue from the mind and go to meet the candle, or swing in mid-air like a bridge between the two? Must it not rather, as a mental state, remain wholly within the precincts of the mind itself? Plainly, the knowledge can be no nearer to the candle than the mind is, and if the candle is distinct from and outside the mind, it must be equally distinct from and outside that modification of the mind which we call knowledge.

Distinct, however, as this modification is from the candle, it is indispensable it should arise in the mind if the candle is to be known. The mere presence of the latter outside is not sufficient. It is necessary to knowledge that the mind should bring forth out of its own resources a mental modification and counterpart of the candle. Nor is it enough that this modification should be a mere state-of-knowledge-or-perception-in-the-abstract, which might derive particularity and concreteness from its relation to this particular concrete candle: it must itself be particular and concrete, it must be *candle*-knowledge as distinguished from lamp-knowledge or table-knowledge, and must therefore contain a detail for every detail of the object that is to be known. In short, if we assume an extra-mental candle, knowledge of it can come about only by the construction of a mental duplicate reproducing every detail of it that is to be known; and what we get is something very like a second candle inside the mind.

Thus, if we start from the realistic assumption of an object existing independently of consciousness, the conclusion to which we are driven is that this object and our perception of it are distinct and separate things. There are really, on this assumption, two candles: the candle that is extra-mentally real, and the candle that is a mental modification. They differ in a variety of ways, one being permanent, the other transient; one made of matter, the other of mind-stuff, etc. Being distinct and separate, each can exist without the other.

Now, which of these candles is it that is immediately known? For it cannot be both; we are conscious of but a single candle. It must be the duplicate candle, the mental modification. It cannot be the real candle, since that is by hypothesis external to the mind. It follows that, if we assume things external to the mind, knowledge of those things cannot be intuitive, but must needs be representative. We are therefore in the following dilemma. Would we have things external to the mind? We must be satisfied with representative knowledge of them. Would we have things intuitively known? We must regard them as mental modifications. By no possibility can the objects we immediately know be extra-mentally real.

That these objects are nothing but mental modifications, may be demonstrated, so to speak, *ad oculos*. Suppose I am looking at a candle; the candle I am conscious of is a mental modification. How may I convince myself of the fact? By the simple process of closing my eyes. Something then ceases to exist: is it the real candle? Certainly not. Then it must be the mental duplicate. By successively opening and closing my eyes I may create and annihilate the perceived candle. But the real candle continues unchanged. Then what I am immediately conscious of when my eyes are open must be the mental duplicate. If an original of that duplicate exists outside the mind, it must be other than the candle I perceive, and itself unperceived.

The idealist winds up his argument with a couple of corollaries. Suppose everything outside the mind to be annihilated, but our perceptions to succeed each other exactly as before. We should never suspect the disappearance of things extra-mental, and should have as much reason to assume their existence as we have at present. Now suppose extra-mental things to continue, but no perceptions of them to arise in our minds. They would be for us as good as non-existent. These corollaries do not, of course, disprove the existence of an extra-mental world; but I think they bring forcibly home to us how true it is that *our* world is the world of our perceptions.

Thus far we have been considering the teaching of idealism as to the manner in which objects exist while perceived. We must now ask how they exist during the intervals between our perceptions. The answer which the idealist must render is plain. If objects exist while perceived only as modifications of consciousness, it follows that when they cease to be perceived they must cease to exist. Here lies the great stumbling-block of idealism for the plain man. That apart from perception objects do not possess their familiar secondary qualities, he might perhaps with a little argument be brought to admit. But a view that dissolves physical reality entirely away, leaving not even a "geometrical ghost" behind, puts quite another strain upon his credulity.

Do you mean to tell me, he asks, that the objects behind my back are non-existent because I do not at this moment perceive them? That when I leave this room the tables and chairs, the pictures on the walls, the clock on the mantelpiece all cease to exist, the walls then having outsides but no insides? Since Berkeley wrote, common-sense has amused itself with picturing the grotesque consequences that must ensue, *e.g.*, in the case of the setting sun, the North Pole, the interior of the earth, the insides of animals, etc.

But the idealist returns a firm answer to the plain man's question. Yes, he says, I mean to tell you exactly that. When they are unperceived, objects do not exist as such, but at most as possibilities of perception, or (it may be) as intentions of the Divine Mind to give us those perceptions.

The plain man next points to a fact which seems

to him to prove the continued existence of objects: that when we reperceive them after an interval we find them changed. Which seems to show that they must have existed during the interval and been undergoing the changes.

But to the quick-witted idealist this reasoning causes no embarrassment. He explains that, when objects are recreated for perception, they are simply recreated changed; which is as easy as for them to be recreated the same.

The Berkeleian view, as thus expounded, is a perfectly logical theory, just because it is an absolutely accurate transcript of the facts. At the same time, its most devoted adherent must admit that it supposes in physical processes a discontinuity, to say the least, rather startling. That the fire in my grate was annihilated brightly burning when I left my room, and recreated in a sinking condition when I returned; that my clock became non-existent at half-past ten, and came into existence again several hours later with the hands marking a quarter to four — all this may be accurate psychology, but it seems impossible physics. Such a piecemeal, fragmentary world seems a long way removed from the continuous and abiding universe of which the latter science tells.

Idealism and Science

How far idealism is consistent with the assumptions concerning matter which underlie physical science, is a controverted question. We have seen that scientific men usually recoup themselves for the discontinuity of the phenomenal world by assuming behind it a world which is continuous and abiding. But we have also seen the untenableness of this assumption. The question is, whether the fabric of science can be disengaged from it, and made to stand solidly upon an idealistic basis.

This is partly a question of terms. We may mean by science either (1) "a series of propositions asserting what, under given conditions, our experience would be,"[1] in short, the laws of the sequence of phenomena; or (2) these laws considered as describing the connections of things in a world existing independently of consciousness. In other words, we mean by it the laws of phenomena either *minus* or *plus* metaphysical realism. Now, there is every reason for restricting the term to the former sense. For all the propositions of science *except* metaphysical realism (supposing that to be a scientific proposition) admit of restatement in terms of idealism, as accounts of the perceptions we should have in case certain conditions were fulfilled, and therefore in no way involve the independent existence of matter. So that by using the term in this sense we conceive science in such a way that it becomes independent of metaphysics, and retains its validity on any metaphysical theory; whereas, by the other usage, we make it responsible for two disparate deliverances which may be of very unequal value. I think there can be no

[1] See Balfour, *Defence of Philosophic Doubt*, pp. 178-193, whose discussion I have in mind in what follows.

doubt which of these usages will be more conducive to clearness and honesty of thought.

The advocate of realism may admit the theoretical separability of science and metaphysics, yet may contend that in science as we actually find it the realistic assumption is not only present, but essential to its full significance. Science, he may say, is understood by its adepts as something more than a mere description of perceived occurrences: it is understood as a genetic explanation of the way those occurrences came about. To explain perceived events by means of preceding events that were not perceived — that is, by means of events which, on the idealistic theory, did not happen at all — is to leave the need for genetic understanding unsatisfied. Thus the piecemeal, fragmentary world which is all that idealists believe in is not only philosophically but even scientifically insufficient.

While I doubt the expediency of this way of stating the matter, I believe the fundamental idea involved to be sound — indeed, that is one of the main contentions of this book. And the need in question can only be met by some form of realism. It does not follow that either the plain man's realism or the realism of the scientific man will suffice for the purpose.

As regards the former, we have seen that the two tenets of which it is made up — the immediacy of our knowledge of objects, and their independent existence — are mutually incompatible. We cannot thus look outside our minds and know immediately things existing there. We can know immediately only our own states of consciousness. It follows that the objects we see and touch exist as states of consciousness; and, if this is so, there is no help for it, they must cease to exist when we cease to perceive them.

But, although the very objects we perceive cannot continue to exist when we no longer perceive them, it is consistent with idealism that they should have extra-mental causes which continue to exist, and of which the perceived objects are symbolic. Of course the plain man knows nothing of such causes, and of course they are not what he means by matter. He means by matter the colored, solid, extended object he immediately perceives, nor does it ever enter his mind that behind the perceived object there may be a second object which he does not perceive. On the contrary, he is convinced that there is absolutely nothing about matter that is not accessible to perception, and would be very much surprised to learn that the perceived matter is not the real matter at all.

This, however, is what the scientific man is obliged to hold in order to have a matter that can continue when perception is over. Thus we get two matters, one capable of being perceived and the other not. But matter, originally and properly, means the thing we see and touch; and the other thing appears to deserve the name only so long as we illegitimately endow it with the sensible qualities of color, length, breadth, and thickness. Hence the likelihood is that, if we come to admit things-in-themselves, we shall have to conceive them as non-material.

Meanwhile, acceptance of the idealistic view as regards perceived objects does not necessarily involve any decision of the question of things-in-themselves. The idealist may be either a phenomenalist or a critical realist. He may follow Berkeley and Kant in assuming extra-mental realities, or he may follow Hume and Mill in rejecting them. He may look upon our perceptions as effects produced in us by action from without, or as states that arise in us spontaneously in virtue of a law of our nature.

Full discussion of the question of things-in-themselves must be reserved for later. But, hypothetically, we may deduce from idealism at once several important consequences concerning them.

(1) If things-in-themselves exist, their existence cannot be immediately known, but only inferred. The broadest of distinctions separates such extra-mental realities, which in the nature of the case can never be immediately given, the hypothesis of which is consequently unverifiable, from the empirical objects and events, such as matter and motion, thoughts and feelings, which we know by immediate experience.

(2) If things-in-themselves exist, the fact that they are not immediately experienced but reached by inference necessarily leaves us more or less in the dark concerning their nature. What they are like in themselves, we have no immediate means of

knowing. Perception cannot inform us, for it tells us (in the first instance at least) only about the characters of perceived objects. We are therefore not justified in transferring to them without further ado those qualities of materiality and spatiality which characterize perceived objects, or in speaking of the extra-mental existence as matter. It may be the very opposite, it may be spirit, as Berkeley opined; or it may, for anything we can yet see, be something unlike either. In a word, its nature has become problematical. On the other hand, we may perhaps legitimately assume that our perceptions, as symbols, convey to us some veiled intimation of its character and doings, if we could be sufficiently nice in our inferences. — But this is to anticipate.

CHAPTER IX

CONSCIOUSNESS

We have reached the conclusion that material objects exist only as modifications of consciousness. Before we inquire whether these modifications stand for realities external to consciousness, we must consider the nature of the necessary starting-point of all trans-subjective inference, consciousness itself. For although the immediate starting-point in this case is not consciousness itself but these special modifications, yet the inference will be found to derive an essential element from consciousness itself. We shall find, namely, that the conception of the thing inferred as real, as a second reality co-ordinate with consciousness, is derived, not from the modifications, but from consciousness itself. Hence an indispensable premise of the proof of extra-mental realities is the proof that consciousness itself is a reality.

But what is a reality? In defining the term we may employ a paraphrase of the definition of substance which Spinoza places at the beginning of his *Ethics*. A reality is something that exists of itself and in its own right, and not merely as a modification of something else. It is consequently something that does not require anything else in order to be conceived. Thus material objects, though in every-day speech we call them real because of their steadiness and independence of our will, are not realities, since they are only abstractions from our consciousness, and require it in order to be conceived. Consciousness itself, on the other hand, would be a reality, an integral part of the universe of things, if it should prove that it cannot be conceived as a modification of anything else, but exists in its own right.

The epistemological change from naïve realism to idealism involves a corresponding ontological change. As naïve realists we supposed ourselves to have immediate knowledge of two antithetical realities, mind and matter. But, since matter exists only as a modification of mind, it results that we have immediate knowledge of but one. Our perceptions prove to be as subjective as our thoughts and feelings, and bring us no more than these into contact with realities other than the mind.

But now, according to a certain school of thought, even this estimate of our cognitive powers is too generous, and the number of realities with which we are immediately acquainted is not one but none. Not even of the mind, so far as it is real, have we immediate knowledge. "All the great realities escape us." "We can know only phenomena" — a train of material and a train of mental phenomena; or rather, since material are now recognized to be in reality mental phenomena, only the latter.

The reality in the case of mind which this agnostic doctrine hints at but declares not immediately knowable need not be a Soul in the scholastic sense, any more than the entity behind matter need be material substance. It may be an Ego, existing only when consciousness exists, yet antithetical in its nature to thoughts and feelings, and not immediately given as they are given. The gist of the view is that thoughts and feelings are essentially phenomena or appearances, existing for the benefit of a something which beholds and enjoys them; that, consequently, in knowing thoughts and feelings we do not know the reality or proper essence of the mind.

Now, it is clear that both the propriety of assuming things-in-themselves and the nature to be attributed to them if assumed will depend on whether the starting-point of inference, the immediate datum of introspective experience, is a train of phenomena or a reality. If it be a train of phenomena, what we must infer will be an entity as their support, or an observer to whom they appear. Whereas, if consciousness be a reality, what we must infer (supposing that we see reason to infer anything at all) will be other realities equally real with consciousness but independent of it. Which, then, of these doctrines is true?

Theory of a Soul

The metaphysical entity called a 'Soul' must not be confused with the 'soul' to which poets and religious teachers refer, nor yet with the 'soul' of empirical psychology and ordinary speech. If we understand by the word, as the Germans do, simply the mind or consciousness however construed, the soul in this sense is a fact, not the doubtful object of a theory. The soul, again, which is a man's most precious possession and whose loss is not to be outweighed by gain of the whole world, is not a man's mental substance but his better self. Even the soul as the subject of immortality is rather a man's consciousness than the mind-atom whose natural indestructibility is supposed to guarantee its continuance. Damnation of the mind-atom without damnation of the consciousness would be a very painless form of retribution, while eternity of the consciousness without eternity of the mind-atom should satisfy the most self-conservative.

If theologians nevertheless cling to a Soul, it is partly because they deem it necessary to responsibility. For this the acts must be the man's; but if the man be no wider than his consciousness, the acts (or at least the thoughts that produce them) appear imposed from without. Again, the Soul is needed as a storehouse for the memories and ideas when not actually in consciousness. The wider man must be either the Soul or the brain; and the latter view is judged materialistic. Finally, to the eye of psychological analysis the thoughts and feelings may appear a bundle, and the mind to share in the mutability and transitoriness of its states till these are given in charge of an underlying entity. Thus arises the theory that consciousness is a mere stream of phenomena; an activity, not an existence; the manifestation or efflux of a Soul.

The first point that calls for settlement is whether the Soul is given in experience or inferred. There can be no doubt as to the answer. The Soul is given introspectively no more than to the senses: it is not an empirical fact, but an inference. This appears from Descartes's argument for it, the famous "*Cogito ergo sum.*" Here the conclusion, the '*sum*,' does not simply mean that 'my thought exists'; that is rather the meaning of the premise, the '*cogito*'; it means that there is a '*res cogitans*,' distinct from the '*cogitatio*,' and not immediately given as the '*cogitatio*' is given. If the Soul were an immediate datum, it would not have to be inferred but merely noted, and the argument would shrink to the observational proposition '*sum*.' The real premise, as Descartes intends it, is not '*cogito*,' but '*cogitatio fit*,' 'thinking goes on,' and the conclusion drawn '*ego sum*,' 'I am': the 'I' thus being given in the conclusion but not in the premise.

Nor can it be maintained that the Soul is in some inscrutable way known "in and through" the states. For then, either it is nothing distinct from them but simply a name for their entirety, or else, if distinct, we know the states but not it. The strong contrast between the two is essential to the theory, and by as much as the states are immediately given, by so much the Soul is a non-empirical entity, that has to be known in some other manner. If the point were still doubtful, we need only consider Berkeley's statement that the "simple, undivided, active being" is apprehended by means of a "notion."

Now, if we were to assume a Soul, what account could we give of the manner in which our knowledge of it had been obtained? It would have to be an inference from the data of introspection. But what could justify such an inference, or even first suggest the thought of it to our minds? Never having experienced the Soul, we ought to be without an idea of it; never having witnessed the manufacture of consciousness, the thought of such manufacture should be wanting to us. The logical conclusion from our experience would be that consciousness exists in its own right. So that, even if a Soul actually existed, no tidings of it could possibly reach our ears, but we should live our lives out in utter ignorance of the fact. The only way to avoid this conclusion is to assume, with Berkeley, that the Soul is known by means of an innate idea or "notion."

But the hypothesis of a Soul involves a second difficulty equally great, in regard to the nature to be ascribed to it if assumed. What could the Soul itself, apart from consciousness, be like? It has been carefully distinguished from and opposed to consciousness, therefore it cannot have the latter's luminous nature. We are forced to conceive it as a dark and mysterious source from which consciousness in some unintelligible manner flows. Insensibly we are drawn to picture it by the aid of that illegitimate notion of matter existing with all its materiality apart from consciousness — in short, as a mind-atom. But, no matter how carefully we define it as immaterial, since we contrast it in nature with consciousness, the origin of the latter out of it is as irrational, as much "the birth of a new nature," as its origin out of matter. Thus the nature of the Soul in itself is as unassignable as our knowledge of it is inexplicable.

Finally, the phenomena-transcending assumption that occasions these difficulties is irreconcilable with the fact that our existence is something of which we are immediately aware. For the existence of consciousness is our existence. If the Soul should continue but consciousness cease, we should be as good as non-existent; whereas, if the Soul should be annihilated but consciousness still go on, we should exist as truly as now. Thus our existence is bound up with that of consciousness, not with that of the Soul; or, as I said before, the existence of consciousness is our existence.

Let us now consider the reasons that are held to justify the assumption of a Soul.

In the first place, there is the felt need of an Ego. Thinking, feeling, and willing, it is argued, as activities, imply a spiritual being whose activities they are. As there cannot be motion without an object to move, so there cannot be thought without a thinker. This may be admitted, but what it proves is not a Soul. For let us transfer the analogy of motion accurately. As the body that moves is given in perception along with the motion, so the being that thinks should be given in introspection along with the thought. And this, moreover, is the actual fact: the 'I' which is the subject of such propositions as 'I think,' 'I feel,' 'I will,' is immediately given in inner experience — not, it is true, at the moment known as such, yet still experienced, given. But, if so, the 'I' cannot be the same thing as the Soul, which is not given, and this particular reason for a Soul falls away.

Secondly, it will be urged that consciousness is empirically a thing so mutable and transitory that we cannot conceive it except as supported by some more durable underlying being, and that our choice lies between making it dependent on the brain and on the Soul. Furthermore, there is the storage of our ideas and the permanence of our characters to be accounted for. But since the brain, as material, cannot treasure up what is spiritual, the treasure-house must be the Soul.

We may admit that consciousness is incompletely self-explanatory, and that other realities have to be assumed in order to explain it. We may grant that there is a certain absurdity in a purely cerebral explanation of memory, if such explanation be understood as ultimate, especially when we consider that the brain exists, on the idealistic theory, only as an actual or possible modification of consciousness. On the other hand, every theory must recognize the empirical fact that permanence of memories is conditioned on intactness of cortical areas, and that memories may be lost piecemeal through lesion of particular areas.

I think we can allow their due weight to these various considerations, and yet obtain the desired 'support' for consciousness without having recourse either to the Soul or the phenomenal brain, if we assume that the brain as the basis of memories not now in consciousness is the symbol of these other realities. This, to be sure, presupposes the proof of things-in-themselves, for which we need the reality of consciousness as a premise. But, assuming this proof to have been given, the line I should take in suggesting a substitute for the Soul would be as follows.

Contemporary psychologists, feeling that physiological dispositions are things of a different order from mental states, assume corresponding to them *psychical* dispositions as the form in which our ideas persist when not in consciousness.[1] This assumption they make 'as a working-hypothesis.' But hypotheses work, or aid us in our work, only by virtue of their elements of truth, which we forbear for the moment to sift from their elements of error. We must therefore raise these hypothetical psychical dispositions to the rank of extra-mental realities; and a system of such realities, neither "simple" nor "undivided," yet quite sufficiently "active," will form our substitute for the Soul.

Since these extra-mental realities are coequal in reality with consciousness itself, the 'support' they furnish is not to be conceived in a metaphysical manner, as a relation of substance and accident, but after the pattern of the relation between the brain-process and extra-cerebral processes; in other words, as a relation of mutual influence and reciprocal

---

[1] Cf. Stout, *Analytic Psychology*, vol. i., pp. 21 ff.

dependence. The theory is offered without proof, merely with the object of showing how the motives that prompt to the assumption of a Soul might have justice done them in another way, more consistent with the facts of brain-physiology.

But, on any theory of its nature, this extra-conscious support of consciousness is only our potential, not our actual self. We exist actually only so far as the thoughts and feelings whose potentialities it enshrines become actualized in consciousness. In the words of Descartes: " I exist — how often? As often as I think. For perchance it might happen that, if I should altogether cease to think, I should at the same time wholly cease to be." What is this but an acknowledgment, from a believer in mental substance, that our essence lies, not in being a mental substance, but in being conscious? Consciousness, then, is a reality. The result of eliminating the Soul is not to degrade it into a mere train of dream-states, as is sometimes fancied, but to secure it in possession of the reality of which it would otherwise have been dispossessed by the Soul.

Theory of a Non-Phenomenal Subject

" Modern psychology," says a recent German writer, " rejects the notion of a mental substance, and puts in its place that of a unitary Subject of our thoughts, feelings, and volitions." The theory of a Subject has two forms, one of which frankly admits the Subject to be a fact of consciousness or datum of introspection, while the other makes it non-phenomenal. The latter form of the theory dates from Kant. By 'Subject' we are to understand the 'Ego as knower' as distinguished from the 'Ego as known,' the 'I' as opposed to the 'Me.' This is conceived as an active spiritual principle (not entity!) to which thoughts and feelings bear the relation of phenomena. It is not itself phenomenal, since it is that to which phenomena appear. It is *that which* thinks, feels, and wills.[1]

The non-phenomenal character of the Subject, on this theory, may be said to be not original, but a consequence of the strong antithesis recognized between the Ego and its thoughts and feelings. What is original is the observation that we do not merely speak of thoughts and feelings as existing, but say, 'I think,' 'I feel,' 'I will,' thus recognizing the peculiar relation in which they stand to an Ego. This relation is conceived after the analogy of that between the eye and the object it sees, and the inference drawn that, as the eye cannot see itself, so the Ego cannot be conscious of itself. But, in deference to the fact that we nevertheless *are* self-conscious, it is added that, although the Ego cannot know itself at the moment when it knows, yet it can turn and know itself the moment after, by means of a representative idea; and then, strangest

---

[1] This is the theory of Professor Ward; see his art. : " 'Modern' Psychology : a Reflexion," in *Mind*, *N. S.*, vol. ii. (1893), pp. 54 ff. For criticism of it, see Mr. Bradley's articles : " Consciousness and Experience," in *Mind*, *N. S.*, vol. ii. (1893), pp. 211 ff., and " A Defence of Phenomenalism in Psychology," in *Mind*, *N. S.*, vol. ix. (1900), pp. 26 ff.

of all, this idea is called, not simply an idea of the Ego, but the Ego — or rather an Ego, the 'empirical' one.

Now, it cannot be too strongly insisted that the existence of an Ego, and even the distinction commonly interpreted as that of two Egos, the 'empirical' and the 'pure,' are in no wise in question. These are indisputable facts. Nor is it my business here to offer a positive theory of them. I am concerned with the Kantian theory solely as an apparent piece of ontology — as positing, or appearing to posit, a non-phenomenal somewhat by contrast with which consciousness becomes a train of phenomena without reality. I ask whether such a theory is consistent with sound metaphysical principles.

Its advocates are inclined to resent the suggestion that their Subject is a non-empirical entity, no better than the Soul. And it must be allowed that there are material points of difference. The Subject is presumably not permanent like the Soul, but exists only when consciousness exists, as (so to speak) its subjective pole. Its function, moreover, is not that of storing ideas no longer in consciousness, but only that of contemplating and influencing ideas actually present. On the other hand, the Soul and the Subject have suspicious points of resemblance. Both are by definition non-phenomenal. Both cause our mental life to appear by contrast a mere train of phenomena without reality. The result of these agreements is that the Subject is exposed to exactly the same difficulties as the Soul.

(1) Granting its existence, it is impossible to give a rational explanation of the manner in which our knowledge of it was obtained. This difficulty is admitted even by its advocates, but they consider the alternative to be the rejection of an Ego altogether, for which they are naturally not prepared. They are unable to conceive a satisfactory phenomenalistic account of the Ego. Kant, for instance, quiets his mind with the remark that the difficulty of understanding how a Subject can inwardly intuite itself is "common to all theories alike"[1]: a palpable error, since it does not exist on the phenomenalistic theory. Whereas, on his own, it is impossible to understand how the thought of a Subject should ever arise in the mind. If the Kantian theory were true, the proper inference from our experience would be that our thoughts think themselves, and do not need a Subject. In short, if the Subject when it acts as such is unknowable, it should be unsuspected, untheorized about, unknown.

(2) But, even if our knowledge of it could be accounted for, it would be impossible to assign it a nature. Since its function makes it antithetical in nature to consciousness, we could only conceive it as an immaterial atom. But how such an atom could take charge of our thoughts and feelings, or they be attached to or fused with it to form a mind, it surpasses the power of human thought to conceive.

(3) Finally, the theory would be inconsistent with the fact that our whole knowledge of the Ego and

---

[1] See the quotation in Professor Ward's article, above referred to.

its function is in truth derived from experience. If we believe in an Ego peculiarly related to our thoughts and feelings, it is because we *find* an Ego so related whenever we think or feel. It is therefore a fundamental error so to conceive the relation as to extrude the Ego from experience and make it non-empirical.

It is not my business to offer a positive theory of the Ego; I am solely concerned to disprove supposititious entities or principles, and thereby vindicate reality for consciousness itself. But, as I have discussed the matter negatively, I may be permitted to say a word about the positive side of the question, especially as the seeming contradiction between the function of the Ego and its givenness constitutes an old philosophical puzzle.

The solution of this puzzle lies in seeing that the very same total experience or field of consciousness may be first 'knower' and then 'known,' according to the moment and aspect in which it is regarded. An experience or state of consciousness may be a vehicle of knowledge, may know, as we see from a memory; nor is there anything else that *can* know. Those who fancy that an indiscerptible entity, whether Soul or Subject, is better fitted to discharge this function than a state of consciousness, must have derived their ideas of knowing from some other source than introspection. The alternative is therefore *not* either to identify the Ego with objects of consciousness or to make it unknowable, but there is a third intermediate course: to make it experienced but not known. The key to the puzzle lies in the distinction between knowledge and experience. The Ego is the fresh experience as it comes, before we have had time to turn round upon it cognitively, and while we — that is, it — are engaged in cognizing other things. Hence, on the one hand, the eternal behind-handedness of cognition, and, on the other, the possibility at the next moment of knowing this knower in memory. This is the solution of the puzzle about the Ego, and no other solution is thinkable.[1]

The Kantian theory arises, as so many erroneous theories do, by giving to this empirical relation a non-empirical value. Because the Ego when it knows is not itself known, it is assumed that it is not even experienced. It thus becomes an eye, seeing other things but invisible to itself. But the eye, apart from seeing, exists as matter: how does the Ego exist apart from knowing? The unanswerableness of this question should teach the Subject-theorist wisdom.

Or, if the thing be not yet plain, his attention

---

[1] Compare with this Professor James's account of the Ego as "the passing thought," *Principles of Psychology*, vol. i., pp. 329-342, and Dr. Stout's contention that the object of thought is always other than the momentary consciousness by which we think it, *Analytic Psychology*, vol. i., pp. 40-46. — I ought perhaps to add that I am able to accept this contention only for the case of representative knowledge; and that what I here call 'experience' and distinguish from 'knowledge,' I later, by a usage which I believe expresses the profounder truth, call 'immediate knowledge' as distinguished from 'representative.'

may be called to certain further deductions from his theory. If there be a Soul or Subject, it is as impossible for me to be immediately conscious of my own existence as of that of other people. Another man's mind is not more inaccessible to me than the inmost essence of my own. I am cut off from myself; an impenetrable veil separates *me* from *me*. Now, this is surely hard. That other people's minds should not be immediately given seems only fitting. That our substitute for the Soul should not be immediately given is no hardship, since it is only our potential, not our actual self. But that our actual self should not be given, that we should be denied true self-consciousness and our essence made to consist in something other than thought and feeling — this, to speak frankly, is so great an absurdity, that I hardly know a greater of which a philosopher can be guilty.

If we reject both the above theories, the stream of consciousness with its empirical characters enters on the reality now vacated by the Soul or Subject. In this reality every thought and feeling shares. A pain, for instance, at the moment when it is felt, is as real as anything can be. It is no mere phenomenon; phenomena that are merely such, and not in another aspect realities or parts of realities, are a delusion. A perception, again, is a phenomenon as the symbol of an extra-mental reality, but in itself, as a state of consciousness, it is real.

Whether each pulse of consciousness has unity,

or is a field or a discrete assemblage, we need not inquire. Even were it an absolute unity, its reality would not lie in this unity apart from the thoughts and feelings, but only as characterized by them.

Of course consciousness is not a *permanent* reality, since it is subject to interruptions. But even the Soul, if we had one, could not make consciousness more permanent than it is found in experience to be. So long as it lasts, it is as real as anything can be. It is the very type of reality, an integral part of the universe of things. Moreover, it is for each of us the *prime* reality — the one part of that universe with which he has immediate contact. And it is surely an excellent thing that in our experience of our own minds we have immediate contact with a little portion of the real universe, instead of being — as on the hypothesis of a Soul or a Subject we inevitably are — cut off from reality at every point.

But, if consciousness is a reality, we have the premise we needed for the inference of other realities beyond it.

CHAPTER X

THINGS-IN-THEMSELVES: THEIR POSSIBILITY

By 'things-in-themselves' I understand realities external to consciousness of which our perceptions are the symbols. This use of language calls for a word of explanation and even defence.

Of course extra-mental realities might exist without being symbolized by our perceptions; and in that case it would be better to call them simply extra-mental realities. But if they not only exist, but have physical things for their symbols, they deserve the name of things-in-themselves: for they are exactly what Kant, in spite of his critical principles, retained under that name, and his successors made haste to throw overboard. The question we must consider is whether the post-Kantians were right in so doing. Or, admitting that their course was a strict deduction from Kantian principles, we must ask whether those principles can themselves be upheld.

The things-in-themselves thus contemplated as possible are perhaps, after all, not exactly those in which Kant believed. It depends on their nature. If by things-in-themselves we understand realities not only not immediately knowable to us, but unknown to any one, unexperienced even by themselves, antithetical to consciousness and quasi-material in their nature — in short, an unknowable, undefinable x — their irrationality and absurdity cannot be too freely admitted. This may seem to some the received and only warrantable sense of the term. But the arguments commonly employed to refute them are based partly on their nature, partly on their relation to our perceptions; and it seems desirable to show that the latter class of arguments is fallacious. On the other hand, he who asserts things-in-themselves is of course bound to give an intelligible account of their nature.

On the question of their existence in the sense defined, philosophers are divided, some treating them as a matter of course, others rejecting them as a delusion and a snare. The latter party even seems the more numerous. It is certainly striking that philosophers of such opposite tendencies as the English empiricists and the Hegelians should agree in rejecting them. If anything in philosophy went by the majority vote, we should have to look upon them as condemned.

The bearing of this question on our problem may be indicated in a word. The relation of mind and body will evidently be an essentially different thing, according as the body is the symbol of a reality external to consciousness, or only a phenomenon within consciousness.

Thorough-going Phenomenalism

By 'thorough-going phenomenalism,' as distinguished from ordinary half-way phenomenalism, I mean the total and consistent denial of the possibility of transcending experience and cognizing realities beyond. This is no uncommon view, though it may be doubted whether its upholders are fully alive to its implications. In a cruder, semi-materialistic form, it asserts that physical phenomena are all. Who has not at moments entertained the notion that perhaps there is no other world but that of the senses? One hears of people who take this notion seriously, and adopt it as a philosophy. Indeed, if we may believe Mr. Balfour, this is no isolated phenomenon, but there is a widespread and powerful 'naturalistic' movement, led by men of science, and representing the most formidable enemy of religion at the present time.[1]

But all Mr. Balfour's critics agree that his definition of 'naturalism' is too narrow. If the world of the senses is to be all, at least the 'internal sense' must be included with the rest, and the thoughts and feelings it reveals placed on a par with the data of touch and vision; otherwise the doctrine would be plainly indefensible. With this correction, the ultimate reality ceases to be the physical world simply, and becomes a sum of physical and mental facts.

But, if the idealistic account of physical facts be accurate, a further correction is necessary. According to that account, physical facts are in reality mental facts. But, if so, the data of the 'internal sense' include all the others, and there is in strictness but one kind of experience, namely, mental.

[1] See his *Foundations of Belief*, pp. 1–8.

With this second correction, the knowable universe ceases to be a sum of physical and mental facts, and becomes a sum of mental facts only; though of course the empirical difference still remains between mental facts which are thoughts and feelings and mental facts which are perceptions of matter.

Now, such a phenomenalism, admitting no existences not capable of being experienced, may seem to the reader the only logical result of the two preceding chapters. For we have resolved matter into our perceptions, and the mind into a series of mental states; and, though we have left it an open question whether our perceptions stand for things-in-themselves, yet the decided way in which we have rejected a non-phenomenal entity behind consciousness suggests a similar phenomenalism in the case of matter. To admit non-phenomenal existences behind matter, but deny them behind consciousness, seems at first sight a curiously one-sided and even materialistic position.

On the other hand, the denial of all knowledge transcending experience — the rejection, not merely of things-in-themselves, but of extra-mental realities in general — would imprison us within our own consciousness and make the latter co-extensive with the universe, thus contradicting our intimate persuasion that we are, mentally as well as physically, not the whole, but an infinitesimal part, of the sum of things. But, if reality in some form extends infinitely beyond us — as on every non-solipsistic theory it necessarily must — then our perceptions *may* be tokens of its nature and operations, as in the theory of Berkeley.

What we mean by empirical facts (using the term in the broadest possible sense) we know perfectly well, we know by experience: the conceptions of physical objects and events and of mental states are perfectly clear. But the conception of non-empirical existences, real yet incapable of being experienced, remains still vague and in the air. The difficulty of assigning to them a nature or accounting for our knowledge of them if assumed, and, moreover, their suspicious resemblance to the scholastic conceptions of material and mental substance, may very naturally incline us to reject them, and to accept thorough-going phenomenalism as the only rational and defensible account of human knowledge.

Nevertheless, phenomenalism is guilty of so monstrous an omission, that the latter needs only to be indicated in order to disarm all opposition and establish extra-mental realities at a stroke as a legitimate category of thought. *Thorough-going phenomenalism makes no provision for knowledge of the minds of other men and animals. They do not exist in its world.* So serious is this omission, that phenomenalism cannot be adjusted to it without admitting extra-mental realities in principle, and so ceasing to be thorough-going.

It seems hardly necessary to offer proof of the proposition that, for each of us, the minds of other men and animals are not empirical facts. We sometimes meet people, it is true, who seem to think that other minds are in some inexplicable way immediately known; but what these people really have in mind is doubtless the certainty of the knowledge rather than its immediacy. It seems clear that another man's mind cannot be a phenomenon for my consciousness. I can see his body; his mind I have to infer. Suppose him, for instance, to be suffering with the toothache: I can see his facial contortions, but the pain is an inference. It is the inference of something real, yet wholly and inevitably out of and beyond my consciousness.

Another man's mind, then, is in the strict sense of the term a non-empirical existence; something real, yet inaccessible to my immediate knowledge; as much so as material or mental substance, and differing from them only in the nature of that which is inferred. In inferring another mind I transcend my experience and make sure of an existence outside my consciousness; and my knowledge is transcendent in exactly the sense in which the post-Kantians rule out such knowledge in principle.

In short, as phenomenalism in the narrowest and crudest sense has to be expanded so as to admit the data of the 'internal sense,' which thereupon swallow up all the others; so this expanded phenomenalism is found to recognize only the data of *my* 'internal sense,' but to ignore those of the 'internal sense' of other people. But the doctrine cannot be expanded a second time without bursting.

The above argumentation neither rests on nor requires the proof of other minds: it takes them for granted. The justification of this belief (if rational justification it has) forms an interesting problem, too much neglected by philosophers. It is customary to explain it as resting on an argument from analogy, thus: other men make movements which resemble those due to thoughts and feelings in myself; consequently they have thoughts and feelings just as I have. That this reasoning is implicitly involved in all assumption of other minds seems undeniable. Nevertheless, the conclusion is in a certain way a *non sequitur;* it does not follow from the nominal premise, except with the aid of a suppressed premise which is not proven but assumed. For the analogy, owing to the peculiar position of the reasoner, is imperfect.

The argument amounts to this, that like consequents (intelligent movements) must have like antecedents (thoughts and feelings). But it is impossible for the antecedents to be perfectly alike, in that the thoughts and feelings which give rise to *my* movements are immediately given, while those which give rise to other people's movements are not given. The question presents itself, whether this essential difference in the mode of existence of the antecedents does not wreck the analogy.

Let us compare the argument with another where the analogy is perfect. Suppose that in the case of one other person I knew intelligent movements to be due to thoughts and feelings which were not given; then, indeed, on seeing a third person execute similar movements, I might argue from them to still other thoughts and feelings which were not given, and the analogy would be perfect. But when I argue from my thoughts and feelings, which are given, to another person's thoughts and feelings, which are not given, the conclusion introduces what is from my point of view a new mode of existence, and therefore contains an element not warranted by the premises.

If I already knew that the movements of other men and animals were due to conscious states, I might argue from the similarity of those movements to my own to the similarity of the conscious states, or from the unlikeness of those movements to my own to the unlikeness of the conscious states. But since I can have no rational ground for assuming that anything whatever exists outside my mind, the basis is wanting on which an argument from analogy might proceed.

It follows that no argument from analogy can possibly prove the existence of things extra-mental. The utmost it can do is to indicate their nature, when their existence is already known from some other source. And, when other arguments for extra-mental things are examined, they will be found to involve the same *non sequitur* and the same suppressed premise. In short, it is in the nature of the case impossible that consciousness should supply rational grounds for the inference of realities beyond itself. We can only find ourselves as a matter of fact inferring such realities, and continue to infer them in the absence of positive reasons to the contrary.

Now, it is surely a striking fact, and one whose

importance for epistemology can hardly be overestimated, that something to which neither the external nor the internal senses lend the slightest testimony may yet be with perfect certainty known to exist. It is strange indeed that so elementary a case of knowledge should not long since have been noticed and anatomized by philosophers. The omission is due to the fact that their attention has been mainly taken up with the question, whether our knowledge of general principles is derived from experience or from an *à priori* source; the emphasis laid on this antithesis having the effect of concealing the no less important antithesis between empirical and transcendent knowledge. Philosophers were so sure that all our knowledge must be derived either from one source or the other, that it never occurred to them that we might have a kind of knowledge less rational than either, a kind founded neither on reason nor experience, but solely on instinct. It never occurred to them that neither experience nor reason can fully account for the knowledge of other minds.

But we have no need to settle the grounds of this belief in order to use it against phenomenalism. The belief is there, unshakable, in the minds of philosophers and laity alike. All men regard other minds as no less certain than their own, nor would a philosopher receive a moment's attention who should call this belief in question. We may therefore (employing a procedure like that of the philosophers of common-sense, but with how far less risk of being challenged!) take the knowledge of other minds for granted, and use it as a test of epistemological principles. According to thorough-going phenomenalism, we can know only physical phenomena and our mental states. But other minds are to be found neither in the one category nor in the other. Then this is the *reductio ad absurdum* of thorough-going phenomenalism.

To conclude: we may call upon phenomenalists to have the courage of their convictions. To deny non-empirical existences is to deny other minds: consequently the consistent phenomenalist should be a solipsist. His principle not only affords him no warrant for assuming other minds, it positively forbids it; his logical position is solipsism. Now *psychologically* solipsism is of course a truism: we can have immediate knowledge only of our own mental states. But *ontologically* it is absurd: through our mental states, which alone are immediately given, we may obtain knowledge of non-empirical existences; as we see from the case of other minds.

Thus our indisputable knowledge of other minds completely refutes the current dogma about the unknowability and consequent irrationality of non-empirical existences. This dogma is no warrantable deduction from idealistic principles. The post-Kantians may be right in rejecting things-in-themselves; they may be right in denying that extra-mental realities have physical phenomena for their symbols, or stand in a relation of cause and effect to those phenomena, or have a nature in themselves like that x.] POSSIBILITY OF THINGS-IN-THEMSELVES 2?

of the phenomena and unlike that of consciousness they are certainly wrong in so far as they base the rejection on the general ground of the unknowability and irrationality of non-empirical existences. On the contrary: as the real world falls apart into two unequal segments, my mind and what is not my mind, the one immediately experienced and consisting in that experience, the other incapable of being experienced: so there are two corresponding kinds of knowledge, empirical and transcendent, knowledge of my own existence and knowledge of other existences.

Perception and Memory as Involving Transcendence

The foregoing refutation of thorough-going phenomenalism is of course not a proof of things-in-themselves, since there may be no extra-mental existences having physical things for their symbols. It only prepares the way for that proof by establishing the legitimacy of the general class to which things-in-themselves belong.

Before proceeding further, let us seek to add precision to our conceptions of empirical and transcendent knowledge by discussing certain cases which appear to be intermediate. For, while our knowledge of our own minds is clearly empirical and our knowledge of other minds clearly transcendent, the former being coincident with our experience and the latter passing wholly beyond it, between these extremes there lie two cases of undoubted knowledge which seem to partake partly of the empirical and partly of the transcendent character. These are perception and memory.

The case of memory, as the simpler, may be considered first. It is clear that what is immediately given, and therefore alone empirically known, is not the entire stream of consciousness but only its present moment. Relatively to that moment, the past experience remembered is in the position of another mind, and the knowledge of it necessarily transcendent; and that quite irrespectively of the subtle question, whether that experience in any sense still exists. Not only is the past experience as inaccessible as if it were in another consciousness, but (except on the untenable theory of a pure principle of identity binding past and present together) it literally *is* another consciousness, although one no longer existent. For memory is not our only means of communication with our past experiences, and reproduces for us but a minimal part of our mental history. In filling in the gaps we are reduced to conjecture, based on inference, the testimony of others, etc. Now, such conjecture presents the closest analogy to the process by which we infer other minds. Memory is therefore as genuine a surmounting of the bounds of immediate experience as the knowledge of other minds. The only difference is, that memory originated in and is in a sense the deposit left behind by earlier experience, while the knowledge of other minds was transcendent even at its origin.

The case of perception is much more difficult.

We do not hesitate to speak of physical objects and events as empirical facts; and, at the moment when our knowledge of them is obtained, they unquestionably are such. So long as actually perceived, they are empirical facts for the reason that they are at the same time mental states.

But, to make this statement perfectly adequate, we must add a qualification. They are empirical facts because they are *my* mental states. For the consciousness to which idealism shows them to be relative is my individual consciousness: every argument which proves them modifications of consciousness at all proves them modifications of my individual consciousness. If other persons perceive them as well, this signifies merely that other consciousnesses are modified similarly to mine, each having access only to its own modifications; the notion that the objects I see are literally *identical with* the objects you see being a gross superstition, refuted, among other things, by the facts of color-blindness. Thus our immediate knowledge of physical objects and events is only one case of our immediate knowledge of our mental states.

But now, the physical objects thus immediately known are invested by the mind with certain attributes very different from those which we ascribe to our mental states. From the fact that physical objects are immediately known because they are mental states, we might be tempted to infer that their reality is nothing more nor less than the reality of our perceptions. This, however, would be an error. When we compare the two, we find that the reality we ascribe to physical objects is an essentially different thing from the reality of our perceptions. The perception is a momentary existence, the object has a certain permanence; the perception ceases when we turn our eyes away, the object continues (or is supposed to continue) whether we perceive it or not. Sometimes we judge the perceived object to be unreal, as in hallucination; which would be impossible if its reality were identical with that of the perception. Now, the question presents itself, whether this enlargement of the object actually seen, this increment which imagination adds to sense, is matter of empirical or matter of transcendent knowledge.

It might be thought that the persisting object which we are supposed to perceive through and beyond our sensations is simply the extra-mental matter of the naïve realist. That this is not so, appears when we consider that the distinction between real objects and objects of hallucination exists equally on a purely phenomenalistic theory. Not only so, but, as idealists, we are obliged to give a phenomenalistic account, an account in terms of perceptions, of that empirical reality of physical objects which has to be recognized by all theories alike.

When, then, we conceive a physical object as real, this signifies that its being is not exhausted in the momentary experience, but extends to other experiences not now actual. Only the smallest part of its being is given in any single experience; the remainder is reserved for possible experiences that are only suggested. These latter are of three kinds. (1) We never experience all the parts of an object at once, but the parts actually experienced imply possible experiences of the remaining parts. (2) Our present experience of the object implies (within the limits laid down by physics — no object is exempt from mutation, or as such eternal) possible future experiences of the same object. (3) If the object is real, it must be perceptible to other persons as well as to myself, and such general perceptibility is implied in my judging it real. In brief, the reality of an object signifies its membership in an order in space and time existing for all similarly organized percipients.

The empirical reality consisting in the implication of these possible experiences must be carefully distinguished from a hypothetical metaphysical reality consisting in the implication of things-in-themselves. If things-in-themselves exist, perception, so far as it conveys knowledge of them, of course involves transcendence. But let us for argument's sake suppose things-in-themselves disproved, and let us ask whether perception involves transcendence so far as it implies other possible experiences.

Notwithstanding the fact that it embraces possible as well as actual experiences, we need not hesitate to speak of physical knowledge as empirical, since (in complete contrast to the knowledge of other minds) it both originates in and refers to experience. In other words, it is an account of what we have experienced, shall experience again, and might experience at this moment. The propriety of this use of language depends on the overshadowing importance, for daily practice, of the distinction between verifiable and unverifiable knowledge. Nevertheless, if we allow ourselves to speak of physical objects and events as empirical facts, we must remember that they are not so in the same sense as mental states, except at the moment of perception; and must therefore recognize a narrower and a broader sense of the word 'empirical,' according as it embraces possible as well as actual experiences, or actual experiences alone.

So far as perception includes the knowledge of possible experiences, it involves a transcending of the present moment of consciousness analogous to that characterizing memory. But while perception and memory, despite the fact that they both originate in and refer to experience, agree in exhibiting such relative transcendence, they differ in this important respect, that memory asserts another existence distinct from the present moment of consciousness, namely, the past experience; whereas perception does not assert real experiences, certain to come in the future, but only possible ones. Its assertions are purely hypothetical, not categorical, and would remain still true and valid even though at the next moment all percipients should be annihilated. While, therefore, we cannot deny perception to be in a sense transcendent, since it holds out to us a whole world of other states of consciousness as possible, yet it does not, like memory or the knowledge of other minds, in any way positively extend the bounds of the real world that environs the present state of consciousness. We must make a sharp distinction between a form of knowledge that merely tells us what *might* now be the content of our consciousness if the conditions were different, and a form that enlarges the bounds of the real world by bringing tidings of other existences, present, past, or future.

Let us bring these observations to a focus by considering a concrete instance of the distinction in question. Let us compare my knowledge of another man's brain with my knowledge of his mind. Both are inferred: I no more perceive his brain than his mind. But his brain is inferred as a possible perception; his mind as a real existence external to mine.

Possibly it may be contended that his mind, although not a possible *perception*, is yet a possible introspective experience for me, the difficulties being purely mechanical, like those which prevent our seeing the other side of the moon; the idea being that, if I could take up my abode in his organism, or strike up a nervous connection between my organism and his, I should have access to his thoughts and feelings.[1] But now, even on this rather venturesome hypothesis, the distinction for which I am contending remains as clear and necessary as ever. For the

---

[1] Such a suggestion is made by Karl Pearson, *Grammar of Science* (1st ed., 1892), p. 60.

point is, that the reality I ascribe to his mind does not, like the reality I ascribe to his brain, consist simply in its being a possible experience for me: *it consists in its being at this moment an actual experience for him.* This is something more, and fundamentally different. It therefore avails not to say that another man's thoughts and feelings might be given to me, so long as in point of fact they are not *and yet exist as actual.* Plainly, their existence as actual lies neither in their being an actual nor in their being a possible experience for me. Hence they are, so far as actual now, wholly and inevitably beyond me.

His brain-process, on the other hand, when not actually perceived, has no real existence at all. It exists solely as a possibility of perception, and the transcendence by which it is known is not categorical but only hypothetical.

Of course no phenomenalist would think of impugning the validity of perception and memory. Yet, so far as these involve transcendence, the one hypothetically, the other categorically, they are clearly inconsistent with the phenomenalistic principle. Thus we see how essential is transcendence to any form of knowledge that is more than simple experience.

But, though perception and memory involve transcendence, only the inference of other minds is transcendent knowledge in the full sense, as conducting us to existences real at this moment, yet neither experienced nor capable of being experienced. Here is the type to which things-in-themselves, if they can be established, would conform. But the proof of non-empirical existences in general is not yet a proof of things-in-themselves.

Metaphysics and Science

We saw in Chapter VIII that all the facts and laws of physical science admit of restatement in phenomenalistic terms, as accounts of the perceptions we should have in case certain conditions were fulfilled; their sole presupposition being that empirical reality of physical objects which has to be recognized by all doctrines alike. This is true not merely of the every-day processes of science, but of its remotest and subtlest theories. Yet we frequently meet with the notion that any inferences going beyond the immediate data of sense — such, for instance, as those involved in the atomic theory — are already metaphysical in their nature; in short, that atoms are non-empirical existences. To show the absurdity of this, and exhibit still more clearly the contrast between such existences and empirical facts, let us consider some examples of both.

The objects in distant and inaccessible regions of the universe — at the North Pole, on the other side of the moon, in remotest space — are not non-empirical existences because nobody has ever experienced them; for the difficulty of experiencing them is purely mechanical, and may in time be overcome. Meanwhile they are conceived as potentially visible and tangible, and as continuous with parts of the universe which are actually so. The same is true of the minute objects which the microscope reveals. Though we searched the entire universe with our unaided eyes, we should nowhere discover them; yet the microscope brings them to light, opening up a new dimension in the direction of the infinitely little. By a slight exercise of fancy, we may follow out this dimension in the opposite direction, towards the infinitely great : we may imagine a macroscope, which should shrink experience as the microscope expands it, thus disclosing to us more and more of immensity at once. But, in whichever direction we go, the facts remain still essentially visible and tangible, and continuous with the middling plane of existence in which we live.

Now, what holds of microscopic facts holds equally of the molecules, atoms, and luminiferous ether that are assumed to lie beyond. These are conceived as essentially visible and tangible, and as continuous with the larger objects that are actually so. We can conceive (even though the thing were optically impossible) a hyper-microscope which should disclose them to the eye. Far be it from me to assert that they really exist, even in this modest empirical sense: the atomic theory may be only a convenient working-hypothesis, or a piece of 'conceptual shorthand,' not a literal tale of facts. But, *if* they exist, they exist as possibilities of perception, not as non-empirical entities. Indeed, if we were to call the atomic theory a metaphysical hypothesis, what name would be left for the theory of material substance? Here comes the real 'passage into another kind.'

Metaphysics is sometimes represented as only empirical science carried further and deeper, in such wise that the validity of science presupposes certain metaphysical principles. Thus we are told that physics assumes a real world, while psychology assumes both this and other minds; assumptions which it is the business of metaphysics to overhaul. Even if this were true, it would not follow that metaphysics is simply a further continuation of empirical science. On the contrary, the two are different in kind and mutually independent; their relation is that of mutual complements, asking unlike questions concerning the same subject-matter. Hence their conclusions can never conflict. Empirical science is a sort of algebra, indifferent to the values which metaphysics assigns to its terms; metaphysics cannot alter or revise the conclusions of science, which must hold good on any metaphysical theory. On the other hand, we shall have to admit a certain reaction of science upon metaphysics, in so far as the data concerning which metaphysics asks its peculiar questions are not natural facts as they impress the uneducated, but natural facts as sifted and guaranteed by science.

To sum up: metaphysics differs fundamentally from empirical science in that it takes cognizance of and investigates a kind of knowledge never dreamt of by the latter, namely, knowledge of the non-empirical. As the real universe falls apart into two contrasted segments, my consciousness and what is not my consciousness, so there are inevitably these two kinds of knowledge, these two opposite positions of the mind towards reality. Empirical science stays at home, and investigates simply the laws of the sequence of phenomena within my consciousness; laws which must hold good even for the solipsist. Metaphysics roams abroad, concerning itself with the inference of those other existences which, together with me, make up the real universe. As chemistry asks how many kinds of elementary substance make up the material universe, so metaphysics asks how many kinds of existence make up the real universe. It distinguishes the legitimate kinds of non-empirical existence, such as other minds, from the illegitimate kinds, such as material and mental substance; and considers how the legitimate kinds are grouped together to form the whole of things.

Refutation of the Kantian Arguments against Things-in-Themselves

He who would establish the existence of things-in-themselves must cope successfully with the Kantian arguments against them.

Kant clung to things-in-themselves irrationally and in spite of his principles; and the first thing his successors found to do was to make away with them. The reality of the physical world, for them, is a purely empirical affair, a matter of objectivity, consisting in the fact that it presents itself independently of our wills, by a law of our mental constitution. This harmonizes well with the fact already mentioned, that what the plain man means by matter is the matter he immediately sees and feels. One of the commonest tasks of philosophy is to strip away the theoretical accretions that often obscure the simplest facts, that we may see these in their nakedness and make our conceptions square with them; and one of its wisest rules is to be economical of assumptions and content with the simplest workable scheme. Considerations of this nature make the rejection of things-in-themselves appear to many a happy deliverance from an ignoble superstition, and nothing will seem to them more retrograde and deplorable than the attempt to reinstate them. But the question is, whether a scheme so simplified is still workable. That one may sacrifice too much to simplicity and economy, is shown by the fact that the simplest and most economical of philosophies would be solipsism.

The principal reason why things-in-themselves are esteemed a superstition is because they are supposed to be necessarily unknowable in nature, to be a mere x. But we may now go a step further. That things-in-themselves are unlikely to have such a nature, appears from the fact that the first case of extramental realities we have recognized is other minds. Possibly things-in-themselves may prove to have a nature equally intelligible. It is not in this sense that they can properly be described as unknowable, but only in the sense that they are inaccessible to perception or immediate experience, like other minds. Yet, even in the latter sense, all that is true is that they are not *immediately* knowable. That we may have mediate yet authentic knowledge of them, is as certain as that we may have such knowledge of other minds.

To justify the assumption of things-in-themselves, we must show that our sensations are to be regarded as effects produced in us by the action of extra-mental causes. Against such a view, the Kantian philosophy interposes its veto on two grounds: (1) that the physical world is not given in our sensations, but constructed out of them by the intellect; (2) that the causal category, which is one of the instruments employed in such construction, is valid and applicable only within the bounds of experience, not as between experience and something non-empirical. Let us take up each of these propositions in turn, and consider whether it is sound in itself and a bar to the assumption of things-in-themselves.

(1) It must be admitted that our knowledge of the physical world is not an affair of the senses alone, and that unless the intellect came to their aid we should have no such knowledge as that which we actually possess. But from this it does not follow that the intellect creates the physical world, and that the latter's order comes from within, not from without the mind. It is evident, in the first place, that if the intellect creates the world it does not do so voluntarily and consciously, but constrained by internal influences as inexorable, as independent of our will and knowledge, as though they came from without. Secondly, it is untrue that the data of sense

are at the outset a manifold without form or order, in such wise that these influences must needs come from within. Though spatial discrimination is an act of the intellect, it is rendered possible by physiological arrangements in the eye and skin, enabling the parts of the object to affect the nervous system separately; and these separate affections of the skin and retina give rise to separate affections of the brain. Now, it is unthinkable that the spatial order thus transferred from the object to the retina and the brain should fail to have its counterpart in the sensation, and have to be subsequently restored by the intellect. On the contrary, we must assume that in the sensation spatial order is somehow implicit, and by the intellect discovered there, not first introduced.

But what holds of spatial order holds of every other kind of order that enters into our conception of the physical world — of temporal, substantial, and causal order.

Let us consider the second of these — that in virtue of which we attribute to the object reality. We have seen that the reality of the object is not identical with the reality of the perception as a mental state; that the reality of the object consists, not in the actual existence of the perception, but in its permanent possibility. Evidently we do not add to an object's reality by deigning to perceive it, or subtract from its reality by turning our eyes away. Its reality lies wholly in the permanent possibility of its perception, not at all in the realization of this possibility in a particular case. But is a permanent possibility a thing that can be experienced or given to sense? Clearly not. It seems to follow that the object is not a datum of sense but a construction of the intellect; and this seems to imply, once again, that we are prompted to construct it by a spontaneous unfolding of mental energy, not by influences acting upon us from without.

But this would be a complete *non sequitur*. It may be shown (*a*) that the object is, after all, a datum of sense, though the reality we attribute to it is not apprehended by sense; (*b*) that the promptings which lead us to attribute reality to it come from sense; (*c*) that the best explanation of the permanent possibility of the sensation is the presence of an extra-mental cause, which by its persistent action on sense makes the sensation permanently possible.

The doctrine that physical objects are not sensibly given offends against our instinctive feeling that something sensibly given is what we mean by physical objects. The argument that they *cannot* be thus given because their reality consists, not in actual sensation, but in its permanent possibility, involves a curiously wire-drawn fallacy. Permanent possibility of what? Surely of the sensation. This doctrine deals in possibilities as if they had reality apart from that of which they are possibilities; but such paper possibilities are worthless except as they are convertible into the coin of sensible fact. The particular givenness of the sensation is one of the specimens and proofs of its permanent possibility. The latter is not something behind and distinct from the particular sensation, like a Platonic idea, but is embodied and exemplified therein. It would therefore be more accurate to say that the reality of the object lies in the particular givenness of the sensation *regarded as a pledge of* its permanent possibility.

To have the matter perfectly clear, we must distinguish between the present existence of the sensation and its future existences. Is it its present existence, or only its future existences, which we assert to be permanently possible? Evidently only the latter. Its present existence, which is yet an essential part of its total existence, has ceased to be a possibility and become an actuality; it is therefore a possibility no longer. The total existence of the object is a chain consisting of many links, most of them merely possible, but one actual. I do not make an object more real by deigning to perceive it, but if it did not change, on my so deigning, from a possible sensation into an actual one, the possibility would not be truly such. So long, then, as there are minds actually engaged in perceiving, the physical world does not consist wholly of possible, but partly of possible, partly of actual sensations. If all its parts were actually experienced, if my mind were so expanded as to take in at once the entire panorama of nature in all its details, the world would consist wholly of actual, and not at all of possible, sensations.

It will be replied that this verges on the absurd, and is a doctrine possible only to the solipsist, since it leaves wholly out of account the fact that the physical world is perceived in common by many minds. Since you and I perceive the same object, and since the sensations by which we perceive it are not identical but distinct, the object cannot be identical with the sensations, but must be a reality, *i. e.*, a permanent possibility, collected from them by both our minds alike. This objection falls to the ground the moment we consider that no two persons ever do or can perceive the same object, but always different parts or aspects of it, their perceptions being complements, not duplicates. This completes the proof that when a possibility is realized it ceases to be a possibility, and that the reality of objects so far as actually given therefore coincides with the reality of our sensations. The difference of mental and physical thus becomes a difference of two orders in which the very same facts are arranged.

But now, it is one thing for the object to be sensibly given, another for its permanence and membership in the physical order to be known. Objects may be sensibly given to very low animals, without their necessarily perceiving them as such. For this the intellect is undeniably necessary. But the work of the intellect is in no wise creative. Because the object's permanence and membership in the physical order are not given in any *single* experience, it does not follow that they cannot be collected from a number. The intellect that does this collecting is no *à priori* faculty, but simply memory and comparison; and what it remembers and compares is simply the sensible experiences. These recur, they come in a certain order, they exhibit a certain permanence: all this the intellect notes and stores away, till it forms at last, by the piecing-together of these remembered data, the conception of a single continuous physical world. Thus the intellect only elicits and realizes in thought an order that was implicit in the stream of sensations from the outset. The physical world is not constructed, but only re-constructed, by the intellect. In its proper essence it is a fact of sense.

But, once more, because there is an order inherent in our sensations, it does not follow that this order was impressed upon them from without. It might still be due to an unfolding of energy from within, not now in the intellectual but in the sensible realm.

The fact, however, that physical things are experienced in common by different persons would be more simply explained on the former hypothesis. The exact agreement between your perceptions and mine, in contrast to the private and personal character of our thoughts and feelings, is an astonishing fact, which calls for some explanation. Phenomenalism must be satisfied to register a pre-established harmony. Yet the agreement would be so simply explained by the hypothesis that the coincident perceptions are so many separate effects of a common cause, external to both our minds and acting in the same manner on each!

(2) This brings us to the second Kantian argument against things-in-themselves, namely, that it is ille-

gitimate to employ the causal category for the purpose of transcending experience.

To state the idea in Kantian language: this is a category which the mind employs to connect its sense-experiences and elaborate them into the perception of an orderly world, and here is its sole legitimate sphere of application; it cannot be legitimately used to connect sense-experiences with something non-empirical. To express the same idea as Hume or Mill would have expressed it: the causal relation is one of whose existence we learn from experience; in experience we always find it connecting empirical events, *i. e.*, actual or possible perceptions; and we have no right to take a relation which in experience has always connected empirical events, and assume it to connect an empirical event with something non-empirical. This is a proceeding to which experience can lend no color. Experience never can afford us a reason for passing beyond experience. The world whose parts are connected by causal relations is a world composed partly of actual and partly of possible perceptions, not a world composed partly of perceptions and partly of things-in-themselves.

The force of this argument is perhaps more strongly felt in the analogous case of space. To assume causal relations beyond the range of experience is like assuming that different minds are in space, and near to or remote from one another. It is clear that the world of which space is the form is a world composed partly of actual and partly of possible perceptions, not a world composed partly of perceptions and partly of things-in-themselves. Space, as a character of perceived objects, is incapable of containing existences that cannot be perceived. Moreover, perceptible objects and events completely fill it out, and leave no room in it for extra-mental realities. But what is true of space is true *mutatis mutandis* of causality.

This argument must be admitted to be logically sound. *Nevertheless, it fails to prove what it is supposed to prove, namely, the impropriety of using the causal category to transcend experience, owing to the fact that in experience two distinct systems of causal relations are given, one real and the other phenomenal, one of which may be legitimately used for this purpose and the other not.* To establish this conclusion, I shall show (*a*) that in certain indisputable cases we recognize causal relations as connecting our mental states with extra-mental realities, and likewise as connecting our mental states *inter se;* (*b*) that in certain other cases we distinguish in an unmistakable way between the real causality that connects our mental states *inter se* and with extra-mental realities, and the phenomenal causality that connects physical events.

(*a*) Suppose I am angry, and strike you a blow that causes pain. Here an event in my mind has been followed by an event in yours, and the sequence is obviously not accidental but causal. Not only so, but since my mind is for yours a thing extra-mental, the pain you feel is an effect due to the action of an extra-mental cause. Or suppose that you thereupon communicate your ideas to me by means of language, in the way of remonstrance. Here an event in your mind is followed by an event in mine, and the relation again is obviously causal. On such inter-mental causal relations all human intercourse depends.

These simple cases completely refute the Kantian argument, and establish in principle the legitimacy of referring events in consciousness to the action of extra-mental causes. They show that there is in consciousness a real system of causality, to which mental states as such are subject, entirely distinct from the phenomenal system that connects our perceptions considered as symbols.

Nor can satisfactory reasons be offered for refusing to regard these relations as causal. It is true that the causation is indirect, and apparently takes place through the medium of matter, thus involving a double interaction. But the parallelist has his alternative account: the causation takes place through the medium of the things-in-themselves for which matter stands. To urge this account at present would of course be to argue in a circle; and we have no need to specify the medium through which the causation takes place, in order to be entitled to assert that the relation is truly causal. The interactionist *must* admit such causal action from without, the parallelist *may* admit it; only the automatist is pledged to reject it.

Nor need we go into the nature of causality, and decide whether it involves a transference of energy or 'real tie,' or only a uniform sequence. On any theory the difference between an accidental and a causal conjunction remains, and in this case the conjunction is clearly causal. Indeed, that it must be causal follows, as we have seen, from parallelism itself. For the brain-event corresponding to the anger is clearly the cause of the brain-event corresponding to the pain; and if the brain-events are active things, the mental states must be active things too; and if the brain-events are causally related, so likewise must be the mental states. So that the parallelist, like the interactionist, not only *may* but *must* admit inter-mental causality; and only the automatist is free to deny it.

Of course such causality is flatly contradictory of those quasi-automatist theories which make of causation a purely or a predominantly physical affair: the theory that the brain-events are active things, but the corresponding mental states mere epiphenomena without causal connection; and the theory that the mental states are active only in conjunction with and, as it were, by courtesy of their accompanying brain-events, not independently and in their own right. The construction to be put upon these theories will depend on whether the brain-events are conceived to exist only as possible perceptions, or somehow independently of the mental states they are said to accompany, as things-in-themselves. In the former case, it is not obvious how a possible perception (since perceptions of brain-events are in fact never actualized) can either assist a mental state or take the causal load off its shoulders. If, on the other hand, the brain-events are supposed to exist as things-in-themselves, there is an alternative to the hypothesis that they are distinct from the mental state and co-operate with or replace it, which I cannot here indicate without anticipating. On the whole, I am content to take my stand on the *primâ facie* fact of such inter-mental causality.[1]

I have put inter-mental causality first because the examples of it are so plain and convincing; not that I expect they will make any immediate impression upon stiff-necked Kantians. The next step in the argument consists in showing that causality is a category applying to mental states in general. Thus, when a pain or ache inhibits thought; when a conscious effort enables us to recall a forgotten name; when one idea suggests another — we have instances of causal action so unmistakable, that only a mind prepossessed by tradition can prevent our recognizing them. This conclusion is avoided on the plea that the antecedent in each case is not the *entire* cause of the result — which is nothing to the point. Or, when a sense-experience leaves behind a mental image or a memory, the two are causally related; the apparent temporal gap being no argument to the contrary, since it is only apparent and requires to be filled out. In sensations, on the other hand, we have mental states which present themselves as distinctly *not* effects (immediately, at least) of anything before in consciousness. And the *rationale* of this

[1] I regret that I cannot consider here the objections to mental causality urged by Royce, in his review of Stout's *Analytic Psychology*, in *Mind, N. S.*, vol. vi. (1897), pp. 379 ff., and by Münsterberg in his *Grundzüge der Psychologie*.

contrast between images and sensations appears when we look at the physical side, and find that mental states which are effects of previous mental states are correlated with brain-events which are effects of previous brain-events, while mental states which are not effects of anything before in consciousness are correlated with brain-events called forth by nerve-currents from the periphery.

(b) If it be admitted that mental states are subject to causality, this would apply to perceptions as much as to other mental states. But now, physical events exist only as perceptions (actual or possible), and physical events also are subject to causality. Whence it apparently follows that our perceptions are at one and the same time subject to two causal orders. The question arises, how this is possible, how these two causal orders can be reconciled with each other. The answer is simple. *These two causal orders are not co-ordinate in value: one of them is real, whilst the other is only phenomenal or symbolic.* Our perceptions are members of the real causal order as mental states: they are members of the phenomenal causal order as symbols, the phenomenal relation being the symbol of a real relation between events external to consciousness.

To establish this distinction, I need only cite every-day instances in which we make it without thinking. Suppose I will to move my arm, and the movement happens. The movement exists only as a perception. Now, while we affirm the volition to be the cause of the movement, we absolutely deny it to be the cause of the perception of the movement. But, if the movement exists only as a perception, why the distinction?

When we turn to the physiological side of the occurrence, we find facts which amply justify the latter. For, physiologically, the movement is one event and the perception of it another, subsequent to the first in time. In order that the movement should be perceived, light-rays must pass from the arm to the eye, and nerve-currents from the eye to the brain, and only then does the perception of the movement arise. Indeed, the notion of the volition causing the perception directly is psychophysically absurd, since the two are correlated with brain-events which are related as cause and effect not directly, but only indirectly, through a loop passing from the brain to the arm, from the arm to the eye, from the eye to the brain. No wonder, then, if we discriminate thus between the movement and its perception!

Let us consider a second case. Suppose one billiard-ball strikes against and communicates its motion to another. Here the motion of the first ball is the cause of the motion of the second, and the causal relation is (if ever in the physical world) directly perceived. Now, these two motions exist only as perceptions. Yet, while we affirm the first motion to be the cause of the second, we absolutely deny the perception of the first motion to be the cause of the perception of the second. Here again, the reason for such a distinction becomes perfectly plain when we turn to the physiological side. For, in order that the two motions should be perceived, light-rays must pass from the billiard-balls to the eye and nerve-currents from the eye to the brain, calling forth three brain-events slightly subsequent to each other, but both also slightly subsequent to the extra-bodily motions for which they stand. Now, it is evident that these brain-events are not causally related to each other. They are merely successive side-effects of a causal process taking place outside the body. But, since the brain-events are not causally related, the corresponding perceptions cannot be; and no wonder, therefore, if we insist that the movements are, while the perceptions are not, causally related.

Here, then, are two plain cases in which we involuntarily distinguish between the causal relations of perceptions and the causal relations of events perceived. And the physiological facts not only warrant but necessitate the distinction. They compel us to recognize that, although physical events exist only as mental states, the causal relations that appear to connect them do not connect the mental states, but have a merely phenomenal value, as symbols of real causal relations which cannot in the nature of the case be immediately given.

To this account of the matter it may be objected that it somewhat falsifies our involuntary judgment, by placing the *real* motions, the motions that *are* causally related, beyond and out of reach of the perceptions. Whereas, though there is unquestionably a distinction between the perceptions and the motions perceived, yet the latter are immediately given as much as the former — in a word, they *are* perceived.

To this I reply that it is not my theory, but the physiological facts, that inevitably place the real motions beyond and out of reach of the perceptions. The relations of things here are a trifle complex, and our only course is to seek to make our ideas a match for them. We are face to face again with that mysterious phenomenon of doubling, that curious repetition of the physical world on a different plane, which we encountered already in an earlier chapter. Physiological psychology, by correlating our perceptions with brain-events, seems to have engendered two physical worlds where but one existed before: the world in which sensory stimuli call forth brain-events, and the world of our perceptions. Of course this is a sort of an optical illusion, an Iceland-spar phenomenon. We need only recur to experience to see that there is but *one* physical world, the world of our perceptions, and that in that world sensory stimulations and brain-events have their place along with extra-bodily motions. Are the perceptions, then, not really accompanied by physiological events at all?

I leave the reader to complete the reasoning: the line of thought is one which we cannot follow out further at present. All we need, as a premise for our argument, is the indisputable distinction between the causal relations of perceptions and the causal relations of events perceived, the real value of the former and the merely phenomenal value of the latter. Equipped with this distinction, we are now in a position to deal with the Kantian argument forbidding the use of the causal category for the purpose of transcending experience; to point out in what sense it is sound, and to show why it nevertheless fails to justify its veto.

The point is, that the causality to which this argument properly refers is the phenomenal kind, the kind that connects physical events *inter se*. With reference to this kind, the argument is sound and the veto valid. The Kantians are perfectly right that this phenomenal kind of causality holds good only within experience, and cannot be legitimately extended beyond its bounds. The world whose parts it connects is a world composed of perceptible events, events that have existence only as actual or possible perceptions. All the parts of this world are potentially accessible to experience, and it is by successively experiencing them and then piecing them together in imagination — much as children do the parts of a dissected map — that we construct our conception of a physical order. Moreover, perceptible events completely fill out this order and constitute it a 'locked system,' in which no room is left for anything non-phenomenal.

But of the real, inter-mental kind of causality — the kind that connects mental states, whether in the same or in different minds — the Kantian argument takes no notice, and indeed completely ignores its existence. Now, with reference to this kind of causality the Kantian veto does not hold good. No valid objection can be urged against our employing it to transcend experience. Indeed, this is precisely what in the next chapter I propose to do.

CHAPTER XI

THINGS-IN-THEMSELVES: PROOFS OF THEIR EXISTENCE

THE result of our reasonings thus far has been merely to establish that things-in-themselves are not antecedently impossible. I have shown (1) that extra-mental existences are a legitimate category of thought; (2) that causal relations may exist between them and consciousness; (3) that the physical order is given in our sensations. But I have not shown that the physical order is symbolic of a real order of which our sensations are effects. For anything I have shown, the universe might consist wholly of individual minds having causal relations with one another; or, if perchance there were existences additional to these, they might not be symbolized by our perceptions. If, then, existences symbolized by our perceptions are to be established, positive proofs must be forthcoming.

Of such proofs we may distinguish three, founded respectively on cosmological considerations, on the facts of physiology, and on the facts of evolution.

First or Cosmological Proof

Let us consider the conception of the universe which would result if things-in-themselves be rejected. Owing to our explicit recognition of other minds as extra-mental facts, this conception would differ essentially from that of the thorough-going phenomenalist. For the universe would consist, not of a sum of physical and mental phenomena, but of a multitude of individual minds. These minds, owing to their internal unity, and to that external separateness in virtue of which they are mutually extra-mental, would appear discrete existences. The greater the stress laid on the apparently non-natural aspects of consciousness — its unity and isolation, its transcendent knowledge — the more discrete would they appear. They would seem to be monads, each self-poised and existing in its own right, and their mutual knowledge would appear miraculous. In a word, the resulting conception would be that of a pluralism. Instead of a single continuous world, a universe, we should have as many little worlds as there were minds.

Why do we recoil from such a conception? Whence our conviction that, despite the separateness of individual minds, the world is yet continuous and one? In the first place, pluralism is hard to reconcile with the every-day relations between minds, the cognitive and the causal. These could be explained only miraculously, by means of a pre-established harmony. On any theory, their effect is to draw the minds together into a larger whole. Moreover, they imply a certain order of arrangement of the minds, since a mind cannot know or act on any other mind it pleases, but only on those whose bodies are next its own — in short, an order in the real world corresponding to that of space in the phenomenal. Thus, even though the minds remain discrete, the relations that connect them give to our conception of the universe a turn in the direction of monism.

But the main source of our monistic prepossessions is the physical world with its continuity and unity. Of this world the minds are in some sort inhabitants; they seem connected by being anchored to bodies lying in its midst; their relations seem carried on, not directly, but through the medium of matter. Monism, then, arises by transferring to the real world, the world of minds, the unity and continuity found to characterize the physical. It is true that the physical world exists only in our perceptions; that we perceive it only piecemeal and in fragments, so that the whole of it never exists at once; and that our idea of its unity is the work of imagination, treasuring up the fragments and piecing them together into the idea of a whole never completely revealed to the senses. The idea of its unity is not on that account the less firmly fixed in our minds, the less necessary to practice, the less essentially true. Its transference to the real world is unquestionably the principal source of our tendency towards monism.

Assuming without further argument the ultimate legitimacy of this tendency, let us inquire whether the materials thus far supplied us are sufficient for the construction of a monistic universe. If the individual minds are to be joined into a compact whole, relations of cognition and causality seem a frail and shadowy bond with which to unite them. But now, we have seen that the minds are not, so to speak, juxtaposed, in such wise that the action of one upon another is immediate, but are separated, as it were, by gaps, and these gaps filled out apparently with matter. The minds are thus like oases dotted over a desert of matter, all communication between them taking place indirectly, by way of the matter. And the question is, whether intervening matter can serve to join separate minds into a universe.

In discussing this question, let us employ again the example of an angry person striking a blow that causes pain. Here the mental state of anger was accompanied or followed by a brain-event that led to muscular contractions and a movement of the arm through space; the impact of the fist upon the other person's skin then aroused nerve-currents, and these then led to a brain-event which was accompanied or followed by the mental state of pain. (I disregard the alternative account offered by automatism, as inconsistent with the now established causality of mental states.) Here we have a causal chain of which the first and last links are mental and the intermediate links physical. Let us consider such a mixed causal chain from the point of view of idealism.

According to idealism, physical events are either actual or possible perceptions in a consciousness. Of the physical events here concerned, obviously only a small part can be actual perceptions, the remainder — *e. g.*, the nerve-currents and brain-events — being hidden away from sight and touch. Let us, however, for argument's sake assume that all are actual, and that for both persons. Both A and B, that is, perceive the entire series of physical events intervening between the anger and the pain. But now, each of these series of perceptions is contained wholly within the mind of A and of B; and neither A's perceptions nor B's can very well serve to bridge the gap between their two minds. Whereas, if the perceptions of both were symbols of a chain of real events outside their minds, by this chain of real events the gap would be bridged.

As we have feigned that all the physical events are perceived by both, we may be permitted to suppose the case in which they are perceived by neither, because both A and B are blind, or because the occurrence takes place in the dark. Here all the physical events are merely possible perceptions. But possible perceptions are not real events either in or out of a consciousness, and are therefore still more obviously unfitted to bridge the gap between the two minds. For gap there is, as is shown by the temporal relations of the events in question. Suppose the whole occurrence to occupy one second, and of this the two mental events to occupy each one-tenth and the physical events the remaining eight-tenths. The phenomenalistic account of the matter then comes to this, that during the first tenth of a second a real event happened, namely, the anger, and during the last tenth of a second a real event happened, namely, the pain, but that during the intermediate eight-tenths of a second nothing happened at all. For a possible perception is nothing, at the moment. A real event caused nothing, nothing then caused nothing, and so on, until finally nothing caused a real event. Such is the inevitable result of attempting to bridge the gap between minds by means of their own states. Whereas again, if we assume these states to be symbols of real events outside the two minds, these real events, being co-ordinate with the pain and the anger, will be fitted to connect them.

Let us consider a second case. Suppose the blow which causes B's pain to be inflicted, not by angry A, but by the falling limb of a tree, detached by a gale of wind. The pain will be none the less real because due to a purely physical cause. But a purely physical cause, it then appears, is able to accomplish the same result as a real extra-mental event! Now, if the physical cause exists only as an actual or possible perception, this is surely a paradox. But, if it stands for a real event outside B's mind, the parity of action is explained.

The reason why most thinkers find no incongruity in an action of mind upon mind through the medium of matter is because they wholly fail to realize the disparity between mental events, which are real, and physical events, which are only actual or possible perceptions. They illegitimately endow the latter in thought with a reality apart from perception which they can properly have only on a realistic theory; or, if they do not so far forget their idealism, at least they yield to the constraint of the facts and acknowledge causal relations between the two, without troubling themselves to inquire what meaning such relations can have when the physical events are interpreted in terms of perceptions.

In the further development of the argument, we may turn to account a certain hypothesis of contemporary psychology. We have seen that the metaphysical incongruity of interaction between mental and physical is felt by psychologists in connection with the phenomena of retention. On the one hand, physiological facts prove that the instrument of retention is not the Soul but the brain; on the other, the brain as a physical fact seems wholly unfitted to serve for the storing-up of mental states. This has led to the theory that to the physiological traces or dispositions which the brain *is* competent to store psychical dispositions correspond. And it is pointed out how recollection, associative suggestion, and even attention involve the co-operation with conscious processes of an extra-conscious factor which is none other than the psychical dispositions in question.

Now, the theory of psychical dispositions may be taken as literal metaphysical truth, or only as a convenient working-hypothesis of psychology. If taken in the latter way, it is wholly superfluous: for the physiological dispositions would have answered just as well, the difficulty about their interaction with consciousness being purely metaphysical. But if it be taken, as in the end it must, as literal metaphysical truth, then it is clearly the assumption at a certain point, and on a very limited scale, of things-in-themselves. And, reasoning from the principles that have dictated this assumption, it is easy to show that the theory requires, in consistency, an indefinite extension.

Psychical dispositions are assumed in order to account for the re-appearance of ideas after an interval, because it is felt that only a portion of the factors at work are given within consciousness. But in how many other cases do events happen in consciousness the factors of which are not given! If we must assume causes for our ideas when they re-appear, why not also for our sensations when they appear? The fact that the former have been in consciousness before, while the latter have not, constitutes no valid reason for discriminating between them. Why not, in short, for every event that cannot be traced directly to a cause within consciousness? If for the re-appearance of ideas, why not for their failure to re-appear, as in amnesia, aphasia, mental blindness? If for the failure of particular states, why not for the failure of consciousness in general, as in sleep or under chloroform, or for its derangement, as in insanity? If for the appearance of particular states, why not for the appearance of consciousness in general, as on waking from sleep or on coming to after anæsthetics? Why not, finally, for its first appearance in the child and in the race? Thus psychical dispositions are to be regarded as only a species of a great genus, comprising all the extra-mental facts which are in immediate juxtaposition with and causal relation to consciousness.

A still further enlargement of the conception is necessitated by the fact that we can discover within the circle of consciousness only a portion of the *effects* of our mental states. Thus attention may increase the vividness of a sensation, or will detain an image in the focus; but, when a volition causes a bodily movement, its immediate effects, if they be more than possible perceptions of brain-events which no human being will ever actually perceive, must be real events happening beyond the pale of consciousness, of which these physical events are merely symbols. Indeed, psychical dispositions themselves are to be numbered among these extra-mental effects when regarded, not from the point of view of the ideas which are their effects, but from that of the sensations which are their causes.

To summarize briefly this first or cosmological proof: things-in-themselves must be assumed in order to fill in the gaps between individual minds, and give coherence and intelligibility to our conception of the universe. Without them, the universe would consist wholly of individual minds with gaps of nothingness between, and our philosophy be one of pluralism. But the fact that causal influences get across the gaps proves that these are filled.

Second or *Physiological Proof*

The physiological and evolutionary proofs result from considering our perceptions in connection with the physical events that accompany them.

Every true sensation involves a train of physiological events consisting of the following three members: sensory stimulation, afferent nerve-current, brain-event. Now, for the interactionist and the automatist, and even for the parallelist, this plainly marks out the sensation as an effect. For the interactionist and the automatist, for they expressly hold the sensation to be the effect of the brain-event. For the parallelist, since the character of the brain-event as an effect must be transferred by analogy to the sensation.

It is an essential part of the parallelist conception that the causal relations of brain-events run parallel to and permit inferences regarding the causal relations of mental states. Thus the order in which images suggest each other corresponds to the order in which the respective brain-areas are excited, and this helps to explain the phenomena of aphasia. But the widest distinction of all is that between brain-events due to previous brain-events and brain-events due to nerve-currents from without; and this is the physiological counterpart of the distinction between events in consciousness due to previous events in consciousness and events due to extra-mental causes. Since sensations, then, of all other states, correspond to brain-events due to nerve-currents from without, they must be effects of extra-mental causes. They cannot be denied the character of effects without limiting and contradicting the parallelism; and if they are effects, they can only be due to extra-mental causes.

Quite apart, however, from the indications furnished by physiology, this character is recognizable introspectively, being what is commonly called the 'passivity' of sensation. This does not mean that sensations are effects but not causes; for every effect becomes in its turn a cause, and sensations are as active as other mental states, *e. g.*, in attracting attention or suggesting ideas. What is meant is rather that *we* are passive in the reception of them; that is to say, that they are not due to those previous events in consciousness whose activity we conceive as our own.

We have, then, both the evidence of introspection and that of the corresponding physiological events, the two bearing each other out; so that sensations cannot be denied the character of effects, due to some sort of action upon the mind, without running counter both to psychology and to physiology. But now, the things that thus act on the mind seem to be sensory nerve-currents or sensational brain-events. But these are only actual or possible perceptions; they have no existence apart from percipient minds, and are therefore incompetent to act on the mind from without, as was shown in the preceding proof. The cause of a sensation, if it have one in any true sense, must be an event equally real with the sensation. Hence, unless we are to deny all true conditioning value to the physiological events which lead up to a sensation, we must look upon them as symbols of extra-mental events.

What lulls the phenomenalist to sleep and prevents his drawing this inference is of course the fact that the physiological events, like physical events in general, can be interpreted as only actual or possible perceptions. He may even deem it a gross *petitio principii* on my part to admit that physical events in general may not be, but insist that physiological events must be, symbols of things-in-themselves. But this is to ignore the peculiar relation in which the physiological events stand to our perceptions, the peculiar knot into which the world of perception here ties itself up, with the result of that strange phenomenon of doubling which we have twice before encountered.

In every actual case of perception, the entire fact is not simply the presence of a physical object to consciousness, but at the same time, and as a condition of that presence, the existence of a (potentially perceptible) train of causes and effects connecting the object with the percipient's brain. If, for instance, I perceive a table, this necessarily involves the presence in the physical world, along with the table, of light-rays passing from the table to the eye and nerve-currents passing from the eye to the brain. Without this train of causes and effects, perception is physically (or shall I say psychophysically?) impossible. All other trains are irrelevant, they may or may not occur: this train *must* occur, or there is no perception.

Again, if we consider a perception closely, we find that it is not merely *of this object* but also *from this percipient organism*; that it has a *terminus a quo* as well as a *terminus ad quem*. We always see along a line whose starting-point is in the eye. Not that we see the line, or anything else but its terminal point in the object; but the object is seen from this particular point of view. Objects arrange themselves into foreground and background, they are visible or concealed, in a manner that appears quite arbitrary until we take account of the physiology of perception.

Now, these are facts wholly overlooked in ordinary statements of idealistic doctrine. The sole fact usually considered is the presence of the perceived object to consciousness. Perception is thought of as a function which the mind possesses quite independently of the body; this function is in effect denied to be physically conditioned at all. But, in a world existing solely as an object of consciousness, why should not all causal trains stand on the same footing, and be equally free to occur or not to occur without endangering the existence of the perception? Why should objects necessarily be perceived from any particular point of view? These are questions which phenomenalism is powerless to answer, but which find a ready solution on the hypothesis of things-in-themselves. If a perception is the last term of a causal train acting upon the mind from without, then the phenomenal train which reveals that action *must* have precisely this unique significance, and the perception *must* appear aimed in a direction opposite to that in which the causal sequence runs.

Not only so, but this hypothesis would explain that mysterious doubling of the physical world which we have repeatedly met with. If we say that the object evokes a brain-event and the brain-event is then accompanied or followed by the perception of the object, the latter, as first the cause and then the datum of the perception, necessarily appears doubled. There seem to be two physical worlds, the world to which extra-bodily objects and brain-events belong, and the world of perception. This, we saw, could not be other than a metaphysical illusion. The illusion is explained, if we assume that the physical train connecting the extra-bodily object with the brain-event symbolizes a real causal train acting upon the mind from without. For, in that case, the physical train that appears to exist in advance of the perception is simply a second manifestation of the constituent links of that real train, acting by means of collateral real trains upon some other mind, or conceivably upon the same mind; whose owner would then be engaged in the delicate task of studying his own nerve-physiology *in vivo*.

To sum up: our perceptions are preceded and conditioned by physiological events, and this marks them off as effects. Any other assumption denudes the psychophysical facts of all real significance. The physical world gets tied into a knot through the existence of this relation of conditioning between certain possible perceptions and an actual perception. This knot, this conditioning, form an *explicandum*. They can be explained only on the hypothesis that the conditioning facts are in reality things-in-themselves. Thus, although our whole report of the occurrence comes in terms of perceptions, we are enabled to triangulate, as it were, to realities incapable of being perceived. The justification of the transcending herein involved lies in the fact that it, and it alone, introduces order and intelligibility into the peculiar entanglement of facts registered by physiological psychology.

But, in my account of the physiological proof thus far, I have cited but half, and that the less convincing half, of the facts. The argument becomes far more impressive when we pass from the moderate stimulations which precede and condition our perceptions to those excessive stimulations which, as we saw in Chapter I, threaten the very existence of consciousness itself. That the physical antecedents of sensation are not mere phenomena, but symbols of realities acting upon the mind from without, is proved conclusively by the fact that, while a moderate stimulus evokes a new content, an excessive stimulus (or, to speak more exactly, excessive action of what was before a stimulus) may abolish consciousness altogether.

Thus chloroform produces at first a certain olfactory sensation, then dizziness and nausea, then unconsciousness. Or a blow on the head may produce either a mere cutaneous sensation, or pain with entoptic phenomena, or loss of consciousness, according to its force. Must not agencies capable of acting on the mind so destructively be co-ordinate with the mind in reality?

The following illustration, which I take in substance from Professor Riehl,[1] deserves to be meditated by phenomenalists. Imagine a philosopher in a burning house, with all means of egress cut off. As the flames approach, he debates whether they be more than phenomena in his consciousness. Surely, the fact that they must soon bring his reflections to a standstill is adapted to throw light on the question — though the light might come too late for use by that particular philosopher.

Or consider the following parable. A fishing-vessel is off the Newfoundland banks in a fog. The skipper thinks he hears the siren of an ocean liner: a moment later he sees a dark shadow outlined on the fog. Is it a real ship bearing down upon him, or only an illusion? The answer depends on what follows. If nothing happens, it was probably an illusion. But if the shadow takes form, comes crashing into his vessel, and sends her to the bottom, then it was a real ship. In the same way, the events that portend the dissolution of consciousness must be more than mere subjective phenomena. If matter can extinguish our minds, be it never so temporarily, it must have some force of its own, some existence in itself. Thus the second group of facts completes the proof begun by the first.

Third or Evolutionary Proof

One of the most pressing duties of philosophy, at the present time, is to effect some sort of reconcilia-

---

[1] *Der philosophische Kriticismus*, Band ii., Theil ii., p. 159.

tion between idealism and the doctrine of evolution. For the latter gives an account of the history of individual minds apparently inconsistent with the former. It is surely a paradox that the physical world should be relative to minds which do not arise until late in the history of that world. On the one hand, idealism seems to involve the consequence that the events described in the nebular theory, or in geology, are not historical fact; it seems to imply that these events only *would have been* perceptible had minds been in existence to perceive them, but that, as a matter of fact, the physical world began to exist as fast as minds arose. On the other hand, neither this pre-existence of matter as a possibility of perception, nor its actual pre-existence as assumed by common-sense, at all helps us to understand the origin of the minds.

For concrete minds are, as we saw in Chapter I, not absolute and eternal things; they have a beginning in time, and are subject to vicissitudes and interruptions. There is a moment when consciousness first begins in the child; there was a moment when it first began in the race. But we need not go so far away to meet with a phenomenon which takes place daily and hourly in the experience of each of us. We cannot awake out of sleep, or come to after chloroform, or collect our thoughts after a moment of listlessness, without consciousness welling up in us anew.

The problem of the origin of consciousness is much too difficult and profound a one to be fully discussed in this book. Many, no doubt, will deem it insoluble, as if we should set out to explain the process of creation; others will declare it meaningless and not really a problem at all. The very notion, they will say, of an individual mind existing in any shape prior to its own origin is absurd; the last word of human wisdom consists in saying that at a certain moment the mind began to be. Without going into the merits of the question, I will merely argue that, *if* the principle '*ex nihilo nihil fit*' applies to the mind and the problem is therefore a real one, it is impossible to take the first step toward its solution without the assumption of things-in-themselves. For the origin of consciousness can be explained, if at all, only by evolution out of antecedent realities of the same order; and such antecedent realities conform exactly to the definition of things-in-themselves. Apart from such explanation, our only choice is between the hypothesis of creation and the crudities of materialism.

This proof is evidently the analogue of the cosmological, except that, instead of starting from the (if I may so say) *quasi-spatial* gaps between simultaneously existing minds, it starts from the *temporal* gaps due to the fact that they had a beginning in time and are occasionally interrupted. Here, as before, the hypothesis of things-in-themselves is necessary in order to avert pluralism and join the minds together into a continuous universe. Here, as before, physical facts are unsuited for the purpose, and we are forced to choose between pluralism and the hypothesis of things-in-themselves.

We may also distinguish, as before, a form of the argument based on general cosmological considerations and a form based on the implications of the physical events with which consciousness is correlated. According to the mechanical theory of life, the brain-process is nothing but an inconceivably complex assemblage of moving molecules, completely explicable by evolution out of simpler physical facts. But consciousness develops *pari passu* with the brain-process, the growth and vicissitudes of the two being an exact match. Unless, then, we are to denude the psychophysical facts of all real significance, we must draw the inference that consciousness too is an evolutionary product; we must hold that, as the brain-process has arisen out of simpler physical facts, so consciousness has arisen out of simpler mental facts. But these simpler mental facts are only another name for things-in-themselves. Either, then, the origin of consciousness is a coming of something out of nothing, or there are things-in-themselves.

We may sum up the first two proofs by saying that a pluralism of individual minds is like a physical world consisting solely of brain-processes. In the same way, we may sum up the evolutionary proof by saying that the phenomenalistic account of the origin of mind is like the view that the brain-process does not arise out of simpler physical facts. Indeed, it is like physiology not only *minus* evolution but *minus* physics and chemistry. It is a sort of psychological vitalism, which not only denies derivation from the inorganic but actually ignores the latter's existence.

Phenomenalism with its logically consequent pluralism gives us a mutilated world, a world without interconnection and inner intelligibility. The individual mind with its unity and isolation becomes the ultimate and final fact, beside which everything else pales. All the most majestic natural facts, the inexorable forces that environ and hem us in — the solid earth, the sea, the sun, moon and stars — are without scruple set down as mere appearance. Agency is degraded into a minor category; for the purposes of action a nothing is esteemed as good as a something; causal chains are held to consist of a procession of alternate somethings and nothings inexplicably mingled. Thus, the better to exalt reason, the world is made irrational.

True, most phenomenalists seek to restore unity to the cosmos by the hypothesis of a universal mind, of which particular minds are phases and with which they at once are and are not identical. Unfortunately this mode of achieving monism is mainly verbal. For, although it would give us a true universe if the relation between the universal and the particular minds could be explained, that explanation is never forthcoming. Considering the apparent unity and isolation of the particular minds, it is not clear how they can be phases of a larger inclusive mind which knows them without their knowing it. The comparison with ideas in a consciousness suggests itself; but it remains to be shown that this is more than a vague metaphor. In truth, these would-be monists are as impotent to define the relation as that of the particular minds *inter se*, and their monism is little better than a pious aspiration. On the other hand, it may be admitted that the existence of things-in-themselves does not necessarily exclude that of a universal mind, or the continuity they bring contradict such unity as might be brought by it. But, even granting such a mind, its unity would be no satisfactory substitute for that continuity of finite things which is impossible without things-in-themselves.

Phenomenalism has its root in an abstract and fictitious conception of consciousness. The consciousness which the phenomenalist has in his mind's eye when he reasons is a sort of absolute fact, ever burning with a steady glow of awareness, sharing none of the mutations and vicissitudes of its content, matter: in short, a very different thing from the concrete human mind of which we heard in Chapter I. This conception is supposed to result from idealism, but in reality the two have no logical connection. Idealism shows matter to be relative to mind, but not to such a mind.

We cannot too often remind ourselves that metaphysical theories never alter facts. Take, for instance, this very theory of idealism. If we fancy that assigning objects to the light and airy category of mental states makes them no longer the gross corporeal things they seem, and that we thus become inhabitants of a world more congenial than before, we deceive ourselves, not the less completely because subtly. The table, on the idealistic theory, still remains the table, hard, heavy, and resisting; for hardness, weight, and resistance — in one word, corporeality — are inalienable characters of certain of our mental states. It is not in an æsthetic or ethical, but only in a metaphysical sense that idealism gives us a spiritual in exchange for a material world.

Now, the fact which phenomenalists fail fully to recognize and take up into their conception is that by this corporeal content, matter, the mind is, even on the phenomenalistic theory, effectually limited and hemmed in. To illustrate: a stone wall bars my passage; a ton is too heavy for me to lift; an object a few feet above my head is out of my reach; an ocean divides me from my friends; I must take food three times a day, and sleep eight hours out of the twenty-four; I can concentrate my mind only for a limited period, and my mental alertness and readiness are subject to great fluctuations; my mental powers may at any moment be inhibited or deranged by bodily facts, such as pain, accident, or disease; a hemorrhage or embolus may deprive me of part of my mental furniture, and chloroform or brain-injury do away temporarily with consciousness itself. In short, phenomenalists have no adequate sense of "how at the mercy of material happenings our spirit is." Such facts as sleep, intoxication, delirium, anæsthesia, aphasia, mental blindness, insanity are lost on them : they think to interpret them as mere changes of content. But it is impossible to interpret experiences in which the degree or the existence of consciousness is affected as mere changes of content. These experiences show that consciousness is a particular fleeting existence in time, and thus imply that it is part of a larger order by which its contents are determined and on which its existence from moment to moment depends.

To sum up: instead of an idealism founded on the mere abstract fact of awareness and ignoring the facts of agency, what we need is one fully alive to mind as it is in the concrete. Such an idealism would take not only the first step of recognizing (1) that physical facts when perceived are modifications of consciousness; but would carry psychological observation farther, and note (2) that the consciousness is *mine*, *i.e.*, that of a particular man or animal; (3) that among its perceptions is that of a body, and that the mutations of consciousness go hand in hand with those of the body; finally (4) that the conciousness, like its associated body, is a strictly limited and non-self-explanatory thing. When psychological observation has thus done its perfect work, we are face to face with the alternative, either to rest content with the mere fragment of reality which introspection reveals to view, eked out by other similar but equally disconnected fragments; or boldly to take the non-rational leap that leads to things-in-themselves.

For this leap must be confessed to be non-rational. *Things-in-themselves cannot be logically demonstrated*, in such a way as to extort conviction from the skeptic; for the simple reason that no argument having only empirical facts in its premises can legitimately have extra-mental existences in its conclusion. But the force of this admission is somewhat attenuated by the fact that the existence of other minds is equally indemonstrable. If children were born solipsists, and had at a certain stage of their education to be brought by reasoning to the recognition of other minds, it is much to be feared (and wished, in the interests of flawless logic) that they would remain solipsists to the day of their death. Not reasoning, but some deep pre-rational instinct, like that on which our faith in memory rests, is the basis of our belief in other minds. Hence the utmost the philosopher can do, but at the same time all he need do, is to show that the inference of things-in-themselves is exactly analogous to that of other minds, and is required in order to give continuity and intelligibility to our conception of the universe. This, to be sure, is somewhat in the nature of an *argumentum ad hominem;* but possibly it will not fail on that account of obtaining the reader's assent.

CHAPTER XII

THINGS-IN-THEMSELVES: THEIR NATURE

SINCE we cannot come at things-in-themselves directly and learn by experience what they are like, it might seem that we can know nothing positive about their nature, and must follow Kant and Spencer in declaring them unknowable. Yet four different lines of inference on the subject are open to us. In the first place, since they manifest themselves through our perceptions, these may throw some light on the matter. Secondly, we may inquire as to the source from which our conception of reality is derived, and approach the question from this point of view. Thirdly, the inference of things-in-themselves is analogous to that of other minds, and this fact may serve as a basis for deductions. Finally, out of things-in-themselves individual minds are evolved, and the former must therefore have such a nature as to permit of the evolution. Let us take up and discuss each of these points in turn.

Relation of Things-in-Themselves to our Perceptions

Our first impulse would doubtless be to look for light on the subject to perception. And, doing this, we might be tempted to transfer to things-in-themselves without further ado the empirical qualities of perceived objects. These may be summed up in the one word 'corporeality.' Many who accept things-in-themselves will insist that they cannot be other than corporeal; that is, soulless, dead, antithetical in nature to consciousness. They will argue that the detailed information about the nature of things which we call physical science cannot be true of the perceptive symbol merely, but must be true of things-in-themselves. Our idea of their nature would thus approximate to the Scholastic and Cartesian conception of matter.

This would be to attribute to our perceptions a maximum of fidelity in reproducing the realities for which they stand, to conceive them as almost equal in knowledge-giving power to intuitions; though they would not actually *be* intuitions, since the knowledge is only mediate and representative. But a little reflection must convince us that the propriety of such transference is, at the very least, open to doubt. While we yet conceived things-in-themselves to be directly intuited, we could trust perception as to their nature, and be sure they were corporeal; but, now that we recognize the subjectivity of physical things and distinguish them from things-in-themselves, it is plain that perception gives us immediate knowledge only of the former, and the nature of the latter consequently becomes problematic. We have no right, in advance of inquiry, to ascribe to them a nature in all respects similar to that of perceived objects. For instance, it would be entirely consistent with the facts of perception if, as

Berkeley supposed, the extra-mental reality were a Divine Mind.

In order to judge whether the transference of corporeality to things-in-themselves is legitimate, we must consider more closely than we have hitherto done the relation between them and our perceptions. This relation is, to begin with, one of representation. Whether the representation is of the nature of portraiture, mirroring the entire being of the thing-in-itself with perfect fidelity, or merely of symbolism, conveying certain of its features by means of signs, still remains to be seen. In any case, the relation does not exclude, but rather involves, that of cause and effect. Perceptions do not arise in the mind spontaneously, in answer to the mere external presence of things-in-themselves, but only by the latter acting on the mind in the way of stimuli. The process is one that may be called imprinting: things-in-themselves imprint copies of themselves on the mind, they call forth in it subjective states that serve as their symbols, and so get themselves known. This may seem romancing, but it admits of proof. For wholly within the physical world — which we now recognize to be in all its parts symbolic of things-in-themselves — there is a parallel and purely phenomenal process of imprinting: namely, that by which the extra-bodily object calls forth the perceptional brain-event. The perceptional brain-event is undeniably at once an imprint and a symbol of the extra-bodily object — " a sort of physical idea," as Professor Huxley puts it. But, since relations between physical facts are always symbolic of relations between things-in-themselves, this phenomenal process of imprinting and symbolization must stand symbolically for a real process of imprinting and symbolization; which is none other than the process by which things-in-themselves evoke perceptions. Thus we have proof that the relation in question is not merely one of symbolism, but one of symbolism resting on causality.

The same line of reasoning shows that the action of things-in-themselves on the mind in the evoking of perceptions is not direct. For, as the extra-bodily object evokes the perceptional brain-event not directly, but through the medium of sense-organs and sensory nerves, so things-in-themselves evoke perceptions only through the medium of those other things-in-themselves for which sense-organs and sensory nerves stand. We are thus led to recognize, behind the body as a phenomenal fact, an extra-mental or real fact for which the body stands, which surrounds consciousness like an outer shell and separates it from the general world of things-in-themselves, in a way parallel to that in which the phenomenal body separates the brain (or, more exactly, the brain-process) from the general physical world.

By following out this line of thought further, we may get light on the question, how far our perceptions are accurate portraits of things-in-themselves and how far mere symbols. For, as the perceptional brain-event is to the extra-bodily object, so must the perception be to the thing-in-itself. Now, it is clear that the perceptional brain-event is very far from being an accurate portrait of the extra-bodily object. In the latter's transference to the retinæ one dimension is largely lost, though the other two may perhaps be retained in its transference from the retinæ to the brain. Despite all similarities, the extreme disparity of the brain-event to the extra-bodily object is perfectly apparent. But, in that case, we must assume a corresponding disparity between the perception and the thing-in-itself, and recognize that the former is not an accurate portrait of the latter but only a symbol.

Clifford compares the relation to that between a map and the country of which it is a map[1]; and the illustration brings out well the immense disparity that is consistent with symbolization. This disparity is twofold. On the one hand, many traits of the reality are necessarily omitted and lost in the representation. On the other, the representation, as made in terms of a certain kind of material, necessarily has qualities of its own to which nothing in the reality corresponds; as words are sounds, yet signify objects in no sense sonorous. To draw the line between what is subjective in our perceptions and what is representative, is no easy matter. Qualities like color, hardness, heat and cold are certainly subjective; though even they, as a rule, vary uniformly with their extra-mental causes, in such

---

[1] *Lectures and Essays* (2d ed., 1886), the lecture "Body and Mind," p. 267.

wise that the same subjective quality regularly stands for the same extra-mental fact, and so are useful as symbols (this follows from what we know in phenomenal terms about the relation between stimulus and sensation). It is a more difficult question, whether and to what extent the space-form stands for a system of extra-mental relations; but, in the end, we shall hardly avoid the conclusion of Mr. Spencer that "there is some ontological order whence arises the phenomenal order we know as space."[1]

This incomplete and partial character of perceptive representation is a consequence of the purely practical function which is its *raison d'être*. We must picture its evolution to ourselves as proceeding parallel with that of sense-organs and brain in the physical world. When organisms were formed in the midst of inorganic nature, evolutionary agencies slowly developed in them a function serving to reproduce within the organism some physical image of the objects and events in its environment, to which it was thus enabled to adjust its relations. In the same way, when minds were formed in the midst of the real world, evolutionary agencies parallel to those at work in the physical developed in them a function serving to reproduce some mental image of the events in the *real* environment. For the struggle of the physical organism with the physical environment is only the symbol of a struggle of

[1] Spencer, *Principles of Psychology* (New York, 1890), vol. i., p. 227.

the mental organism with the real environment, a struggle in which adjustment is as essential to survival as in the physical world. But, in order that they may serve for such adjustment, it is not necessary that our perceptions should photograph reality; it suffices that they reproduce its main features and habits symbolically. A map, to recur to Clifford's illustration, involves enormous simplification, roads being represented by lines and cities by dots, yet it serves usefully to guide the traveller's course; in the same way, the symbolic character of our perceptions in no way detracts from their practical usefulness.

If this be true, it is absurd to find fault with perception for not being intuitive, and to complain that it gives us no knowledge worthy of the name. This complaint re-appears in an argument sometimes urged against things-in-themselves, that they make the phenomenal world unreal by contrast, and perception a nugatory function that conceals instead of revealing reality. The facts may be admitted, but they do not constitute a valid argument. It is perfectly true that perception does not give us a full and authentic account of reality, but in a measure falsifies and hides it; indeed, this is a truth on which the deepest philosophers have always insisted. It does not follow that our perceptions give us about reality no knowledge at all. Though they do not reveal its essential nature, they give us all the knowledge about its character and habits that we need for every-day use. In Berkeley's system, for instance, they give us a great deal of information about the habits and intentions of the Creator. So that, if perception is a screen, it is at least not an opaque screen, but one that reality shines darkly through.

That the plain man does not conceive perception as such a screen, is perfectly true. While physical objects are perceived, he never suspects an existence behind them, but supposes himself directly to contemplate reality itself. Yet his naïve realism is not so out of harmony with the doctrine of things-in-themselves as it might at first sight appear. To understand it, we must bear in mind that it is intended, not to satisfy the intellect, but for the needs of practice. It arises by a sort of fusion of things-in-themselves with perceived objects, in which the latter contribute the qualities and the former the continuity and permanence. This fusion proves very convenient from the point of view of economy of thought, since instead of having two more or less duplicate things to deal with the mind has only one. Despite the philosophical absurdity of such a theory, it works well enough in practice; for things-in-themselves may be safely ignored provided their continuity and permanence are transferred to physical objects, and the fact that sensible qualities are not really permanent can never be discovered, since objects never re-appear without them. So it comes about that propositions may be asserted with impunity of the fused product which in reality hold true only of one or the other of the elements. Yet, now and again, the plain man's judgments show peculiarities which prove that things-in-themselves, though in words denied, are yet woven into the very tissue of his thought; as, for example, the distinction already discussed between the causal relations of perceptions and the causal relations of events perceived — a distinction hardly to be construed except on the hypothesis of things-in-themselves.

To sum up this account of the relation between things-in-themselves and perceptions: the latter may be compared to shadows thrown on a curtain by persons moving behind, where one dimension is lost and all the shapes and colors are represented by variations of light and shade. As the perceptional brain-event is a sort of shadow thrown upon the brain by an extra-bodily object, so the perception is a sort of shadow thrown upon the mind by a thing-in-itself. It lies in the nature of such adumbration that the shadow-symbol should be in important respects unlike, and should to that extent misrepresent, the reality symbolized. And we may well ask ourselves whether the soullessness and deadness of physical objects — their corporeality, in one word — does not arise in this manner; whether a symbol must not, as such, be more or less soulless and dead, even though the reality symbolized were never so soulful and alive.

Source of our Conception of Reality.

The foregoing considerations merely raise the doubt whether things-in-themselves be corporeal, without settling the question in one sense or the other. The result of idealism, with its splitting of physical objects into perceptions that are given and things-in-themselves that are not given, is, first of all, to make the nature of the latter problematic. But now, when we reflect further on the matter, we find that the result of idealism is not merely to raise the question whether things-in-themselves are corporeal, but to decide that question in the negative. For it will be admitted that we are dependent for our conceptions of the nature of reality upon experience. Now, so long as we supposed physical objects to exist independently of the mind, we were legitimately (from our own point of view) in possession of the conception of a reality corporeal in its nature, since that conception could be shown to rest on experience. As naïve dualists, we supposed ourselves to have immediate experience of two antithetical kinds of reality, material and mental. The result of idealism is to deprive us of the first of these conceptions, by withdrawing its empirical basis. Instead of having experience of physical objects that are independently real, we find that we have experience only of physical objects that are modifications of mind. Matter being a modification of mind, we have not the conception we thought we had of a reality corporeal in its nature. This conception is shown to involve a combination of incompatible attributes: corporeality with independent existence; for our experience now affords us no example of a reality at once corporeal and independently existing. Since material things, so far as our experience goes, are always at the same time modifications of mind or perceptions, the only way to conceive things-in-themselves as still corporeal would be to conceive them as duplicate perceptions, supposing another mind outside our own of which they were modifications. Since the would-be dualist is not likely to take this course, the practical outcome is that things-in-themselves are not and cannot be corporeal.

In order nevertheless to keep them as corporeal as possible, the dualist will next maintain that their nature is unknown, but in any case very different from the nature of mind. This was Kant's view, who taught that the thing-in-itself is " weder Materie noch ein denkend Wesen." But Kant's premises were essentially different from ours, in that he held not only physical facts but also mental states to be phenomena, and assumed things-in-themselves to lie indifferently behind both. This degrading of mental states to the level of mere phenomena and placing of them on a par with physical facts is one of the gravest errors of the Kantian philosophy. It would follow from such a view that we do not come in contact with the reality of things at any point; that we ourselves, so far as known or given to ourselves, are unreal; that the reality which appears both as matter and as mind is unknowable; and that we therefore have no sample in our possession of what reality is like.

Our chapter on Consciousness contained the antidote to this error. It was there shown that the essence of our mental being, the Ego, is not something distinct from all thoughts and feelings and more real than they, so that by contrast with it they deserve the name of phenomena; but that, on the contrary, they are integral parts of the mind and its reality their reality, in such wise that when they disappear the mind disappears with them. Since we exist only so long as we are conscious, it follows that the essence of the mind is consciousness. Thus our reality is the reality of consciousness: nothing can be more real than a feeling at the moment when it is felt. It follows that consciousness is an actual fragment and specimen of the reality of things, and that in it we have a sample of what reality is like.

Physical facts, on the other hand, are unreal, they are merely phenomena. As shadows are unreal in comparison with the objects that cast them, so physical facts are unreal in comparison with the things-in-themselves for which they stand. At the same time, as a shadow is such only in relation to the object that casts it, but in itself a piece of black ground, equally real with other visible objects; so physical facts are unreal only as symbols, but in themselves, as perceptions, they are equally real with other mental states. Thus even phenomena must be in another aspect realities, otherwise they would not exist to serve as symbols. The view that both mental and physical facts are phenomena is therefore absurd.

Now, if both physical and mental facts were phenomena, it might fairly be held that their divergent reports about reality mutually cancel each other and leave the latter's nature unknown. A reality that manifests itself indifferently through mental and through physical facts need not in itself be either physical or mental. And since experience, on this view, supplies us with no sample of reality, we have no alternative but to acknowledge the nature of things-in-themselves unknown.

It is otherwise when we recognize mental states to be real. For, in that case, they belong to the same category as things-in-themselves; and, indeed, this follows from the fact that they are effects of which things-in-themselves are causes, and causes of which things-in-themselves are effects. But, if mental states are real, in experiencing them we enjoy a sample of what reality is like, and it is at least possible that things-in-themselves resemble this sample, and are accordingly mental in nature. On the other hand, it must be admitted to be also possible (for anything we have yet seen) that they are of different nature from consciousness. And the question is, whether the data at our disposal afford any indications that permit us to decide between these possibilities.

In the first place, continuing the previous line of argument, it may be questioned whether the hypothesis of a reality of different nature from consciousness is consistent with the principle that our conception of a reality must be based on experience. If the only reality of which we have any experience is consciousness, we have no material out of which to form the conception of a reality of different nature, and that conception is consequently perfectly groundless and arbitrary. It would follow that the only legitimate conception of a reality which we possess is that of a reality mental in its nature, and that if we conceive things-in-themselves as realities we are bound to conceive them as having that kind of nature.

This general principle about the nature of reality has been insisted on by every idealistic school, but often with a falsifying twist due to the peculiar type of the idealism. We may distinguish three different types of idealism, calling them idealism of thought, idealism of perception, and idealism of feeling. All three insist that reality must be interpreted in terms of consciousness. But by consciousness each means a different thing. The first takes as its specimen of consciousness the apprehension of relations — that is to say, one of the more difficult feats of the adult human intellect — and to this specially chosen form of consciousness it concludes all existence to be relative. But it is unable to construe the dim feelings of the lower animals, or our own non-intellectual states. Pleasure, pain, and will do not exist merely so far as we reflect upon and analyze them, they do not exist merely *for* thought; nor do they exist merely *as* thoughts, unless we broaden the term so as to include all mental states. The second type of idealism takes as its specimen of consciousness our perception of physical objects, and its fundamental maxim is '*esse = percipi*.' But it has equal difficulty in construing our sensational experiences and the minds of animals. Both of these types rest on an illegitimate antithesis between consciousness and its objects; the one conceiving reality not as existence *of* but as existence *for* thought, the other not as existence *of* but as existence *for* perception. Both thus involve a fallacy which may be described as the 'eye theory' of the mind. They divide the mind into two opposite poles, a seen and a seeing, an objective and a subjective, corresponding to the difference between the knower and the known. They do not see that this is to apply the idealistic principle but half-way round the circle. If realities behind physical phenomena that exist neither for themselves nor for any one else are an absurdity, then so is a Subject or Ego or Spiritual Principle behind mental states existing neither for itself nor for any one else. From all such errors and delusions we are saved by our grasp of the truth that consciousness is the essence of the mind, and that consciousness is something empirically given.

Reality cannot be existence *for* thought or perception, because the antithesis between consciousness and its immediate objects is fallacious. The things we are immediately conscious of are always modifications of consciousness itself, and the existence of consciousness is their existence. The existence of things immediately known is simply the existence of the knowing state.[1] Hence reality is not existence

---

[1] As I have said before, I am able to accept Dr. Stout's position, *Analytic Psychology*, vol. i., pp. 40–46, only for the case of representative knowledge.

for but existence *of* consciousness ; or, to express the same thing otherwise, all existence *for* consciousness is existence *of* consciousness, consciousness being in its very nature existence *for itself*. The principle regarding the nature of reality which results from idealism therefore is, not that reality must be interpreted in terms of *objects* of thought or of perception, but that it must be interpreted in terms of thoughts, perceptions, *or other mental states.*

For perceptions and thoughts are but particular cases of mental states in general, and the essential insight of idealism is that the prime reality is our mental states. Moreover, they are specially chosen cases, the cases in which human consciousness attains to its maximum of cognitive grasp. But, besides these highly evolved states, there are a vast number of dim and inarticulate ones, states of feeling rather than of thought, out of which the higher states may have been evolved. Since these lower states are just as real as the higher, it is just as consistent with idealistic principles to interpret reality in terms of them as in terms of the higher states. Idealism merely requires that we should interpret reality in terms of consciousness, and it is just as consistent with it to take as our sample the consciousness of an earthworm or a polyp as that of a human being. It is perfectly true that our only key to the nature of reality is our own consciousness : but it is equally true that this is our only key to the nature of the polyp's consciousness; and if, in forming some faint notion of the latter, we take our start rather from our dumb feelings than from our more intellectual states, how much more in forming a notion of the realities that underlie inanimate matter!

Thus the only type of idealism consistent with psychological facts is idealism of feeling; and this only bids us attribute to reality a nature like that which all forms of mental life have in common. Berkeley's Divine Mind would satisfy the requirements of the case, but so also would Professor Clifford's Mind-stuff.

Analogy of Other Minds

Another ground for holding things-in-themselves to be mental in their nature is the fact that inference of them is analogous to, and may be conceived as a further extension of, the inference of other minds.

Some thinkers, indeed, seek to demonstrate their existence by showing that the argument from analogy which underlies the assumption of other minds requires in consistency of thought to be extended to inorganic matter. They maintain that the movements of particles by which a crystal is formed, or those by which minute portions of water in falling gather themselves into globules, are, despite their vastly greater simplicity, strictly analogous to animal movements, and hence to be regarded as manifestations of feeling. They even hold the same of the very simplest motions, those of molecules and atoms, thus breaking down the barrier between the organic and the inorganic and making mind omnipresent in nature.[1]

[1] Cf. Paulsen, *Einleitung in die Philosophie*, pp. 105-106.

This would harmonize well with the fact that living and animate beings appear to have originated out of inanimate and lifeless matter, and it is of course precisely the conclusion at which we have above arrived. At the same time, the argument seems somewhat lacking in cogency. The analogy on which it rests is too frail and dubious to carry conviction by itself alone. For biology has taught us to think of feeling as presupposing an organism whose movements are adjusted to the environment in a way contributory to its survival, and we cannot feel sure that the movements of the particles of a crystal or a water-drop are to be conceived in this manner. We are in the habit of contrasting the end-seeking and intelligent movements of living beings with the brute necessity that governs the motion of inanimate matter, and we cannot readily give up the habit and revise our notions. On the other hand, we do not feel called upon actively to contest the analogy; we feel that we might err in denying it as much as in asserting it. We can only say that it is too precarious for the argument to have demonstrative force.

Origin of Minds out of Things-in-Themselves

An absolutely conclusive reason for holding things-in-themselves to be mental in their nature is the fact that individual minds arise out of them by evolution. The worst difficulty of materialism was to explain how in the midst of a purely material world such things as minds could ever arise. Now, if we make things-in-themselves either material or unknown in their nature, we perpetuate this difficulty. If, on the contrary, we conceive them as of like nature with consciousness, the difficulty disappears. Our doctrine would then be that, as in the phenomenal world the brain-process arises out of simpler physical facts, so in the real world consciousness arises out of simpler mental facts.

Thus three different lines of reasoning — from the source of our conception of reality, from the analogy of other minds, and from the evolution of minds — concur to the same result, that things-in-themselves must be mental in their nature.

To complete the demonstration, it would be necessary to discuss the mental nature of things-in-themselves in detail, showing how it is consistent with the fact that they form a continuous world, and explaining how out of such a world individual minds characterized by unity and isolation can be evolved. The internal difficulties of such a theory seem at first sight immense, not to say insuperable: yet it is astonishing how many of them can be overcome. But adequate discussion of the subject would fill a volume, and we cannot go into it now.

SUMMARY OF THE PRINCIPLES ESTABLISHED IN THE LAST FIVE CHAPTERS

1. The assumption that material objects exist independently of the mind involves a series of difficulties. In the first place, the immediate perception of objects so existing at a distance from the body is inconsistent with the fact that they call forth perceptions only by acting on the body.

2. The assumption that perception acquaints us with the nature of such objects is inconsistent with the fact that certain at least of the qualities of objects are secondary and subjective.

3. The notion of perception as a function that takes us outside the mind and gives us immediate intuition of realities existing there involves a psychological (or epistemological) impossibility. We can have immediate intuition only of our mental states.

4. Material objects, being immediately intuited, therefore exist as mental states. If there are realities outside the mind, they can be known only through the medium of our mental states, that is, representatively.

5. Phenomenalism, or the denial of such realities, is a perfectly logical theory of perception; the fact that it makes objects cease to exist when we cease to perceive them being no valid argument against it. But it gives us a mutilated and incoherent conception of the universe, and it leads logically to solipsism.

6. To restore unity to the world, to fill out the causal order, to explain the evolution of minds, we must assume things-in-themselves.

7. The prime reality, the only reality ever immediately given, is consciousness. Matter is not a reality, but a phenomenon. As such it symbolizes things-in-themselves, whereas mental states as such symbolize nothing.

8. Since consciousness is not in space, things-in-themselves are not, strictly speaking, *outside* or *beyond it*, but only *other than* it; and the world composed of consciousness and things-in-themselves is not in space, though it may be in something of which space is the symbol.

9. Since consciousness is the only reality of which we have any immediate knowledge, and therefore our only sample of what reality is like, we have no other conception of a reality. Hence we must assume things-in-themselves to be mental in their nature; and this is the more necessary, that individual minds arise out of them by evolution.

Book IV

APPLICATION OF THE FOREGOING PRINCIPLES TO THE PROBLEM — CRITICISM OF THEORIES

CHAPTER XIII

INTERACTIONIST THEORIES

ULTIMATE or metaphysical theories of the relation of mind and body, to which we now turn, are distinguished from causal theories by the facts (1) that they do not confine themselves to the causal issue, but discuss the problem in all its breadth, seeking even to explain why mind and body are associated at all; (2) that in solving it they call to aid metaphysical considerations, and, in particular, undertake to appraise the comparative reality of the two associates. Thus there are dualistic theories which make mind and body equally real, materialistic theories which attribute greater reality to the body, idealistic theories which attribute greater reality to the mind, phenomenalistic theories which deny reality to both, etc. If the metaphysical principles which we have worked out in the last five chapters are sound, they should enable us to decide between these theories and solve the problem.

Metaphysical theories may be divided into two classes, according as they rest on a phenomenalistic or a realistic view of matter. If our principles are correct, phenomenalistic theories must be rejected simply as such. But, on every realistic theory, an important question arises to which no reference has been made hitherto. This is as to the relation between the mind and the things-in-themselves symbolized by the brain. Here comes the decision by which theories are made or marred. There are two possibilities: either the mind is distinct from the things-in-themselves symbolized by the brain, and associated with them as we commonly conceive mind and brain to be associated; or else it is identical with them, and itself the reality which appears as the brain-process. The choice between these alternatives is a choice between dualism and monism. For, if we conceive the mind as distinct from and additional to the system of realities that appear as the physical world, our conception is dualistic. Whereas, if we regard the mind as a member of this system and as necessary to its completeness, our conception is monistic. As the assertion or denial of causal relations between mind and body marks the widest divergence of empirical theories, so the alternative here presented marks the widest divergence of metaphysical theories.

In classifying the latter it will be better, however, to divide them, first, into three groups, according as they arise as metaphysical interpretations of interactionism, automatism, or parallelism.

Interactionism in its most typical form involves and necessitates dualism, since matter must exist separately from mind for the latter to act upon it. The matter which thus exists separately may be the matter of the naïve realist, or it may be the reality that appears as phenomenal matter. In either form we may call the theory *psychophysical dualism*, distinguishing the two forms as naïve and critical respectively. There is also a third and subtler form of interactionism which is not necessarily dualistic, since by the matter on which it asserts the mind to act it means simply phenomenal matter. This form we may call *psychophysical phenomenalism*.

Coming next to automatist theories, it is at least as necessary that matter should exist separately from mind to be its cause as for the latter to interact with it. And again, the matter which thus exists separately may be the matter of the naïve or that of the critical realist. In either case we have a doctrine which, since it makes mind arise out of matter, is fairly entitled to the name of *psychophysical materialism*. If, on the other hand, the matter which is held to be the cause of mind is simply phenomenal matter, the materialism of the doctrine is neutralized, and we shall perhaps do best to call this form of theory also *psychophysical phenomenalism*, distinguishing it from the interactionist doctrine of the same name by means of the epithets *interactionist form* and *automatist form*.

Coming finally to parallelist theories, a dualistic form of doctrine is conceivable, since it might be held that matter must exist separately from mind in order to run parallel with it. But, among theories actually held, two call for special notice. The first looks upon mind and body as of equal reality or rather unreality, and interprets them as parallel manifestations or aspects of a single real being: to this we may give the name of *psychophysical monism*. The second regards mind as alone real and matter as phenomenal, and by means of this hypothesis explains their connection: this we may call *psychophysical idealism*.

We must now take up each of these forms of theory and discuss it in detail, asking what are the conceptions of matter and mind underlying it and how far it satisfies the requirements which may legitimately be made of any ultimate theory. These requirements are three in number. (1) An ultimate theory should explain the connection of mind and body, and make clear to us how two such disparate things come to be associated. (2) It should pave the way for an explanation of the origin of consciousness. (3) It should — if possible — vindicate the efficiency of consciousness.

Average Current Interactionism

Both here and under the head of automatist and parallelist theories, we may begin by inquiring as to the metaphysical conceptions underlying average current interactionism, automatism, and parallelism, meaning by these phrases the forms of doctrine in which the metaphysics is unavowed or unconscious. For the fact that a writer has made no express declaration of principles or has formulated none in his own mind is no proof that he has none, but a definite set of principles may be implied unmistakably in all that he says.

What, then, are the conceptions of matter and mind underlying average current interactionism? A little examination of interactionist arguments shows that they are those of naïve realism and dualism. They are simply the common-sense conceptions of every-day life, which the writers have taken over uncritically. Not that most interactionists are not professed idealists; but they forget their idealism when they discuss the relation of mind and body. Their whole way of speaking shows that they think of matter as equally real with mind, and as existing alongside of it; as something on which mind might naturally be expected to act, and on which it is a shame that it should not be admitted to act.

A few quotations will illustrate this habit of arguing as if matter were real and efficient and the only question were whether mind was to be real and efficient too. "If feelings are causes," says Professor James, "of course their effects must be furtherings and checkings of internal cerebral motions. . . . It is probable that for years to come we shall have to infer what happens in the brain. . . . The organ will be for us a sort of vat in which feelings and motions somehow go on stewing together. . . ."¹ After all allowances have been made for metaphor, does this passage betray the slightest consciousness of the fact that motions exist for us only as feelings, or the least effort to reconceive the relations of feelings and motions in deference to that fact? Is it not plain that all thought of idealism is leagues away from Professor James's mind, and that he is working away at the problem of the relation of mind and body in naïvely dualistic terms? Or take the following passage: "It is to my mind quite inconceivable that consciousness should have *nothing to do* with a business which it so faithfully attends."² Is not the dualism perfectly clear? The same dualistic atmosphere clings to the statement from which a phrase was quoted in an earlier place: "The ultimate of ultimate problems . . . is to understand . . . how such disparate things are connected at all."³ Dear interactionist, the whole trouble is that you do not conceive them as disparate enough! You make them disparate in nature, but equal in point of reality, whereas they are disparate in both respects. A little further on we read: "I confess . . . that to posit a soul influenced in some mysterious way by the brain-states and responding to them by conscious affections of its own . . ."⁴ But if the brain-states exist only as actual or possible conscious affections?

Of course I know how Professor James would

---

[1] *Principles of Psychology*, vol. i., pp. 137, 138.
[2] *Ibid.*, p. 136.   [3] *Ibid.*, p. 177.   [4] *Ibid.*, p. 181.

reply to this arraignment. He would represent his assertions as made from the natural-science point of view and as subject to metaphysical revision. But how does he know that, after such revision, matter would still exist alongside of mind for the latter to act upon it? How does he know that metaphysics would not revise the duality, and therewith the interaction, quite out of existence? The fact is that, the moment you pass beyond observed facts of co-existence and sequence, the relation of mind and body is essentially a metaphysical question, and there are but two courses open to one: either to discuss it with the aid of critical conceptions, or not to discuss it at all.

On the other hand, it is but fair to recall that, in the controversy to which Professor James's paper [1] was a contribution, he was not the aggressor. His protest was called forth by Professor Huxley's (real) and Professor Clifford's (supposed) denial of the efficiency of mind; and what he protested against was the untimely dogmatism with which that denial was put forward. He deserves credit for not putting forward his own interactionism as absolute and final truth; for foreseeing that automatism (as yet undistinguished from parallelism) might prove to be true in some translated form; and for holding obstinately fast only to the one conviction, that in the final re-adjustment consciousness would be found to be of use, to be somehow effective and influential. In virtue of these previsions, we must acknowledge

---

[1] Art.: "Are We Automata?" in *Mind*, vol. iv. (1879) — see especially pp. 21, 22.

him to have looked forward with a true prophetic sense to the theory which in Chapter XV we shall recognize as affording a solution of the problem.

I think it must now be plain that the first duty of the interactionist is to give a clear and unequivocal answer to the question: *What do you mean by the matter on which you assert that the mind acts; how does it exist, and what is its nature?* Without such an answer the doctrine is ambiguous, and should not be urged upon the acceptance of thoughtful persons.

Now, by matter the interactionist may mean either the matter of the naïve realist, or the phenomenon, or the thing-in-itself. If he means the first or the third, he is a naïve or a critical psychophysical dualist. If he means the second, he is a psychophysical phenomenalist. Most interactionists, as we have seen, are to all intents and purposes naïve psychophysical dualists. But, the moment their attention is drawn to the point, we may be sure they will abandon a doctrine resting on naïve realism, and make choice either of the second or the third form of theory; so that these are the only forms we need consider.

Psychophysical Phenomenalism, Interactionist Form

This is the theory that what the mind acts on or influences is matter regarded as a modification of consciousness or phenomenon. The interactionist will hold that it is not necessary for matter to exist separately from mind in order to be acted on, since action does not imply a real tie or influence but only a uniform succession.

Suppose I will to move my arm, and the resulting movement is perceived. The doctrine then comes to this, that one mental state, a volition, causes another mental state, a perception. To this the interactionist will doubtless demur, feeling that he means something a little different; but he will find difficulty in revising the statement, since it follows logically from idealism. The first thing that occurs to him may be that at least the causation is not direct, since between volition and perception there are intervening events, the motor discharge and the out-going nerve-current. But this will not suffice to right matters. Whether the volition causes the perception directly or indirectly, the causal relation is not really a thing between mental and physical, but between two mental states. As against such an interpretation, what the phenomenalistic interactionist feels prompted to hold is that the volition's effect is not the perception of the movement but the movement perceived — a distinction which does not at first sight appear to exist on his doctrine. The distinction is the more necessary, since before the movement can evoke the perception light-rays must pass from the arm to the eye and nerve-currents from the eye to brain. But his critic may return to the attack, and inquire whether the movement is not something immediately perceived? To which the phenomenalist can only reply that it is. But, in that case, since what is immediately perceived is a modification of consciousness, the theory amounts, once again, to the statement that a volition evokes a perception, that one mental state causes another.

To metaphysical experts of the Hegelian school this will seem very crude; and incomplete it undoubtedly is, since it overlooks certain necessary qualifications and reserves for the sake of insisting on a core of truth. The experts, of course, avoid the difficulty by distinguishing between the psychic being of a mental state and its content or meaning, matter being the latter, and thus succeed in making out the interaction to be, after all, between mental and physical. It cannot be denied that this account of the matter harmonizes well with certain facts omitted from view in the other, such as that the volition's effect may be indifferently an actual or only a possible perception, and is a possible perception not for one mind only but for all minds. If we were content to formulate these facts without explaining them, we might do so by saying that what the volition causes is not so much the particular perception as a psychic fact, as the character this and other like perceptions will have in case they exist. Which is, of course, just what the experts mean by their distinction between mental state and content.

But, having given the experts their dues, let us go on to note the limitations of their distinction as applied to this particular case. In the first place, how a volition can get at and influence the content, not only of other states of the same mind, but of states of other minds, is something of a mystery. In the second place, since content, however distinct from the mental state which is its vehicle, is brought home to us only by that mental state and has no other foothold in reality, it is hard to see how the volition can influence the content of a perception without at the same time influencing the perception. If it does not actually cause the perception to arise in a given case, this may be because it is only one of several necessary factors, of which others (such as opening the eyes, looking towards the object, etc.) are wanting. But if the volition influences the content only by influencing the perception, we were right, after all, in arguing that the interaction is a thing between mental states.

Finally, it might be thought a difficulty to this view that the volition influences the content of the perceptions *of all minds*. It will be held, on this and other grounds, that the content is a 'universal,' something whose fortunes are quite distinct from those of the mental state in which it is momentarily incarnated, and indeed an altogether superior kind of thing. Those who speak adoringly of 'universals' are apt to forget that they exist only by being incarnated in mental states, and (in the present case) only by different minds having similar perceptions. But, what is more to the point, it will be found on examination that the minds actually influenced are those only of persons physically near, and that the possible perceptions of other persons are as a matter of fact impossible. By no amount of volition can we influence the minds of persons out of reach of the post or the telegraph. The fact, therefore, that the movement is perceived in common by different minds does not alter the problem from what it would be for one mind only. We have simply to trace the causal connection between the volition and the several perceptions, instead of tracing it between the volition and a single one. The fact that this form of theory makes the interaction a thing between mental states would be no objection to it, provided these causal connections could be traced.

But such tracing of causal connections (as we saw in Chapter X) is a thing that phenomenalism cannot do, either between different minds or between not immediately successive states of the same mind. It can trace them in terms of possible perceptions, but it cannot trace them in terms of real events. This, of course, is only to say that the defects of phenomenalism, and, chief among them, its discontinuity, inevitably cling to a phenomenalistic theory of the relation of mind and body; but it is none the less sufficient to condemn such a theory.

For the benefit, however, of readers whom our proofs of things-in-themselves may not have convinced, let us waive this fundamental difficulty and consider the further working-out of the phenomenalistic theory. Thus far, it has given a perfectly accurate and straightforward account of the facts, erring only by incompleteness; for on all three theories (as we have seen) there is a uniform sequence of the arm-movement upon the volition. In other words, we have not yet come to close quarters with the interactionism of the theory. Nor shall we do so till we investigate the relation, not between the volition and the arm-movement, but between the volition and the brain-event which precedes and conditions the arm-movement.

In discussing this matter, we may continue to assume (a point irrelevant to the main question) that between the volitional brain-event and the motor nerve-current there is a motor discharge in cells of the brain which are 'insentient.' To the motor discharge and the motor nerve-current, the same considerations apply as to the arm-movement; all three happen subsequently to the volition, and the theory gives a correct account of the facts. But when we come to the volitional brain-event, the case is different. Some interactionists will hold that it also happens subsequently to the volition — this, indeed, is the typical interactionist view — and, until the two can be shown empirically to be simultaneous, their theory must be allowed to stand, and can only be attacked on general metaphysical grounds. Other interactionists, however, will admit the two to be simultaneous, and a word may be said regarding the complications of theory which then ensue.

Since simultaneous events cannot be causally related, and since the volitional brain-event as much as the volition must have something to do, the conscientious interactionist — Mr. Bradley, for instance, in Chapter XXIII of his *Appearance and Reality* — concludes that the two must be joint causes of the motor discharge. This is as if the reader of an interlinear translation should deem it the height of philological acumen to construe the Greek noun and the English noun together as joint subjects of the English verb.

But even this simile fails to do full justice to the case. Let us compare these two joint causes. The volition is an actual mental state, it is metaphysically real. The brain-event is only a possible perception, without metaphysical reality at the moment. Notwithstanding the innumerable occasions on which volitions have been followed by movements since the world began, never once has this brain-event, or for that matter the motor discharge or the motor nerve-current, been actualized in any human consciousness. This being so, it is difficult to see what help it can render the volition in effecting the movement. To harness the two together is like assuming that a horse's shadow, since it accompanies him so faithfully and duplicates all his efforts, must assist him in drawing the cart.

On the other hand, we must remember that the movement, equally with the brain-event, is a mere phenomenon, the cart to be drawn merely a shadow cart; and perhaps a shadow horse would amply suffice for this purpose. Indeed, the hypothesis that the real horse draws the shadow cart — which is the equivalent of the view that the volition causes the movement — seems curiously supererogatory and futile. The real horse draws the real cart, and the shadow horse appears to draw the shadow cart, but there is no interchange of rôles between them.

The foregoing illustration may prove to be more than mere simile, since on a certain theory soon to be expounded the volitional brain-event is just the shadow thrown by the volition upon another consciousness. But a doctrine which, like phenomenalism, makes realities act on each other through the medium of shadows might have been expected on occasion to make shadows and realities co-operate. It is to be noted, finally, that this notion of joint causation follows entirely from admitting the simultaneity of the two events; though the view that the volition is the sole cause would be more characteristically interactionist and would harmonize better with our instinctive feeling.

We can now appreciate for the first time the true meaning of the parallelist argument which denies interaction between mental and physical events on the ground of their heterogeneity. Interactionists take this to mean that mind and matter are simply unlike in nature, while still separate realities: they take it, in other words, in a dualistic sense. For them the argument means: How can a spatial material thing and an unspatial spiritual thing have causal relations with each other? But, thus understood, the argument retains but a fraction of its force. It still remains true that the notion of sentiments of amity serving to couple railway carriages (to quote Clifford's illustration) puts a certain strain on the mind; it still remains true that, if causal relations existed, no such phenomenal continuity and quantitative equivalence could be demonstrated as between physical events. On the other hand, so long as the two realities remain, so to speak, moored alongside of each other, mutual influence between them is not only possible but presumable; and interactionists are perfectly right in seeing no particular cogency in the parallelist contention as they understand it. It is otherwise when the heterogeneity is taken in its true sense, as signifying not merely oppositeness of nature but *disparity in point of reality*. Only when the contrast between mental and physical is recognized as that of reality and phenomenon, of substance and shadow, does the absurdity of a volition giving rise to a brain-event begin to dawn on the mind.

Aside, however, from the incongruity and unintelligibility of a world in which able-bodied mental states are on terms of intimacy and co-operation with ghostly possibilities of themselves, it must be admitted that psychophysical phenomenalism, in the form we are now considering, formulates accurately the facts it is willing to recognize. For it makes the volition and the volitional brain-event simultaneous and uniformly followed by the motor discharge, and it may also admit that the latter is connected with the volitional brain-event by quantitative relations which do not connect it with the volition, in such wise that there is no infringement of the principle of the conservation of energy. But interactionism, thus interpreted, differs from parallelism (as we saw in Chapter VII) only by the arbitrary claim that the volition is still in some unexplained sense the cause of the motor discharge. The two theories agree in their accounts of the facts, and differ only by this irresponsible addition.

Let us, in conclusion, ask how far the phenomenalistic theory satisfies the three requirements above formulated. Does it explain the connection of mind and body? Evidently not. For a brain composed of naïvely conceived matter it substitutes a brain composed of phenomenal matter, and there stops. How the two come to be associated, it makes not the slightest attempt to explain. Indeed, Mr. Bradley, whose view this appears to be, frankly tells us that in his opinion the connection of mind and body is inexplicable.[1] I confess that the philosophy of the Inexplicable makes very much the same kind of impression on me as the philosophy of the Unknowable. In neither case can I admit the conclusion of mental impotence to be justified. Indeed, if on certain principles the connection of mind and body is inexplicable, I should regard that as demonstrating the inadequacy of the principles.

It goes without saying that psychophysical phenomenalism makes no provision for an explanation of the origin of consciousness. That it vindicates, or rather would like to vindicate, the efficiency of consciousness, may be admitted.

Psychophysical Dualism

If, to escape the pluralism and discontinuity of a phenomenalistic theory, we assume the existence of things-in-themselves, then what the mind acts on

[1] *Appearance and Reality*, pp. 295, 336.

may be the things-in-themselves with which it is, so to speak, immediately contiguous. This, to be sure, would be no longer an interaction with matter, the term being properly applicable only to the phenomenon, and the assertion that the mind interacts with things-in-themselves therefore tantamount to the withdrawal of the claim that it interacts with matter. If, now, we assume that the matter on which parallelism asserts that the mind does *not* act means phenomenal matter, and that the matter on which interactionism asserts that it *does* act means things-in-themselves, we shall perhaps have recognized the element of truth in both theories and reached a basis for reconciliation between them. For parallelism itself, when interpreted in terms of the realistic theory, asserts just such interaction, holding that, as the volitional brain-event causes the arm-movement, so the volition causes the extra-mental event for which the arm-movement stands. Only automatism is irretrievably committed to the denial of such interaction.

Everything depends, however, on the further working-out of the theory. The case of the motor discharge is like that of the arm-movement: parallelism holds that, although the volition does not cause the motor discharge, it causes the real event for which the motor discharge stands. But the case of the volitional brain-event is different. Here, as under the head of psychophysical phenomenalism, the question arises whether volition and volitional brain-event are simultaneous or successive; and here, as before, the typical interactionist will hold them to be successive. The result is as genuine a psychophysical dualism as if what the mind acted on were the matter of the naïve realist. For the real event that appears as the volitional brain-event is then not the volition but something distinct from it, and the mind a reality additional to the entire system of realities that appear as the physical world, a sort of stranger from another sphere.

The dualism is equally plain if the two be held to be simultaneous but distinct. In that case their co-operation as joint causes is not subject to the difficulty that existed before, where one of the joint causes was an actual and the other only a possible state, since both are now real. It is true that such joint causality deprives the volition of the credit of being the *sole* cause of the motor discharge, as the interactionist would like to believe it; but he may think half a loaf better than no bread. On the other hand, just so far as the volition co-operates, there is a breach of the principle of conservation.

The objections to psychophysical dualism are the same as those to naïve dualism apart from its naïveness. In the first place, no dualistic theory can explain the connection of mind and body, and tell us why two such disparate things are associated. For dualism regards the association on the phenomenal plane as only the symbol of a real association equally difficult to understand, and thus perpetuates the problem instead of solving it. In the second place, no dualistic theory can explain the origin of mind. For, though the interaction makes it intelligible *why* consciousness has been evolved, namely, because of its use, the dualism leaves it absolutely unintelligible *that* it should have been evolved. In a self-sufficient world of things-in-themselves as much as in a world purely material, no reason appears why consciousness should ever have arisen at all. If the mind is not a member of the system of realities that appear as the physical world, it cannot have been evolved out of them, and we lose our reason for assimilating it to them in nature. Thus at one stroke the origin of mind is made unintelligible and the nature of things-in-themselves unknowable.

If, on the other hand, we regard the mind as a member of the system of realities that appear as the physical world, and as, in particular, the reality that appears as the brain-process, at a stroke both the problem of the relation of mind and body and that of the origin of mind are solved. The latter, for the mind, in that case, is evolved out of the things-in-themselves that appear as the rest of the physical world, in the same way that the brain-process is evolved out of other physical facts. The former, for the empirical duality of mind and brain is then explained by the two points of view from which one and the same reality is regarded, the relation of mind and body being subsumed under that of thing-in-itself and phenomenon. But, with the choice of this better alternative, psychophysical dualism passes over into the parallelist theory which we are to consider under the name of psychophysical idealism.

CHAPTER XIV

AUTOMATIST THEORIES

We pass now to theories which arise as metaphysical interpretations of automatism. Automatism, it will be remembered, is our name for the doctrine that mental states are in all cases effects of brain-events, never causes. Not satisfied with regarding mental states as impotent to cause brain-events, this doctrine goes farther, and makes them impotent even to cause each other. It would be impossible to emphasize more strongly the helpless dependence of mind, or to contradict more flatly that desire for its efficiency which is the main-spring of interactionism.

Since our examination of the arguments for automatism in Chapter V, we have undertaken in Chapter VII an analysis of the causal relation as actually employed in physical science. Let us, before entering on the discussion of particular theories, apply to automatism as a causal doctrine the results at which we there arrived. Automatism asserts a one-sided causal relation in which brain-events are always causes and mental states always effects. Let us consider whether the position thus assigned to mental states accords with correct views of causality.

The position is a peculiar one. Causal relations are held to connect physical events but not mental states. Physical events not only cause each other, but they cause mental states as well. Each brain-event has two effects: a physical event, which becomes in its turn the cause of another physical event, and a mental state which does not cause anything further. We cannot exactly say that mental states are not subject to causality, since they are effects; but, as effects which do not in their turn become causes, they are subject to causality, so to speak, *à parte ante* but not *à parte post*. Is the conception of an effect which does not in its turn become a cause, of what we may call a *pure* effect, a legitimate one?

It will be admitted that at least there are no such effects in the physical world. There are no physical effects in which the causal influence exhausts itself and becomes finally extinguished. Thanks to the principle of the conservation of energy, every physical series is gifted with an endless life. Nor do these statements necessarily imply that causation consists in anything but uniform sequence with equivalence. Now, if causation in the physical world implied power or a 'real tie,' our inability to discover power in mental states might be a reason for denying them to be causes. But physical events and mental states are in this respect exactly on a par. The real difference between physical and mental causation lies in something wholly different: the demonstrability of equivalences in the one case, and not in the other. But, while this might be a reason for holding physical events but not mental events to be causally connected *inter se*, it cannot be a reason for admitting physical events to be causes of mental but denying mental events to be causes of physical. Since equivalences are in both cases impossible, either both relations are consistent or both are inconsistent with causal principles. If, on the other hand, a less perfect form of causation be admitted consisting in uniform sequence *without* equivalence, the sequences of physical events upon mental are as uniform as those of mental events upon physical, volition being as regularly followed by movement as stimulus by sensation. So that nothing in the abstract principles of causality justifies our attributing to physical events a power to produce mental which mental events have not to produce physical, or entertaining for the mental realm a notion of effects that do not in their turn become causes which we should not think of entertaining for the physical.

Automatism might, however, be true for reasons of fact: because empirically the volition can be shown to be subsequent to the volitional brain-event and without effects of its own. But we have seen that empirically this cannot be shown. It is an assumption due partly to an arbitrary transference to the case of volition of the temporal relation assumed to exist between sensational brain-event and sensation, partly to a loose inference from the general fact of the apparent dependence of mind on brain. We have seen that the exact temporal relation between brain-events and mental states is difficult or impossible to determine empirically, and that we are forced to look for light on the subject to metaphysical theory. But, in the dearth of empirical evidence, the only natural assumptions are those of typical interactionism and typical parallelism. Either common-sense is right in asserting causal relations between mind and body, and, if so, we must trust appearances in both cases and recognize that the causation of the volitional brain-event by the volition has exactly as much evidence for it as that of the sensation by the sensational brain-event; or else in both cases we must reject the testimony of appearances, and hold brain-event and mental state to be simultaneous. Thus the view that mental states are always subsequent to and effects of brain-events appears a perfectly arbitrary assumption, warranted neither by the principles of causality nor by empirical facts.

But now, the final possibility remains that automatism may be capable of establishment on metaphysical grounds. This would mean that, when we consider what matter and mind are in ultimate analysis, we find that the hypothesis that the brain-event brings the mental state into existence affords the best explanation of their observed connection. The question thus resolves itself into this: Is mind, metaphysically, the sort of thing that can best be understood as an effect of matter? Or, to put the question conversely: Is matter, on a critical view, the sort of thing that can rationally be conceived to give rise to mind? To answer this question, we must study the metaphysical theories that arise as interpretations of automatism.

Average Current Automatism

Let us begin by considering the metaphysical conceptions underlying average current automatism. In discussing the empirical arguments for the theory, we admitted that its causal thesis is conceivably separable from the metaphysical or creationist thesis which the former might seem necessarily to imply — that it is possible to hold that matter, as an empirical fact, is the cause of consciousness, without necessarily holding that it gives birth to consciousness. Actual automatists, however, continually overstep this line, and describe consciousness not merely as an effect but as a product of matter.

"The whole of the *causae cognoscendi*," says Mr. Shadworth Hodgson, "of all phenomena whatever lies in consciousness — the whole of their *causae existendi*, so far as we have any means of positively tracing it, lies in matter."[1] A very pretty antithesis; but the conception of matter causing the existence of consciousness certainly needs clearing up. Even granting that a material event is the uniform antecedent of a mental state, "we do not possess the organ, nor apparently any rudiment of the organ," that would permit us to pass in thought from one to the other. If this be true where matter merely influences mind, how much more where matter is assumed to give birth to mind!

Even on dualistic principles the foregoing remark

[1] *Brain*, vol. xvii. (1894), review of Flournoy's *Métaphysique et Psychologie*, pp. 103 ff.

holds true. The incomprehensibility becomes greater when we reflect that the matter which is supposed to work such wonders is itself, according to idealism, only an actual or possible mental state. How a mind can be brought into existence by the action of previous states of some other mind (for they cannot very well be states of its own), is sufficiently hard to understand; how it can be brought into existence by previous states that are not actual but only possible, is scarcely harder. If the actual or possible states were symbols of a reality existing antecedently to the mind in question, the case would be different. But the conditioning of a mind by previous possible mental states would seem more aptly describable as *un*real than as what Mr. Hodgson calls "real conditioning."

Mr. Hodgson holds his view partly constrained by the facts, partly lest a worse thing befall. " Previous to the rise of physiological psychology, there were two claimants in the field for the office of being the really conditioning agent or agency in generating, sustaining, and governing the phenomena of consciousness. One was the Soul, Mind, or Spirit: the other was the Ego, or some other form or mode of consciousness itself. . . . The value of physiological psychology consists, therefore, in the fact that the neuro-cerebral system is a new and rival claimant for the office. . . ."[1] If this be meant simply as a statement of empirical fact, I have nothing further to say. But it looks suspiciously like a piece of metaphysics. For " generating," " sustaining," and " governing " are

[1] Loc. cit.

metaphysical words; they carry us far beyond the uniformities of co-existence and sequence which are the sole concern of natural science, and exhibit matter in a relation to consciousness only to be described as parental. Now, as to the power of matter to "sustain" and "govern" consciousness opinions may possibly differ; but its obvious incapacity to "generate" it not only refutes this form of automatism, but would seem, on Mr. Hodgson's showing, to throw the door as widely open to the Soul as it was before the advent of physiological psychology. If this is not so, if the door is finally closed, it is partly because things-in-themselves are at hand to generate and in a measure also to sustain and govern consciousness, partly because the latter is able in a measure, by a judicious utilization of the realities that appear as food and drink and by a wise control of the attention, to sustain and govern itself.

The painful ambiguity of statements like those just quoted makes it perfectly plain that the automatist, no less than the interactionist, is in duty bound to tell us precisely what he means by matter. Unless he be a naïve realist, he must mean either phenomenal matter or the extra-mental reality that appears as matter. If he means the former, he is a psychophysical phenomenalist of the automatist type. If he means the latter, everything depends on how he conceives the nature of the extra-mental reality. If he conceives it as still material, we have no choice but to call him a psychophysical materialist. If, on the other hand, he conceives it as neither mental nor material, or feels constrained to declare it simply unknowable, his doctrine approximates to the parallelist view which we were to call psychophysical monism, of which we should have to designate it as an automatist form. Such an unknown reality, to be sure, no longer properly deserves the name of matter; and automatism is the view that consciousness depends on matter. So it comes about that psychophysical phenomenalism and psychophysical materialism are the two typical metaphysical interpretations of automatism, and it will be better perhaps to reserve psychophysical monism for discussion under the head of parallelist theories.

Psychophysical Phenomenalism, Automatist Form

This is, by implication, the theory of Professor Huxley. It furnishes an interesting example of the positive and experimental character of Professor Huxley's mind. He saw clearly that matter, so far as our experience goes, is merely a phenomenon in consciousness. He thought he saw clearly that mental states are, empirically, uniform consequents of bodily antecedents. On the supposed testimony of experience, he firmly held both of these propositions, undisturbed by the paradox which results when they are combined.

For the view that consciousness is existentially dependent on what, metaphysically considered, is only one of its own states, is surely a paradox. Locke's Hindoo fable about the earth resting on an elephant, the elephant on a tortoise, and the tortoise on "something I know not what," would be quite outdone if the earth rested on the tortoise and the tortoise meanwhile walked the earth. Matter a phenomenon of consciousness, yet consciousness at the same time an epiphenomenon of matter: here is surely a *circulus in philosophando*. A serpent with its tail in its mouth would be the fit emblem for such a philosophy.

The theory becomes more paradoxical still when we go backward into the past and apply it to the problem of the origin of consciousness. So long as there are human minds with developed perceptions, the terms it employs may still seem to exist. But, as we proceed, the minds grow more rudimentary and the perceptions less developed, and what must ultimately happen is typified by the case of the snake. Suppose no physical obstacles opposed themselves to its continued swallowing of its tail. When the process reached what mathematicians call the limit, there would remain neither a head to swallow nor a tail to be digested. So, previous to the dawn of consciousness, there is no matter to 'cause its existence' because there is no mind to which the matter could be phenomenal. Unless the phenomenalist is satisfied to hold that the existence of mind is caused by previous perceptions that are not actual but only possible!

Thus the great drawback of phenomenalism is the necessity we are under, in view of the facts, of making mental states arise out of physical facts, realities out of shadows. Whereas, on the hypothesis of things-in-themselves, they arise out of the real facts for which physical facts stand. These real facts both ante-date and fill in the gaps between individual minds, thus doing away with the discontinuity and incompleteness that characterize the universe on the phenomenalistic theory.

To sum up: psychophysical phenomenalism, in this automatist form, is not only inconsistent with causal principles and wholly unsupported by facts in so far as automatist, but, as a metaphysical theory, it fails most lamentably in all that such a theory might reasonably be expected to perform. It finds the connection of mind and body an empirical fact; it leaves it a metaphysical paradox. In its application to the problem of the origin of consciousness, it stretches this paradox to the bursting-point. And then, as a slight token of our appreciation of these failures and absurdities, it asks us to give up our belief in the efficiency of consciousness. Truly, a more unsatisfactory theory could hardly be conceived.

Psychophysical Materialism

I do not feel sure where to classify the theory of Mr. Shadworth Hodgson. His recent encyclopædic work [1] shows him to be a realist rather than a phenomenalist, the background of his philosophy being filled in with an Unknowable which recalls that of Mr. Spencer. Yet he is never weary of asserting that consciousness is a dependent thing, and that matter is the thing on

[1] *The Metaphysic of Experience*, London, 1898 — see especially vol. i., chapter viii.

which it is dependent; and it is difficult to suppose that he means by matter this unknown reality, rather than phenomenal matter.

Thinkers enough will be found, in any event, to maintain that the extra-mental reality is material, or at least that its nature must be assumed to be more like matter than like consciousness, and that consciousness is its pure effect. Now, a view which makes matter a reality and consciousness dependent on it is fairly entitled to the name of materialism — a name which I have not felt justified in applying to the phenomenalistic form of theory simply in virtue of its automatism. If, on the other hand, the nature of the extra-mental reality be declared unknowable, some such name as 'psychophysical realism' would perhaps be juster; but I have no wish to multiply names beyond necessity.

On either view, the dependence implied in such a one-sided causal relation is evidently absolute. The thing-in-itself that appears as the brain-process becomes more real, or at any rate more fundamental, than its offshoot and dependency, consciousness. The latter sinks from a reality into a mere appearance. It is conceived, to be sure, as additional to the system of realities that appear as the physical world, yet as something so tenuous and shadowy that it can find room for itself in the crevices of things — in short, as a 'mere epiphenomenon.'

Now, thinkers who hold this view, or would be forced to it if they defined their doctrine metaphysically, are led to it originally by the assumption that the dependence of consciousness on something distinct from itself is an indubitable empirical fact. Were it not for this assumption, it would never occur to them to propound such dependence simply as a metaphysical theory. Nevertheless, it is as a metaphysical theory that we must here consider it; and, since we have recognized that dependence cannot be upheld as an empirical fact, it only remains for us to examine its merits in this rôle.

In conceiving the supposed empirical dependence on the brain-process as only the symbol of a dependence on things-in-themselves, psychophysical materialism has at least the merit of making consciousness dependent on a reality, not a shadow. Thus it is not chargeable with the preposterous inversion of rôles of which the phenomenalistic form of theory is guilty. On the other hand, its conception of consciousness is nothing if not obscure. If it conceived consciousness as a reality co-ordinate with that symbolized by the brain-process, it could hardly fail to admit interaction between the two, and so pass over into the form of interactionist theory which we have called psychophysical dualism. Hence it seems condemned to conceive it as a mere series of phenomena, co-ordinate with the phenomena of matter and inferior in reality to the extra-mental events of which it is the pure effect. What still distinguishes the theory from psychophysical monism is, first, its automatism, and, secondly, its irrational assumption that the reality symbolized by the brain-process is still material or quasi-material.

Having discussed its metaphysical premises, let us ask how far it explains the relation of mind and body, and tells us why the two are connected. Evidently it does not explain this relation at all, but assumes the empirical connection to be only the symbol of a real connection which is ultimate and inexplicable. Why a series of mental phenomena should be attached to the quasi-material events that appear as the brain-process, remains an enigma. And not less so, how in the midst of such a quasi-material world consciousness should ever arise. Thus neither regarding the connection of mind and body nor regarding the origin of consciousness do we get any the least ray of light.

Let us now recall the two alternatives presented to the believer in things-in-themselves when he approaches the relation of mind and brain: either the brain — or, more exactly, the brain-process — is the symbol of a reality distinct from the mind, or else the reality that appears as the brain-process is the mind itself. Psychophysical materialism has chosen the less excellent of these two alternatives, the one which perpetuates instead of solving the problems of the relation of mind and body and of the origin of consciousness. It may now be observed, as a legitimate concession to materialism, and the only legitimate one, that even those who choose the opposite alternative are forced by the facts to recognize a dependence of consciousness on the things-in-themselves that surround it, corresponding to the empirical dependence of the brain-process on the rest of the bodily processes. This dependence bears, it is true, a certain resemblance to that asserted by psychophysical materialism between consciousness and the things-in-themselves that appear as the brain-process. But the former is a transcript of the empirical facts, and makes consciousness partially dependent on a reality co-ordinate with it and resembling it in nature; while the latter is based on an erroneous version of the facts, and makes consciousness totally dependent on something more real than it and different from it in nature. This more excellent hypothesis we are to consider in the next chapter under the name of psychophysical idealism.

CHAPTER XV

PARALLELIST THEORIES

PARALLELISM is, no more than automatism or interactionism, an ultimate or philosophical account of the relation of mind and body, as its advocates are apt to suppose. It merely formulates the empirical connection without attempting to explain it, and thus belongs rather to physiological psychology than to metaphysics. The conception of concomitance or parallelism, on its positive side, involves the two elements of simultaneous happening and invariable connection — in one phrase, uniform co-existence: elements both of the empirical order. But the parallelist who would be also a philosopher may rightly be called on to specify the real relation which makes such simultaneous happening and invariable connection possible. The attempt to do so gives rise to the metaphysical interpretations of parallelism now to be considered.

As under the head of interactionist and automatist, so under that of parallelist theories we may ask first as to the metaphysical conceptions underlying the average current form of the doctrine.

It can hardly be denied that parallelism is conceived by some of its more popular advocates in what are practically dualistic terms. The material events to which consciousness is held to run parallel are more or less dimly conceived as independently real. The doctrine thus receives a twist in the materialistic direction, notwithstanding the pains its advocates take to distinguish it from materialism in the strict sense. But this is in no way logically necessary. There is something in interactionism, as the doctrine of common-sense, more harmonious with, if it does not actually necessitate, dualism; whereas, to a philosophical mind, the doctrine of the two parallel series can hardly fail to suggest that one is real and the other only apparent.

We need not waste time in discussing a form of parallelism based on naïve realism. Obviously the exact correspondence of the two series would be an insoluble enigma. Let us pass at once to the typical forms in which the theory is currently held. The first of these makes the physical and the mental series co-ordinate in point of reality, and regards them as parallel manifestations of a single real being: this we were to call *psychophysical monism*. The second makes the mental series alone real and the physical merely phenomenal, and our name for this was *psychophysical idealism*.

Psychophysical Monism

This must not be confused with metaphysical monism, or the doctrine that the universe is fundamentally one. Psychophysical monism seeks to explain the empirical parallelism by holding that mind and body are opposite sides or manifestations of a single reality. It has two forms, according as this reality is conceived to be given in and with the two series of phenomena, or to be distinct from and underlie them. We may say that the first form makes mind and body *aspects*, the second *attributes*, of the One Substance. It is characteristic of both forms to co-ordinate mind and body, regarding them as equally real or equally unreal, as equally good or equally bad specimens of what the reality of things is like.

The first form appears to have been the theory of Spinoza, who regarded extension and thought as distinct but co-ordinate modes of reality. It was reserved for Leibnitz to subordinate extension to thought by conceiving the latter as real and the former as only phenomenal. The crucial question, of course, for the monist is how the two co-ordinate modes hang inwardly together. The monist of the first type either boldly affirms their identity, or else resorts to similes. Thus he compares the relation to that between the two sides of a shield, which from one point of view appears convex, from another concave. But, unfortunately, this is an explanation which does not explain. For we readily comprehend how the two sides of a shield, being both material, are fitted together to form the material object; but how things of opposite nature, and belonging in fact to disparate worlds, can be joined into one, or rather truly *be* one, the simile in no way helps us to understand. When we try to unite them in thought, they refuse to be joined, and remain obstinately separate in spite of all our efforts. Thus the 'identity' of the psychophysical monist of this type is a word that conveys no idea, or none adequate to the situation. Apart from the word, the theory is simply a sort of phenomenalistic dualism on a parallelist basis.

The second form of psychophysical monism has sounder claims to the monistic title, since, instead of trying to fuse the two kinds of phenomena, it assumes a substance or thing-in-itself behind both. This was the theory of Kant, who seems to have been a psychophysical monist without being a parallelist. Kant (as we already know) regarded not only physical facts but also mental states as phenomena, and assumed things-in-themselves behind the latter as well as behind the former. He even hazarded the conjecture that the things-in-themselves behind physical phenomena and the things-in-themselves behind mental phenomena might be identical. And, since mental phenomena, on this view, are not specimens of reality, but reality manifests itself through them and through physical phenomena indifferently, he naturally concluded that we have no ground for supposing reality to be like either, but must conceive it as " neither matter nor a thinking being."

In other words, psychophysical monism in this form is the theory of the Unknowable. Or perhaps the One Substance it assumes is, after all, not negatively unknowable, since from its indifferent manifestation through physical facts and through mental states we may fairly conclude that it is unlike either. Thus it becomes a sort of *tertium quid*. But now, such a conception is inconsistent with sound metaphysical principles. If (as we saw in Chapter XII) we possess no conception of a reality material in its nature, à fortiori we possess none of a reality neither mental nor material, of a *tertium quid*. The notion is a perfectly arbitrary and baseless invention, having the same status in metaphysics as that of a centaur or chimæra in zoölogy. Nor will it help matters to be entirely non-committal, and call it the Unknowable. It were much to be wished, in the interests of philosophical progress, that the Unknowable were at the same time the Unthinkable and the Unmentionable.

Perhaps the psychophysical monist may think to remedy the difficulty by making the One Substance mental in nature. But such an hypothesis would be inconsistent with the fact that consciousness is held to be its attribute. For the essence of mind is consciousness, and, if the One Substance is mental, it can only be another consciousness; but one consciousness cannot stand to another in the relation of substance and attribute. Two consciousnesses must needs be co-ordinate, be joint members of the world of reality.

Again, quite apart from the nature assigned to the One Substance, the relation in which it is held to stand to our thoughts and feelings is enough to condemn it. For the affiliation of our thoughts and feelings upon an entity distinct from themselves, whether this entity be a private Ego or a universal Substance, necessarily deprives them of reality. But this is inconsistent with sound metaphysical principles. Our thoughts and feelings may be transitory and ephemeral, but so long as they last they are as real as anything can be.

Finally, let us ask how far the monistic theory in this second form explains the connection of mind and body. The explanation it offers seems at first sight plausible: the two series are held together by their common relationship to the One Substance. Assuming that a reality can project, so to speak, into space manifestations of itself or phenomena, no reason appears why it should not project two different kinds, and project them in parallel series. But once cast doubt on the reality of such projection, and the theory collapses. Now, the conception of projection — or, to abandon metaphor, the old-fashioned idea of the relation of substance and accident — is perhaps the weakest point in the theory. Collapsing, it leaves on our hands *three* associated things, in place of the two whose association we set out to explain, with never a hint as to the mode of their connection.

In this it is not alone. The interactionist theory of psychophysical dualism and the automatist theory of psychophysical materialism likewise make this highly superfluous addition to the elements of the problem. They make it through their assumption that the reality symbolized by the brain-process is distinct from the accompanying consciousness, and it is the inevitable result of this assumption. The theory which remains to be considered, and of which psychophysical monism is little better than a grotesque parody, rests on the assumption that the reality symbolized by the brain-process is consciousness itself.

Psychophysical Idealism

This view, based on the hypothesis of things-in-themselves and belonging thus to the realistic rather than the phenomenalistic type of theory, holds that the thing-in-itself symbolized by the brain-process is the accompanying consciousness. Thus it explains the connection of mind and body by subsuming the relation under that of thing-in-itself and perception.

Suppose that by means of a surgical operation, and with the aid of microscopes far more powerful than any yet invented, I were enabled to see the molecular changes in another person's brain. On the realistic hypothesis, we are bound to regard these changes as the manifestation of an extra-mental fact. What is this fact? Is it a reality distinct not only from my perception but also from the other person's consciousness? Is there, intermediate between his consciousness and my perception of his brain, a real brain sustaining peculiar relations to his consciousness; or is there no such intermediate reality? May it not be that his perceived brain — or, to speak more exactly, his brain-process — is in some sort the manifestation of his consciousness, and his consciousness accordingly the thing-in-itself that appears as his brain-process?

It might seem that consciousness, as something

immediately given, is the very opposite of a thing-in-itself. But if we consider, first, that consciousness is a reality; secondly, that from the point of view of other minds it is an extra-mental reality, we shall see that it needs only to be symbolized by the brain-process in order to be a thing-in-itself. Thus, if psychophysical idealism be true, other minds are not merely extra-mental realities, they are the first case of things-in-themselves.

But, if consciousness is a reality and the brain-process a phenomenon, a perception in another mind, what more natural than to assume that the former is the reality symbolized by the latter? Is not the brain-process truly, when we come to think of it, a manifestation of the accompanying mind? If men's thoughts and feelings are manifested by their words, facial expressions, and acts, how much more by the brain-events from which all these external changes proceed!

Nay more, the law of psychophysical correlation itself, with its seemingly materialistic implications, proves our best helper in establishing this idealistic dependence of the brain-process on consciousness. Disparate as the two things at first sight appear, and unlike as their component elements must always remain, this law assures us that in their main outlines they are constructed on the same plan. The amount of correspondence thus guaranteed is amply sufficient to serve as the foundation of a relation of symbolism. A somewhat unexpected turn of the argument, surely! The law of psychophysical correlation, which seemed to bind the mind to the brain as a mere epiphenomenon, is now seen to bind the brain to the mind as the latter's adequate external expression, its apparent materialism being converted as by magic into idealism. The only possible question is, whether the manifestation of the mind through the brain is indirect and roundabout, by way of a real brain given neither to its owner nor to the spectator, or direct and immediate. I need hardly point out the greater simplicity and economy of the latter hypothesis.

No solution of the problem, in fact, could be simpler or more economical. We have two things, the brain-process and consciousness, and the question is as to their relation. The brain-process is a phenomenon, and every phenomenon symbolizes a reality, and consciousness is a reality. Therefore, conclude the psychophysical materialists and monists, the brain-process symbolizes a reality of which consciousness is the manifestation or on which it is dependent. They actually go out of their way to avoid the solution! For, if the reality symbolized by the brain-process is distinct from consciousness, then the two are loosely and externally attached as we commonly conceive brain and mind to be attached, and the problem is simply transferred to another sphere and perpetuated. Whereas, if the reality symbolized by the brain-process is consciousness itself, their connection is explained and the problem solved. Indeed, this is the only conceivable solution of a problem which all other hypotheses necessarily perpetuate.

On every other hypothesis, the duality of mind and body is either a duality of existences or a duality of disparate phenomena; in either case their connection is a new fact, not provided for in their nature, and consequently inexplicable. On this hypothesis, the duality is that of a reality and its phenomenon; this, for believers in things-in-themselves, is a *vera relatio*, and the connection is therefore explained by being subsumed under the relation of phenomenon and thing-in-itself.

So far, we have been considering the relation between another man's consciousness and *my* perception of his brain, conceiving the brain-process as the way one mind manifests itself to another. Let us now consider the case in which the perception is the man's own, supposing such a thing to be possible. This case is attended with peculiar difficulties not attaching to the other. It is essentially a test case, and if the theory is able to construe it satisfactorily, that will be strong confirmation of the theory's worth.

A man's brain is evidently not a thing perceptible solely to other people. Like physical facts in general, it is a potential object for all similarly constituted minds, and therefore for its owner among the rest. Even the mechanical difficulties of getting a glimpse of one's own brain-process are scarcely greater than those of observing other people's. In the experiment before suggested, we have only to suppose, after the laying-bare of the brain-tissue and the application of the hyper-microscope, an arrangement of mirrors to be brought to bear, in such wise as to reflect the light-rays traversing the microscope into the subject's eye. This happy mortal would then, if the parallelist hypothesis be correct, be simultaneously conscious of a feeling and of the accompanying brain-event. This suggests a curious deduction. Suppose the feeling happened to be a perception, and the perception that of the very brain-event in question; then mental state and correlated brain-event would apparently for that mind be fused into one!

But this has a suspicious look. A reality and its symbol can hardly be identical, even where both are states of the same mind. Attentive consideration of the matter suggests the following important question: If the brain-process is the way one consciousness appears to another or to itself, can it be true, as the parallelists are wont to assume, or in what sense, if any, is it true, that reality and symbol are simultaneous? Is there not rather, on this theory, between mental state and symbolizing brain-event a relation of cause and effect, due to the fact that the brain-event is a perception called forth by the action of the mental state on another or on the same mind? And, if so, does it not follow that there is a temporal relation between the two, different from that assumed by the parallelists, and the exact opposite of that asserted by the automatists, the brain-event being uniformly *subsequent* to the mental state?

This is a delicate matter, and we shall need to recall some of the subtler aspects of the metaphysics of perception in order to do it justice. Everything depends on what we mean by the brain-event. Conceived in one way, the latter is manifestly subsequent to the mental state. Conceived in another, it may be asserted to be simultaneous with it, and the assumption of simultaneity made by the parallelists to be essentially correct.

If by the brain-event we mean the actual modification of another or the same consciousness — and this is the only natural or strictly defensible meaning of the word — there can be no doubt whatever that this modification is subsequent to the mental state it symbolizes, and that the two are related as cause and effect. This results clearly from the manner in which the perception of the brain-event is obtained: by means of light-rays passing through the microscope and into the observer's eye, and nerve-currents passing from his eye to his brain. These are processes occupying time, and they necessarily intervene between the mental state and the perception of the brain-event. Of course, on the hypothesis of things-in-themselves, what really intervenes and enables the consciousness to act on another or on its later self is not these physical processes as such, but the extramental processes for which they stand; but the temporal gap between mental state and symbolizing perception is none the less real.

But this is not the last word of the matter. Possibly the reader may recall the curious distinction we found the plain man making between the perception of a physical event and the physical event perceived ; as where he insists that what his volition causes is not the perception of the arm-movement but the arm-movement itself. Inconsistent with idealism as this distinction appears, it is yet fully justified by the fact that light-rays must pass from the arm to the eye and nerve-currents from the eye to the brain before the movement can excite the perception. But its only intelligible interpretation is, that it is really a distinction between the perception considered as a symbol and the extra-mental event symbolized. This subtle point we can now turn to account. What if the parallelist, by the brain-events which he asserts to be simultaneous with mental states, means not the perceptions but the events perceived, the only intelligible explanation of the latter being that they are events-in-themselves? What if the simultaneity he asserts is really between mental states and the real events for which the brain-events stand?

But these real events, the reader will reply, are simply the mental states over again, and the simultaneity asserted is therefore that of the mental states with themselves; in other words, it is not a simultaneity at all, but an identity. Hence one of two things : either by the brain-event the parallelist means the perception, in which case the latter is subsequent to the mental state, and its effect; or else he means simply the mental state itself regarded from the point of view of the perception, in which case there is no simultaneity at all but an identity — no parallelism but a single series.

The deduction is unassailable. And it helps to bring out a corollary of psychophysical idealism which one must appreciate in order fully to understand the doctrine : namely, that when the parallelism of mental and physical events is metaphysically interpreted, no real parallelism remains. For — quite apart from the temporal difference just referred to — one of the two series is not real but only phenomenal, it is a shadow cast by one consciousness on another or on its latter self, and having no existence apart from the two; and the parallelism necessarily shares the phenomenal character of its physical member. Secondly, under existing conditions the phenomena composing the brain-process, being hidden away in a corner of the physical world where they cannot be got at, are never actualized in consciousness but remain merely possible; so that up to the present moment in the history of the race this shadow has never been cast upon any human mind. Possibly it may be a comfort to the reader to know that there are no two series going on in him at this moment, any more than in the writer of these lines.

Psychophysical idealism is thus, at bottom, a doctrine of identity rather than of parallelism. It realizes intelligibly the postulate of one reality with two aspects set up but not realized by psychophysical monism. By making the physical series merely phenomenal, it does away completely with the absurd dependence of the mental on the physical asserted by psychophysical materialism, while acknowledging the undeniable dependence of the mind on the other realities which with it appear as the body. Subordinating the physical to the mental and conceiving the latter as alone real, it accords as neither the materialistic nor the monistic doctrine does with the fundamental principle of all idealistic philosophy, and is therefore justly entitled to its name.

Besides explaining intelligibly the association of mind and body, it deals no less successfully with the connected questions. If consciousness is the thing-in-itself symbolized by the brain-process, then consciousness occupies a position in the real world exactly analogous to that of the brain-process in the physical world. Here is a proposition fertile in theoretical consequences. In the first place, it logically involves the efficiency of consciousness; in the second, it enables us to explain its origin; in the third, it supplies the basis for a philosophy genuinely and thoroughly monistic.

As regards the efficiency of consciousness, it has already been pointed out that, if the parallelistic conception be correct, our mental states must stand in causal relations to each other analogous to those which connect brain-events. This is a proposition which must hold true even for the phenomenalist. But, on phenomenalistic principles, the causal chain appears incomplete; for, while an earlier mental state may be the cause of a later, yet, since sensory stimuli and voluntary movements are merely phenomenal facts, our sensations appear to be effects without real causes and our volitions to be causes without real effects. The real causes and effects required to make the causal chain complete are supplied the moment we admit things-in-themselves, since the sensation's cause and the volition's effect are in that case the real events for which sensory stimuli and voluntary movements stand. Thus, according to psychophysical idealism, the phenomenal causal relation between sensory stimulus and sensational brain-event is the symbol of a real causal relation between an extra-mental event and the sensation, the phenomenal causal relation between volitional brain-event and voluntary movement the symbol of a real causal relation between the volition and an extra-mental event.

Psychophysical idealism thus affords as complete satisfaction to the demand for the efficiency of consciousness as any interactionist theory. Indeed, the satisfaction it affords is in a certain way more complete, since, instead of resting efficiency on mere dogma or intuition, as the interactionists do, it offers as evidence for it the analogy of the relation between volitional brain-event and voluntary movement. On the other hand, the efficiency thus guaranteed is entirely consistent with the empirical truth of parallelism. Parallelism forbids us to assume causal relations between mental states and physical events: psychophysical idealism upholds the prohibition, allowing their assumption only between mental states and the real events for which physical events stand.

In the second place, by its assumption that consciousness and other things-in-themselves are of the same nature, it paves the way for an explanation of the origin of consciousness. For the evolution of the brain-process out of simpler physical facts is now the symbol of the evolution of consciousness out of simpler mental facts. This, to be sure, is only the beginning of a solution, and, to make it complete, it would be necessary to explain how things-in-themselves despite their continuity can be mental in nature, and how consciousness despite its unity and isolation can be evolved out of them; matters which it will be impossible for us to consider in this book. But psychophysical idealism differs from its materialistic and monistic competitors in being able to offer at least this beginning of a solution.

Finally, the theory is genuinely monistic, and that in a double way, both as regards the stuff of the universe and as regards its form. It is monistic as regards the stuff of the universe, for, unlike both psychophysical materialism and psychophysical monism, it holds the universe to be in all its parts mental in nature. It is monistic as regards its form, for it conceives individual minds and other things-in-themselves as together constituting a single system, whose continuity and order are symbolized by the continuity and order of the physical world.

It may be interesting to compare psychophysical idealism with the theory of Berkeley, to which it is more closely allied than might at first sight appear. The two doctrines agree in conceiving the physical world as an impression produced on our minds by the action of a reality outside them. But Berkeley sets the Divine Mind and the finite minds over against each other and makes them mutually exclusive; he allows to the finite minds no share in the action of imprinting, supposing them merely to receive and the Divine Mind alone to communicate impressions. So long as finite and Infinite remain thus *vis-à-vis* and unincluded, the system is plainly no monism, but a pluralism of one large and many smaller minds. To correct this error, the finite minds must be conceived as integral parts of the Infinite and as sharing in its action of imprinting. Moreover, this action must be conceived as performed, not by the Infinite acting as one whole on its part — for action of a whole on its part is impossible in logic — but by the parts acting in turn on each other. In other words, my mind, which is such a part, sometimes receives impressions from other parts, sometimes in its turn produces impressions on them. Thus Berkeley's theory needs only to have its pluralism corrected in order to pass over into psychophysical idealism.

But, to make the foregoing account strictly accurate, we must add a couple of restrictions. In the first place, while all parts of the mental universe are capable of such action of imprinting, not all parts are capable of receiving from others those impressions which we call perceptions, but only those parts which have the form of individual minds, and only those individual minds in which the faculty of perception has been evolved. This faculty is not an inherent property of all reality because all reality is mental, but only a late evolutionary product in those parts which are individual minds. This statement is, of course, only a translation from symbolic into real language of the biological fact that perception presupposes sense-organs and a brain. As has already been pointed out, wholly within the physical world there is a process of symbolic representation by which extra-bodily objects call forth perceptional brain-events. It follows that in the real world there must be a parallel process, by which parts of the mental world are symbolized to those other parts which are individual minds. Minds and other things-in-themselves, then, are manifested by means of perceptions, not to other minds and other things-in-themselves, but only to other minds. Secondly, so far as there are physical facts too minute or too recondite to be appreciable to sense, we must recognize a converse restriction, and say that there are details of the real universe not capable of symbolization, directly at least, to human minds.

CONCLUSION

WE set out on our metaphysical inquiry with the object of obtaining light upon the controversy between the interactionists and the parallelists. Let us consider how far the theory just set forth is adapted to serve as basis for reconciliation between the two schools.

A theory which preserves a formal parallelism, while guaranteeing efficiency to the mind, would seem admirably adapted for this purpose. For the supposed denial of efficiency was clearly the great stumbling-block of parallelism, to persons whose interest in the physiological explanation of mental events would otherwise have inclined them to accept it. The blunder of the parallelists lay in turning the physical inefficiency of mind into a general inefficiency, and putting this paradox forward as the most interesting and valuable result of their doctrine. Epiphenomenalism once cast to the winds and consciousness restored to its rightful position as a cause, it would certainly seem as though the remaining concomitance need have no terrors for conservative minds — were it not for the determinism necessarily implied in it.

Let us compare the theory, regarded as a basis for mutual understanding, with the interactionist proposals made by Professor Stumpf in his address before the Congress of Psychologists at Munich.[1] One of these was that we conceive consciousness as a sort of by-product of physical evolution, arising without the expenditure of energy and therefore consistently with the principle of conservation, yet for all that as causally related to its physical antecedents and consequents. Our earlier comment on this was that, while interactionist in form, in substance it differs from the most epiphenomenalistic type of parallelism only by its arbitrary claim that, despite the non-transference of energy, the relations of mind and body are still causal. We may now note that it leaves both the connection of mind and body and the origin of consciousness wholly unexplained. For the proposal to conceive consciousness as a by-product of physical evolution will surely not be regarded as such an explanation. Yet the proposal errs mainly by defect. Fill in the phenomenalistic gaps with things-in-themselves, give to mind and brain their true relation of reality and phenomenon, substitute real causal ties for these verbal ones, and the proposal becomes identical with our own.

A more genuinely interactionist proposal, yet one having certain points of resemblance with psychophysical idealism, is that we conceive the physical order as incomplete and the *lacunæ* as filled out with consciousness. Consciousness thus becomes, not a by-product, but an actual *product*, of physical evolution, a form of energy subject to the law of con-

[1] *Dritter Internationaler Congress für Psychologie in München* 1896, pp. 11–13.

servation and "equivalent" to its physical causes and effects. As one link in the causal chain, it has efficiency. At the same time, it constitutes with the other physical links a single orderly system, and the conception is therefore formally monistic.

Before we can pass judgment on this proposal, we must know exactly what Professor Stumpf means by physical events. Is he a naïve realist, or a phenomenalist, or a critical realist? Not the least surprising feature of his address is his failure to inform us on this point. From his assertion of interaction and his view that consciousness is a product of physical evolution, we are bound to attribute to him some form of realism. We can hardly suppose him to be a naïve realist; then he must be a critical one, a believer in things-in-themselves. But his rejection of panpsychism shows that he does not conceive these as mental in nature; and that is perhaps why he refers to them as physical. His view, then, would seem to be that which we have called critical psychophysical dualism.

The advantages of this proposal are its upholding of efficiency and its formal monism. But psychophysical idealism equally upholds efficiency. And Professor Stumpf's view, while formally monistic, is dualistic as regards the stuff of the universe, since it recognizes two distinct and irreducible natures. But how can consciousness be a product of physical evolution, even "occasional," if physical and mental facts are radically unlike? The only view consistent with an explanation of the origin of consciousness is the view that things-in-themselves are mental in nature.

When Professor Stumpf comes to the question of the reality that appears as the brain-process, he takes for granted that it is distinct from the accompanying consciousness. Holding the two to be distinct, no wonder the inability of consciousness to act on something with which it is so closely connected appears to him incredible. To him, as to Professor James, it seems " quite inconceivable that consciousness should have *nothing to do* with a business which it so faithfully attends."[1] Neither to Professor Stumpf nor to Professor James has the possibility occurred that consciousness may itself be the reality that appears as the brain-process. Yet this hypothesis would admit consciousness to a place in the causal order and guarantee its efficiency as surely as the other. At the same time, this hypothesis alone explains the connection of mind and body and the origin of mind. This hypothesis alone, by conceiving the relation between consciousness and other things-in-themselves as the counterpart of that between the brain-process and the rest of the physical world, admits consciousness to a place in the causal order without making it a form of energy. This hypothesis alone, by making the physical world disappear, so to speak, in the individual minds, offers us a monism of stuff as well as of form.

As we have considered the advantages of psychophysical idealism, it is right that we should also take

[1] *Principles of Psychology*, vol. i., p. 136.

note of its difficulties. If the theory solves the problem, these cannot of course be insuperable. Nevertheless, they may be sufficiently serious to prevent impartial readers from accepting the theory, and it will be better to state them frankly than to slur them over, even though little or nothing can at present be done to remove them.

In the first place, there is the doubt whether the empirical characters of the brain-process adapt it to be the manifestation of a consciousness — a doubt only partially removed by the law of psychophysical correlation. The trouble is that consciousness appears so very much simpler a thing than the brain-process.[1] When we reflect, the disparity between the two seems immense: the brain-process a concourse of moving molecules inconceivable in its complexity; consciousness a tangle of half-a-dozen feelings, or at most a mosaic of a few hundred. To remove this difficulty, since the brain cannot be made simpler, consciousness must apparently be made more complex. It must apparently be shown to have a histology, a microscopic structure invisible to the naked eye of introspection. But is not this to falsify the record, to contradict the principle that the *esse* of consciousness is *percipi?*

Secondly, there is the conception of things-in-themselves as mental in nature. This is the difficulty which

[1] It is of course to be borne in mind that we have been using the term 'brain-process' in a special sense, to signify only such part of the total brain-process as forms the immediate correlate of consciousness, and that we are very far from knowing exactly what that part of the brain-process is.

leads Professor Stumpf to reject panpsychism. How, he asks, can we conceive a crystal, a dewdrop, or a molecule as possessing anything analogous to sensation and will as we know them in ourselves? How, I may add, can we conceive a motor nerve-current or a muscular contraction as having a mental counterpart? How can we conceive the sound-waves that irritate the ear as having a mental existence in themselves? How can we conceive a mental equivalent for electric currents, for the Röntgen rays, for the shot-off particles of radio-active substances? Or, to present the same difficulty in another aspect: since the real world is presumably, like the physical, continuous, how is its continuity consistent with its being mental? Does it consist of as many separate feelings as there are atoms, or of one great feeling or consciousness, or of something between the two, a sort of mental fluid universally diffused through quasi-space? Before we can admit the mental nature of things-in-themselves — which is practically to say, before we can admit their existence, since with any other nature they were better unassumed — we must have some positive conception of what their mental nature can be like.

Finally, there is the evolution out of things-in-themselves of individual minds. We commonly conceive an individual mind as something unitary and isolated. If things-in-themselves form a continuous world, how out of such a world can something unitary and isolated be evolved? To say that both are mental is to solve the problem with a word. Or is the individual mind less unitary and isolated than we commonly imagine?

These difficulties all centre in the question of the nature of consciousness. To deal with that question properly, it would be necessary to take up, one after another, such forms of consciousness as memory, discrimination, perception, will, to analyze it, and to ask wherein its unity consists. The plural side of consciousness is evidently correlated with processes in locally separate brain-areas, and is therefore itself in a certain way spread out, so that it opposes little obstacle to evolutionary explanation: all the difficulty is on the score of the unity.

Such an investigation of consciousness as it appears from within would take too long, and would carry us too far from the external relations of consciousness with which alone we are immediately concerned in this book. I propose, therefore, to reserve it for another.

WORKS BY
EDWARD BRADFORD TITCHENER
M.A. (OXON.), PH.D. (LEIPZIG),

*Member of the Aristotelian Society and of the Neurological Society of London;
Associate Editor of Mind and of the American Journal of Psychology;
Sage Professor of Psychology in the Cornell University*

AN OUTLINE OF PSYCHOLOGY
Third Edition, revised and enlarged.   Cloth. 8vo. $1.50 net

IN many ways it is the most serviceable text-book of psychology from a modern scientific point of view that has been written; ... [it is] clear, exact in expression, systematic, methodical. The work is thoroughly good and useful.— Professor J. JASTROW, University of Wisconsin, in *The Dial*.

A PRIMER OF PSYCHOLOGY
Third Edition, revised and enlarged.   Cloth. 8vo. $1.00 net

THE reader for whom the book is specially intended, and others for whom it is not specially intended, may derive from it a substantial body of knowledge and a real increase of clearness and insight. ... For systematic lucidity and easy mastery of exposition, Professor Titchener's book has no rival on its own ground.— DR. G. F. STOUT, Oxford University, in *Mind*.

EXPERIMENTAL PSYCHOLOGY
A Manual of Laboratory Practice

VOLUME I.— QUALITATIVE EXPERIMENTS
PART I. — STUDENTS' MANUAL.   Cloth. 8vo. $1.60 net
PART II.— INSTRUCTORS' MANUAL.   Cloth. 8vo. $2.50 net

VOLUME II. — QUANTITATIVE EXPERIMENTS
(*In Preparation*)

THE MACMILLAN COMPANY, 66 FIFTH AVE., NEW YORK

AN INTRODUCTION TO PSYCHOLOGY

By MARY WHITON CALKINS

PROFESSOR OF PHILOSOPHY AND PSYCHOLOGY AT
WELLESLEY COLLEGE

Cloth. Crown 8vo. $2.00 net

PLAN AND PURPOSE

THIS book is, in the first place, a text-book for college students in psychology, and constant effort is made to stimulate students to independent and careful observation of their own consciousness. It is clear and simple in style, but the attempt is made to avoid the inevitable dogmatism of unduly simplified assertions. For this reason the work contains careful statements of the theories on important topics of psychology, which are opposed to those of the writer.

In preparation for early issue:

OUTLINES OF PSYCHOLOGY

By JOSIAH ROYCE, PH.D., LL.D. (Aberdeen)

PROFESSOR OF THE HISTORY OF PHILOSOPHY
IN HARVARD UNIVERSITY

Cloth. *12mo.*

THE MACMILLAN COMPANY
66 FIFTH AVE., NEW YORK